"Searching for a timely and comprehensive book on cyber law? If so, *Cyber Law & Ethics* should be for you. For this book is for anyone interested in all the major legal and ethical cyber issues, including freedom of online speech, privacy, IP and gaming. Also covered are a number of evolving and emerging topics such as AI, cyborgs and drones. Although it centers on U.S. law, the book is refreshingly global. Mark Grabowski and Eric Robinson pay discerning attention to international and comparative law. What a remarkable contribution to understanding cyber law."

Kyu Ho Youm, *Jonathan Marshall First Amendment Chair, University of Oregon, USA*

Cyber Law and Ethics

A primer on legal issues relating to cyberspace, this textbook introduces business, policy and ethical considerations raised by our use of information technology.

With a focus on the most significant issues impacting Internet users and businesses in the United States of America, the book provides coverage of key topics such as social media, online privacy, artificial intelligence and cybercrime as well as emerging themes such as doxing, ransomware, revenge porn, data-mining, e-sports and fake news. The authors, experienced in journalism, technology and legal practice, provide readers with expert insights into the nuts and bolts of cyber law.

Cyber Law and Ethics: Regulation of the Connected World provides a practical presentation of legal principles, and is essential reading for non-specialist students dealing with the intersection of the Internet and the law.

Mark Grabowski is Associate Professor of Communications at Adelphi University, USA.

Eric P. Robinson is Assistant Professor at the University of South Carolina, USA and is "of counsel" to Fenno Law, LLC.

Cyber Law and Ethics

Regulation of the Connected World

Mark Grabowski and Eric P. Robinson

Routledge
Taylor & Francis Group
LONDON AND NEW YORK

First published 2022
by Routledge
2 Park Square, Milton Park, Abingdon, Oxon OX14 4RN

and by Routledge
605 Third Avenue, New York, NY 10158

Routledge is an imprint of the Taylor & Francis Group, an informa business

British Library Cataloguing-in-Publication Data
A catalogue record for this book is available from the British Library

Library of Congress Cataloging-in-Publication Data
A catalog record has been requested for this book

ISBN: 978-1-032-02309-0 (hbk)
ISBN: 978-0-367-46260-4 (pbk)
ISBN: 978-1-003-02778-2 (ebk)

Typeset in Bembo
by Deanta Global Publishing Services, Chennai, India

Contents

Preface

For most of us, the Internet simply exists and we take it for granted. Every day, we do things like send text messages, post comments on Facebook, upload photos to Instagram, find dates on Tinder, stream music on Spotify, shop on Amazon, bank online, publish blog posts, play video games or get around town using Uber.

Without even knowing it, we are licensing content, exercising free speech rights, utilizing artificial intelligence technology, sharing personal information and, sometimes, perhaps being victimized by cybercriminals or even breaking laws ourselves. Legal issues relating to cyberspace are becoming more and more important to everyday people as the world becomes more connected. With technology rapidly upgrading and changing, the issues are in constant flux and impact everything from what we buy to what we know about governments and elections.

Therefore, in modern society, understanding the nuts and bolts of cyber law is useful for anyone and everyone, but especially people who work in fields such as the media and tech, or aspire to. But there's seemingly no good textbook suited for such a necessary subject. The existing books are narrowly focused, written for law students or out of date. But this textbook is different. Co-written by two journalists-turned-lawyers-turned-professors, this book's appeal lies in its succinct, informative and easy-to-understand style. Its goal is to engage modern college students who want a practical, "bottom line" presentation of legal principles, rather than a complex, legalistic approach more suited to law students and attorneys. Having taught courses such as media law, cyber law and blockchain to undergraduates, the authors know how to explain complicated terms in a way that laypersons can understand.

This book examines many of the legal, policy and ethical issues raised by our use of cyberspace and information technology. It is not meant to be interpreted as legal advice, nor is it an exhaustive listing of every cyber law in the world. Rather, it provides a primer on the most common and important legal and ethical issues impacting cyberspace, particularly Internet users and businesses in the United States. Some of the topics include: social media, online privacy, artificial intelligence, cybercrime, intellectual property, online gaming, network neutrality and Internet governance. This book also covers novel and emerging issues that other books do not, such as catfishing, doxing, ransomware, sexting, revenge porn, data-mining, drones, cybernetics, Bitcoin, WikiLeaks, e-sports and fake news.

Each chapter ends with a "Closing Arguments" section that includes a question to provoke further thought and discussion.

Turn the page and start upgrading your legal knowledge!

About the Authors

Mark Grabowski is an associate professor of communications at Adelphi University on Long Island, where he teaches courses on web journalism, cyber law, digital ethics and cryptocurrency. He is also a columnist for the *Washington Examiner* and frequently writes about tech policy. Grabowski's previous book, *Cryptocurrencies: A Primer on Digital Money*, was published by Routledge in 2019. He has also published in top law journals such as *Yale Journal on Regulation, Stanford Law & Policy Review, Harvard Journal of Sports and Entertainment Law, Communication Law Review* and the *Journal of Law, Technology & the Internet*. His work has been cited by many major media outlets, several top law journals, the National Constitution Center and renowned federal Judge Richard Posner. It has also been translated and republished in Korean and Romanian. Grabowski is frequently invited to give talks around the world, which includes a 2014 TEDx talk on "The Battle for Control of the Internet" in Shanghai. He won the 2015 James Madison Prize for Outstanding Research in First Amendment Studies and a 2020–21 Fulbright award to study cryptocurrency regulations in the Philippines. The former newspaper reporter holds a J.D. from Georgetown Law. His website is markgrabowski.com.

Credit: Stan Foxworthy.

Eric P. Robinson is an assistant professor in the School of Journalism and Mass Communications at the University of South Carolina, where he teaches media law and ethics. He is also "of counsel" to Fenno Law, LLC in Charleston/Mount Pleasant, South Carolina, which focuses on media and Internet law. He was previously co-director of the Press Law and Democracy Project at Louisiana State University, and deputy director of the National Center for Courts and Media at the University of Nevada, Reno. He was also an affiliate scholar with the Digital Media Law Project at Harvard Law School's Berkman Klein Center for Internet & Society, a staff attorney at the Media Law Resource Center and a legal fellow at the Reporters Committee for Freedom of the Press. He recently published *Reckless Disregard: St. Amant v. Thompson and the Transformation of Libel Law*, and oversaw a complete revision of *Internet Law: The Complete Guide.* He is also the monthly media law columnist for the South Carolina Press Association. He earned his J.D. from Syracuse University, and his Ph.D. from Louisiana State University. His website is ericrobinson.org.

Acknowledgments

The authors would like to thank the following individuals for their assistance: University of South Carolina student Anna Bennett, who served as a research assistant and proofreader; Parsons School of Design associate professor William Bevington, who designed the book's cover; and artist Debjani Bhattacharya, who created the illustrations inside the book.

1 Origins of the Internet

> When we look at the Internet, and where it came from, and where it's arrived today, and where it's headed, I think it's quite clear that the engineers didn't really realize just how much this was going to change things.
>
> — Edward Snowden

Things were so different before the Internet that it's inconceivable for today's university students to appreciate how much the Internet transformed our existence.

Before we had things like social media and dating apps, meeting a new person happened organically: through our family, neighborhood, school or events. There were also clubs for everything: garden clubs, game clubs, clubs for collectors. They were a way for people to connect with others with similar interests. Communications occurred through letters, phone calls and in-person meetings, not e-mails, text messages or Zoom meetings.

If you wanted to meet up with a friend, there was no Skype or FaceTime: you had to make plans over landline telephones to rendezvous at a specific time and a precise location. If the person was outside your local calling area, it was a "toll call," which could be expensive. Phones were strictly for talking and didn't have contact lists, cameras or any other capabilities. Phone numbers needed to be memorized or looked up in a "phone book" which was often thick enough to double as a child's booster seat. There was no GPS: either a paper map or handwritten directions were necessary to get to the meeting place. And you better not run late or get lost because there was no way to inform your friend to wait for you.

If you needed to buy something, you'd go to a store or the mall — there was no Amazon. If you couldn't find what you were looking for, you ordered it from a catalog and would wait six to eight weeks for delivery. Payment was made with checks, not PayPal or online banking. Looking for a good place to eat? You'd ask someone for a recommendation and hope they were right, since there was no crowdsourcing via review sites like Yelp. Reservations were made over the phone, not online. And having your own car or taking a taxi or other public transportation was the only way to get from place to place as there was no Uber or Lyft. If you needed to fly somewhere, you visited a travel agent or called the airline to make your reservations and mail you your plane ticket.

If you wanted entertainment, you'd religiously watch your favorite TV shows at a set day and time each week, or else you were likely never be able to see them. There was no such thing as "On Demand" or DVRs. At a certain time at night, many TV channels would play the national anthem or disco music and then just go off the air, showing a blank screen. Before Netflix and streaming, you had to rent a VHS tape or DVD from Blockbuster Video. People bought music in the form of records, cassette tapes and CDs from a store or listened to their AM / FM radios. One of the first commercial video games, Atari's *Pong*, was a far cry from today's visually stunning, role-playing, online video games. Later, *Super Mario Bros.* on Nintendo was a huge breakthrough, as were the first affordable home computers like the Commodore 64. But until the release of user-friendly software such as Microsoft's Windows operating system, only geeks with programming knowledge knew how to operate a computer.

There was no Google. If you forgot a fact like the name of a film or who starred in it, you would head to the local library building, during the hours it was open, and hope that the book you needed wasn't already checked out. For more general knowledge, you'd look things up in a big book or series of books known as an encyclopedia, which was the analogue of Wikipedia, or perhaps ask a wise elder. Want the news? *The New York Times* and other physically printed newspapers could be delivered to your doorstep each morning and provide coverage of the previous day's happenings. TV news was generally limited to local news shows at 6 and 11 p.m., plus the networks' national news broadcasts. CNN began in 1980, but its 24/7 coverage of the Persian Gulf War in 1991 was a game-changer.

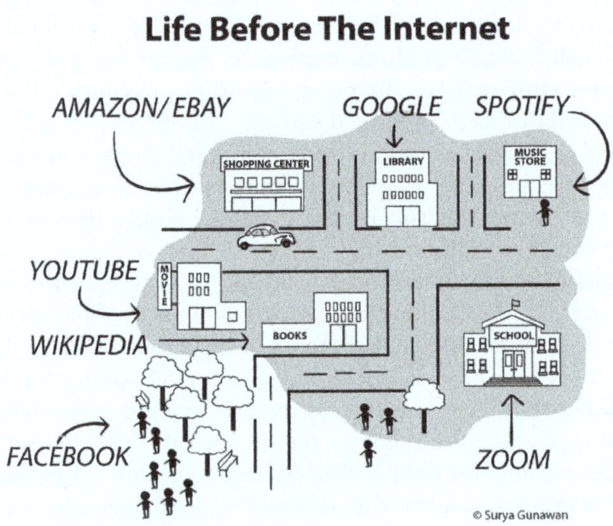

The Internet changed all of that, along with virtually every aspect of modern American life, whether it's ordering a pizza, buying a TV, sharing a photo with a friend, going to school and even finding a romantic partner. It has revolutionized communications, expanding our access to information, people and ideas from around the corner and around the world.

The Internet itself has also been transformed. It's not your father's Internet anymore. Heck, it's not even your older sister's Internet anymore. In its early days — which from a historical perspective are still relatively recent — it was a static network designed to shuttle a small amount of data or a short message between two terminals and store information published and maintained only by expert coders. Today, however, immense quantities of information are uploaded and downloaded over this electronic leviathan every moment. And the content is both created and accessed by everyone, for now we are all commentators, publishers and creators online.

A few visionaries had some insight into how the Internet would change our lives forever. But most people, including many scholars, had no idea how far-reaching this technology and its impact would become. For example, in a 1998 article about the pitfalls of making predictions about technological progress, Paul Krugman, later a *New York Times* Pulitzer Prize-winning columnist and Nobel Laureate of Economics, wrote, "By 2005 or so, it will become clear that the Internet's impact on the economy has been no greater than the fax machine's."[1]

The Internet has become necessary for survival, a trend which reached new importance during the COVID-19 pandemic. With most businesses and schools closed due to government-imposed lockdowns, many important aspects of everyday life shifted online. Governments also used it to controversially monitor and track citizens for the stated purpose of preventing further virus outbreaks.

The technological advancements offered by our modern, connected world haven't necessarily always translated into progress. The rapid and unexpected rise of the Internet has outpaced social norms and has sparked a debate about how it should be used, and how it should not be used. It has also outpaced the law, and has left courts, legislators and regulators playing catch-up. This book, which describes the laws and regulations applicable online right now, should thus be considered a work in progress, just like the law itself is.

But before covering the legal and ethical implications raised by the Internet, it is important to first understand how it developed, how it works and how it's used. Knowing the history, architecture and uses of the Internet will help inform us about the creation and appropriateness of laws and social norms for it.

1 Krugman, Paul, *Why Most Economists' Predictions Are Wrong*, Red Herring, June 1998, archived at https://web.archive.org/web/19980610100009/http://www.redherring.com/mag/issue55/economics.html.

How the Internet Works

The Internet is a world-wide network of computers linked together by telephone and fiber optic wires, satellite links and other telecommunications infrastructure. The essential components of the Internet can be divided into two categories: servers (computer hardware) and software applications. Servers house most of the information on the Internet: they are specialized computers which store information, share information with other servers and make this information available online. Software applications, such as browsers and mobile applications ("apps"), are what people use to access the information available on the Internet, using a computer or mobile device. Google Chrome, Mozilla Firefox, Apple Safari and Microsoft Edge are the most commonly used browsers. Popular apps include Uber, Tinder, Spotify, Instagram and various mobile video games.

When you connect your computer or mobile device to the Internet, you are connecting to a special type of server which is provided and operated by your Internet service provider (ISP). The ISP is the entity that provides your connection to the Internet; examples include Verizon, AT&T, a library or your university. The job of this "ISP server" is to provide the link between your device and the Internet. A single ISP server can handle the Internet connections of many individual devices. When you use a browser or app, there may be thousands of other people connected to the same server that you are connected to.

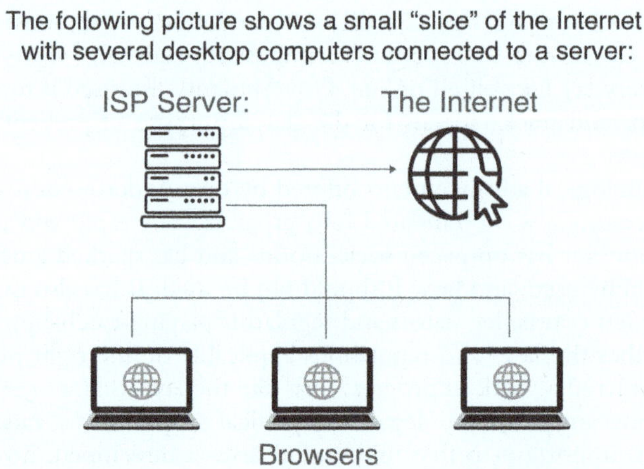

ISP servers receive requests from devices to view webpages, check e-mail, utilize apps and use every other Internet function. Since each individual server can't store all the information from the entire Internet, in order to provide users' devices with the pages and files they request, ISP servers must connect to other Internet servers known as "host servers."

But first they must determine which host server contains the relevant information. It does this by accessing a database that is stored in various copies at several servers, known as name servers. The database is known as "WhoIs," which is short for the question "Who is responsible for this domain name?" It translates web addresses into numerical codes that indicate where online the information can be found.

The numerical codes correlate with host servers, which are the computers where websites and apps "live." The host server's job is to store information and make it available to other servers. Every website and application in the world is located on a host server somewhere. For example, harvard.edu is hosted on a server on Harvard's campus. The textbook authors' personal websites, markgrabowski.com and ericrobinson.org, are both hosted on servers in California.

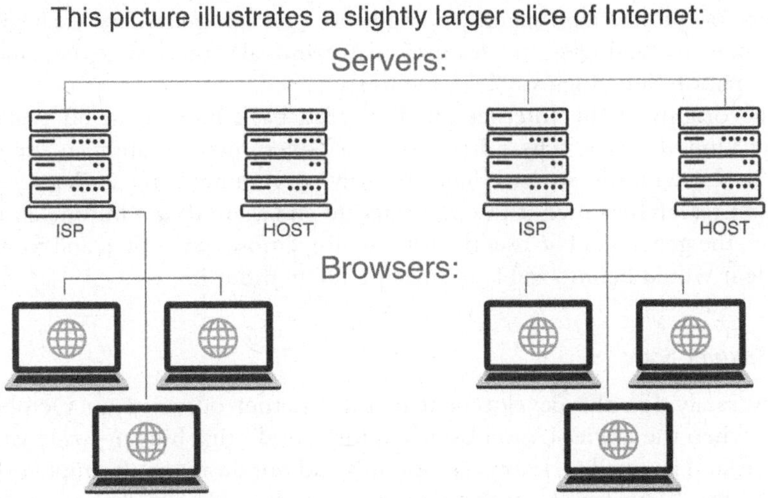

To view a web page from your browser, the following sequence happens:

1. You either type a website address, also known as a uniform resource locator (URL), into your "address bar" or click on a hyperlink that includes a URL for the website.
2. Your browser sends a request to your ISP server asking for the page.
3. Your ISP server looks in the WhoIs database to find the exact host server which houses the website you requested, then sends that host server a request for the page contents.
4. The host server sends the requested page to your ISP server.
5. Your ISP sends the page to your browser and you see it displayed on your screen.

This entire process takes mere seconds, so that most websites can be easily and quickly accessed. And the Internet includes built-in redundancy, so that the system may use various routes through servers and connections in order to supply the data.

This underlying architecture serves as the first level of what is effectively a sort of "regulation" of online behavior. Much like how humans must operate within the confines of the laws of physics in the real world, Internet users are restricted to the code the Internet and its applications are built on and can only work within its limits.

History of the Internet

Choosing a "birthday" for the Internet is a rather arbitrary task since someone didn't just flip a switch and send the whole thing into existence. Unlike technologies such as the light bulb or the microwave, which resulted from an inventor's "eureka" moment, the Internet has no single "inventor." Instead, dozens of pioneering scientists, engineers and programmers each developed new technologies and features that eventually merged to become the "Information Superhighway" we use today.

The origins of the Internet can be traced back more than 60 years ago in the United States, where it began as a government weapon in the Cold War rivalry with the Soviet Union. Initially, government and academic scientists and researchers used it to communicate and share data with one another. Today, the general public uses the Internet for almost everything, and for many people it would be impossible to imagine life without it.

The Sputnik Scare

A key catalyst in the development of the Internet occurred on October 4, 1957, when the Soviet Union launched the world's first human-made satellite into orbit. The satellite, known as Sputnik, did not do much. It simply orbited around the Earth for about three months, sending blips and bleeps from its radio transmitters until its batteries died. Still, the beach-ball-sized Sputnik provided an alarming wake-up call: while the brightest minds in the U.S. had been designing bigger cars and better TV sets, it appeared the Soviets had been busy focusing on less frivolous things. And, Americans feared, they were going to win the Cold War because of it. "The Soviets had caught us with our pants down," said Leonard Kleinrock, a UCLA professor who helped build the Internet. "We were behind in technology."[2]

Sputnik's launch galvanized Americans to think more seriously about science and technology so that the nation could regain ground it appeared to have lost to its feared rival. Schools added courses on subjects like physics, calculus and chemistry. Corporations received government grants to conduct scientific research and development. And the federal government itself created agencies, such as the National Aeronautics and Space Administration (NASA) and the

2 National Geographic, The Internet Revolution and Digital Future Technology Documentary, 2018, https://youtu.be/V9xZFZ07UbA.

Department of Defense's Advanced Research Projects Agency (ARPA), to develop space-age technologies such as rockets and computers.

The Birth of the ARPAnet

Scientists and military experts were especially concerned about what might happen in the event of a Soviet attack on the nation's telephone system. They feared that just one accurately targeted missile could destroy the whole system of physical lines and wires that made efficient long-distance communication possible. In 1962, a scientist from Massachusetts Institute of Technology and ARPA named J.C.R. Licklider proposed a solution to this scenario: an "intergalactic network" of computers that could talk with one another.[3] Such a network would enable government leaders to communicate if the telephone network was destroyed. Thus, Licklider developed the first practical schematics for the Internet.

In 1965, researchers developed a way of sending information from one computer to another known as "packet switching," a process which breaks data down into message blocks, or packets, before sending it to its destination. Each packet takes its own route in cyberspace and is then reconstructed into the message at its destination. Without packet switching, this ingenious computer network — known as the ARPAnet — would have been just as vulnerable to Soviet attacks as the phone system, which can't reroute data transmission when a line is down because it relies on circuit switching.

"LOGIN"

In 1969, ARPAnet delivered its first message: a "node-to-node" communication from a computer at UCLA research lab to a computer at Stanford University. (Each of these computers was the size of a small house.) Though short and simple, the message — "LOGIN" — crashed the fledgling ARPA network. Stanford's computer only received the first two letters. Two years later, ARPA computer programmer Ray Tomlinson perfected the messaging system into what we know today as e-mail. He also made the decision to use the "@" symbol to separate the user name from the computer name (which later on became the domain name).

3 Whitall, Susan, *How Michigan Man Helped Map Path to the Internet*, Detroit News, Oct. 14, 2015, https://www.detroitnews.com/story/opinion/2015/10/14/internet-michigan-nsfnet-douglas-van-houweling-university-michigan-merit/73959878/.

UCLA professor Leonard Kleinrock helped develop "packet switching" and sent the first message over ARPAnet using the device he's pictured with. Credit: UCLA.

The Network Grows

The virtual world grew steadily during the 1970s, expanding beyond the four computers in the continental U.S. to include the University of Hawaii's ALOHAnet, London's University College and the Norwegian Seismic Array near Oslo, Norway. The network was then expanded beyond military and academic use. In 1975, the first commercial ISP was born with the introduction of a private-sector version of ARPAnet known as Telenet. It enabled tech companies and computer hobbyists to connect to cyberspace and would later be acquired by later-day telecom giant Sprint.

Michael Hart, a data processor at the University of Illinois at Urbana-Champaign, published the first e-books and founded the first digital library, known as Project Gutenberg, by manually typing the U.S. Declaration of Independence, the Bible and other texts into a computer to transmit to other users on the network. Just as quickly, the new technology started to be abused, as Gary Thuerk, a marketing executive for a computer company, sent the first spam e-mail to 400 ARPAnet users in 1978. While the e-mail campaign did result in over $12 million in sales, Thuerk received many complaints from those he contacted, and a strict rebuke from the government.[4] Little did he know that his stunt would set a bad precedent for decades to come.

4 Bonazzo, John, *This Week in Tech History: First Spam E-mail, Hindenburg Explosion*, Observer, May 2, 2016, https://observer.com/2016/05/this-week-in-tech-history-first-spam-e-mail-hindenburg-explosion/.

Traveling throughout the cyberverse still wasn't easy. It wasn't like it is today, when users can just enter a web address in their browser and get taken there automatically. To access one of those early networks, users had to either be logged into a device hardwired directly into the network or gain access remotely through a modem, which sends computer data over a phone line. If they wanted to go to a different network, the process would have to be repeated each time. As these separate, packet-switched computer networks multiplied, it became more difficult for them to integrate into a single worldwide network.

By the end of the 1970s, Stanford University computer science professor Vinton Cerf and government scientist Robert Kahn remedied this problem by developing a way for all of the computers on all of the world's mini-networks to communicate with one another. They called their invention "Transmission Control Protocol," or TCP. Later, they added an additional protocol, known as "Internet Protocol," or IP. Today these protocols are better known by the acronym TCP / IP. The term "Internet" also began to be used for the entire network.

The World Wide Web

Cerf and Kahn's combined protocol, as one writer put it, is "the 'handshake' that introduces distant and different computers to each other in a virtual space."[5] And it transformed the Internet into a worldwide network. To this day, TCP / IP remains the standard protocol for the Internet.

By the 1980s, there were more ordinary citizens accessing the Internet than government officials and academic researchers, due to the introduction of IBM's personal computer and telephone modems. Cyberspace exploration also became much easier thanks to Jon Postel and Elizabeth Feinler, who developed the Domain Name System (DNS), which established the familiar .edu, .gov, .com, .mil, .org and .net systems for naming websites. This was easier to remember than the previous numeric designations for websites, such as 216.58.213.78 (the IP address for google.com). Users formed virtual communities by using "Usenet groups," which allowed them to post messages to an electronic bulletin board. Although few people participated (interactions were limited to text and response times could take weeks or longer), these groups were a primitive form of social media. The Internet was now thought of as being its own place, albeit a virtual one, and novelist William Gibson coined the term "cyberspace" in *Neuromancer*, a 1984 book that added the cyberpunk genre to science fiction.

At the same time, government officials began to worry that connecting computers could lead to harm. The 1983 techno-thriller film *WarGames* — in which a young teenager breaks into a U.S. military supercomputer and unwittingly almost starts World War III — prompted Congress to enact the first cybercrime law. Under the 1986 Computer Fraud and Abuse Act, hacking became a federal felony. The law was used to prosecute an offender just two

5 Wenkart, Michael, 50 Scientific Discoveries That Changed the World, 2014, 160.

years later when a Cornell University student unleashed an Internet virus that caused millions of dollars in damage, rendering 10% of all computers worldwide useless.[6] Using the Internet now posed serious risks. So, a year later, John McAfee formed the first antivirus company, which later became part of Intel. Still, the Internet remained an obscure technology, as less than 1% of the world's population had Internet access at that point.[7]

That changed in the 1990s, when the Internet transformed into the online environment we inhabit today. In 1991, Tim Berners-Lee, a British computer programmer working at the European Organization for Nuclear Research (known as CERN for its French acronym) on the France–Switzerland border, introduced the World Wide Web: an Internet that was not simply a way to send files from one place to another but was itself a "web" of information that anyone on the Internet could retrieve. Unsurprisingly, CERN is credited with having the first website. A search tool called "Gopher," developed by University of Minnesota computer programmer Mark McCahill, helped users find and retrieve information they were seeking. These developments served as a crucial step in developing the vast trove of information that most of us now access on a daily basis.

In 1992, a group of students and researchers at the University of Illinois developed a browser they called Mosaic (which later became Netscape) that offered a user-friendly way to search the web. For the first time, users could see words and images on the same page and navigate using scrollbars and clickable links.

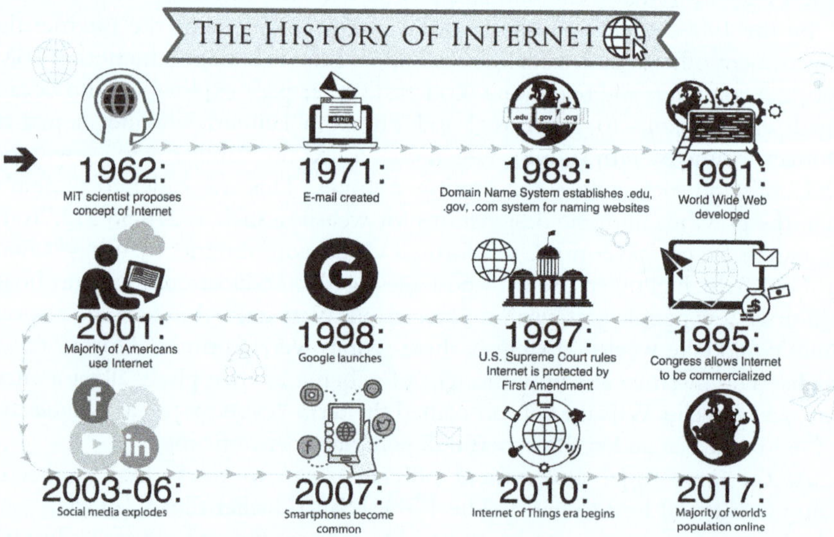

6 Vaughan-Nichols, Steven J., *The Day Computer Security Turned Real: The Morris Worm Turns 30*, ZD Net, Nov. 2, 2018, https://www.zdnet.com/article/the-day-computer-security-turned-real-the-morris-worm-turns-30/.

7 Roser, Max et al., *Internet*, Our World in Data, 2015, https://ourworldindata.org/internet.

The Internet Goes Mainstream

In 1995, the Internet became commercialized. After Congress decided that the web could be used for commercial purposes, companies of all kinds hurried to set up websites, and e-commerce entrepreneurs began to use the Internet to sell goods directly to customers. Giant ISPs such as CompuServe, Prodigy and America Online (AOL) provided e-mail, instant messaging and web browser features to millions of Americans nationwide. Netscape's development of Secure Sockets Layer (SSL) encryption made it safer to conduct financial transactions, such as credit card payments, online. Banks began to offer online banking to customers. Amazon and eBay commenced business. Users could shop online for books, food, wine, travel deals and real estate. Craigslist offered online classified ads for jobs, apartments, personals and more. And Match.com enabled people to find romantic partners online. Bill Gates decided to redefine Microsoft as an Internet company, beginning a browser war against Netscape with his unveiling of Internet Explorer.

The Internet also changed traditional media in many ways. RealAudio Player's creation in 1995 made it possible to stream audio and video over the Internet. Newspapers — including *The New York Times* in 1996 — created websites and began breaking news online. Eventually journalists started getting scooped by upstart bloggers. In 1998, Matt Drudge broke arguably the story of the decade when he revealed that President Bill Clinton had an affair with a 22-year-old White House intern, which led to his impeachment. 1998 also gave birth to Google, which today is the second-largest Internet company, behind only Amazon, thanks largely to its search engine and advertising platform. As the decade approached its end, Napster opened up the gates to mainstream peer-to-peer file-sharing of media over the Internet.

Suddenly, the Internet looked like it could be as revolutionary as the printing press; maybe even more so. No longer was it just for computer geeks. The new digital frontier spawned a "dot-com" boom that reinvigorated America's lagging economy and revolutionized the way people communicated. By the end of the 1990s, almost half of the U.S. population was online.[8]

But this new communication and convenience caused casualties. E-commerce and online banking caught the attention of criminals who saw a new frontier. Facing increased competition from blogs for audiences and from Google and Craigslist for advertising dollars, newspapers struggled to survive. Movie and music revenues also suffered as Napster made it easy to pirate entertainment. Companies such as Microsoft were able to establish monopolies by using anti-competitive business practices to crush competitors. And pedophiles utilized the web to spread child pornography and prey on unsuspecting children.

8 Real Time Statistics Project, *Internet Live Stats*, accessed Oct. 5, 2020, https://www.internetlivestats.com.

The Internet was quickly devolving into an "Old Wild West" environment. Lawmakers tried to play catch-up but had mixed results. An attempt by Congress to censor "indecent" and "offensive" speech online was struck down by the Supreme Court, which declared in the 1997 landmark case *Reno v. American Civil Liberties Union* that the First Amendment's freedom of speech clause protected content on the Internet.[9] The U.S. Department of Justice was successful, however, in reining in Microsoft. The tech giant avoided being split up by agreeing to pay an enormous settlement to Netscape's parent company and curb its anti-competitive practices. Meanwhile, a federal court ordered Napster to shutter.

Many other Internet companies didn't survive either, but for different reasons. The dot-com bubble collapsed in 2000 as hundreds of Internet-based companies failed to make profits and closed. The NASDAQ Composite, a stock market index which includes a large number of tech companies, lost 10% of its value in a single day, and finally hit bottom in October 2002.[10]

But the industry quickly rebounded, thanks to the emergence of "Web 2.0," a term coined by web designer Darcy DiNucci to describe websites that enabled users to share content and socialize. While this wasn't a new technology, it hadn't been popular to use the Internet in such a collaborative way until then. The amount of data created on, with or by the Internet in 2003 alone was more than all the data created in human history up to that point.[11] Between 2003 and 2006, MySpace, Facebook, YouTube, Twitter, LinkedIn, Reddit, WordPress, Flickr and Skype were all born, spurring massive growth and adoption. Video games became both a social affair and a spectator sport. Nintendo, Sega and Microsoft released Internet-ready gaming consoles that allowed online multiplayer modes. E-sports grew tremendously, both in viewership and prize money, and the number of tournaments grew from about 10 in 2000 to 260 by the end of the decade.[12] Meanwhile, smartphones, such as the BlackBerry and Apple iPhone, became ubiquitous, creating a culture of constantly being online.

But this expansion of online activities came with many caveats and qualifiers. Psychologists such as Kimberly S. Young broached the concept of Internet addiction.[13] Unsolicited commercial e-mail, known as "spam," was another

9 *Reno v. American Civil Liberties Union*, 521 U.S. 844 (1997).

10 McCullough, Brian, *A Revealing Look at the Dot-com Bubble of 2000 — And How it Shapes Our Lives Today*, TED, Dec. 4, 2018, https://ideas.ted.com/an-eye-opening-look-at-the-dot-com-bubble-of-2000-and-how-it-shapes-our-lives-today/.

11 Siegler, MG, *Eric Schmidt: Every 2 Days We Create As Much Information As We Did Up To 2003*, TechCrunch, Aug. 4, 2010, https://techcrunch.com/2010/08/04/schmidt-data/.

12 Popper, Ben, *Field of Streams: How Twitch Made Video Games a Spectator Sport*, The Verge, Sept. 30, 2013, https://www.theverge.com/2013/9/30/4719766/twitch-raises-20-million-esports-market-booming.

13 Young, Kimberly S. *Internet Addiction: A New Clinical Phenomenon and Its Consequences*, American Behavioral Scientist, Dec. 1, 2004, https://journals.sagepub.com/doi/10.1177/0002764204270278.

growing problem, accounting for nearly 90% of e-mail traffic by the beginning of the 21st century.[14] In 2003, 25 years after the first spam e-mail, Congress finally took action, making it a crime to send spam. But the government failed to address the other major problem that developed with all of this online activity: less privacy. As the Internet became more entrenched in society, businesses began to harvest users' data, which created a trade-off. Data-mining allowed websites to create a better user experience, but also required users to sacrifice potentially sensitive private information for the sake of convenience.

Other nations worried that connecting to cyberspace was also requiring them to sacrifice their culture and values. The Internet was no longer an American phenomenon, but it was still very Americentric. By the end of the decade, nearly one-third of the world's population — 2 billion people — had Internet access, and China had twice as many Internet users as the U.S.[15] Yet, American companies dominated the Internet business. They dominated web browsing, search, e-mail and social networking on computers, smartphones and tablets. Chinese officials worried their society might become infected by decadent American culture. So, they banned some platforms, placed onerous restrictions on others and developed their own homegrown competitors that could reap the economic benefits for China — and keep the Chinese government in control.

By 2010, even more things or objects were connected to the Internet than people, giving birth to the term "Internet of Things" (IoT).[16] Besides computers and phones, TVs, appliances, door locks, baby monitors and many other everyday objects were now "smart gadgets." Refrigerators, for example, could be programmed to stream music, share notes with household members and order food online when supplies are running low. The Internet also began to play a major role in politics. Presidential candidates started doing much of their fundraising, advertising and campaigning via the Internet and much of the public's political discourse happened on social media apps instead of in the town square. Social media also began shaping Hollywood. Kim Kardashian, Justin Bieber, Kate Upton and countless others went from obscurity to celebrity thanks to the Internet.

At the same time, the Internet became a more perilous place. A handful of tech companies, including Google, Apple, Facebook and Amazon essentially established monopolies in their industries, making serious competition from startups nearly impossible. Critics grew especially concerned about the implications for free speech, as Silicon Valley giants began heavily censoring

14 Clement, J., *Spam: Share of Global E-mail Traffic 2007-2019*, Statista, May 14, 2020, https://www.statista.com/statistics/420400/spam-e-mail-traffic-share-annual/.

15 Real Time Statistics Project, *supra* note 8.

16 Evans, Dave, *The Internet of Things: How the Next Evolution of the Internet Is Changing Everything*, Cisco White Paper, Apr. 2011, https://www.cisco.com/c/dam/en_us/about/ac79/docs/innov/IoT_IBSG_0411FINAL.pdf.

their platforms to curtail what they considered hate speech and disinformation. Even a sitting U.S. president, Donald Trump, was censored and permanently banned by some platforms. But some politicians insisted more censorship was needed to prevent social media platforms from being weaponized to spread disinformation and incite violence. Social media also came under attack from educators and psychologists, who blamed it for a rapid rise in cyberbullying, depression and school shootings. Cybercrime rates skyrocketed, as miscreants weaponized the Internet in new and cruel ways to harass others, such as revenge porn and "swatting" (harassing someone by reporting false emergencies at their home, provoking a response from first responders). Criminals managed to weaponize the IoT to temporarily shut down popular websites in 2016.

The Internet, particularly social media, has also been utilized against governments. Twitter and Facebook played a large role in the Middle East revolts of the early 2000s, eventually leading to the overthrow of dictators in Egypt and Libya in 2011. Meanwhile, Russia attempted to interfere with the 2016 U.S. election by spreading disinformation online. The U.S. government also found itself embroiled in controversy when Edward Snowden, a National Security Agency contractor, revealed that officials were using the Internet to secretly spy on its citizens and other countries. That scandal led to the U.S. agreeing to abdicate its long-standing control of key Internet infrastructure to an international multi-stakeholder group. In response to these crises, many governments began heavily censoring the Internet to avoid being the next to lose control.

In 2010, a group of scientists working as part of the Pentagon's JASON project concluded that the Internet is complex far beyond modern understanding. In their report they stated that many of the Internet's behaviors cannot be explained well and that a better understanding of the science behind cybersecurity was needed. "When we look at the Internet, and where it came from, and where it's arrived today, and where it's headed, I think it's quite clear that the engineers didn't really realize just how much this was going to change things," Snowden said.[17]

THE INTERNET BY THE NUMBERS

The Internet has become almost a full-time job for the average American, who now spends more than six hours online per day using it for almost any activity imaginable. Consider the numbers:

- Worldwide, about 59%, or 4.5 billion of the 8 billion people in the world, have access to the Internet. A majority (51%) of all Internet

17 The Internet Revolution and Digital Future Technology Documentary, *supra* note 2.

users worldwide are in Asia; only about 7% of Internet users reside in North America.[18]

- Of those worldwide users, 96% access it daily and about half actively use social media.[19]
- More and more Americans are accessing the Internet through smartphones instead of computers. 81% own a smartphone and 37% of all Internet users go online mostly using their phones, and not using another device such as a desktop or laptop computer.[20]
- 89% of Americans get at least some of their news online — more than any other medium, including traditional TV, radio and newspapers — and 37% prefer to get their news online than via analog media.[21]
- There are more than 1.5 billion websites worldwide.[22]
- Every day, 169 billion e-mails are sent, 4 billion Google searches are made, 4.6 billion YouTube videos are viewed, 500 million tweets are posted, 4 billion blog posts are written, 82 million photos are uploaded on Instagram, 3 million smartphones are sold, and 90,000 websites hacked per day.[23]
- More than 80% of the U.S. population has used the Internet to purchase something. Domestically, online sales are growing by 15% annually and account for nearly $517 billion per year. Amazon is the most popular online retailer.[24]
- Approximately 40% of American heterosexual couples and 60% of same-sex couples now first meet online.[25] About 40% of single adults have used online dating. Nearly half of online relationships end through an e-mail.[26]

18 Miniwatts Marketing Group, *Internet World Stats,* accessed Oct. 5, 2020, https://www.Internetworldstats.com/stats.htm.

19 Kemp, Simon, *Digital 2019: Global Internet Use Accelerates,* We Are Social Inc., Jan. 30, 2019, https://wearesocial.com/blog/2019/01/digital-2019-global-Internet-use-accelerates.

20 Anderson, Monica, *Mobile Technology and Home Broadband 2019,* Pew Research Center, June 13, 2019, https://www.pewresearch.org/internet/2019/06/13/mobile-technology-and-home-broadband-2019/.

21 Mitchell, Amy et al., *For Local News, Americans Embrace Digital but Still Want Strong Community Connection,* Pew Research Center, Mar. 26, 2019, https://www.journalism.org/2019/03/26/nearly-as-many-americans-prefer-to-get-their-local-news-online-as-prefer-the-tv-set/.

22 *Id.*

23 Real Time Statistics Project, *supra* note 8.

24 Young, Jessica, *US Ecommerce Sales Grow 14.9% in 2019,* Digital Commerce 360, Feb. 19, 2020, https://www.digitalcommerce360.com/article/us-ecommerce-sales/

25 Kopf, Dan, *Around 40% of American Couples Now First Meet Online,* Quartz, Feb. 12, 2019, https://qz.com/1546677/around-40-of-us-couples-now-first-meet-online/.

26 Thottam, Isabel, *10 Online Dating Statistics You Should Know,* 2018, https://www.eharmony.com/online-dating-statistics/.

What Comes Next?

With the arrival of the 2020s, and with them a global pandemic, Internet access has practically become a necessity for survival in the U.S. and much of the developed world. Those who didn't lose their jobs due to the pandemic started working from home. Schools went entirely online. And due to social distancing, dialog and expression occurred almost entirely through digital communication. The average U.S. adult spent a whopping 16 hours a day with digital media during "shelter in place" orders, according to an analysis by Activate Consulting.[27] Governments worldwide rolled out intrusive surveillance systems to ensure citizens were obeying lockdown orders and to trace transmission of the virus. The COVID-19 pandemic exposed the digital divide like never before as those without Internet access, particularly in Africa (where 70% lack a connection), became more vulnerable.[28] It also widened an existing rift between the U.S. and China, which now find themselves engaged in a digital "Cold War," with both sides banning each other's top tech companies and popular apps.

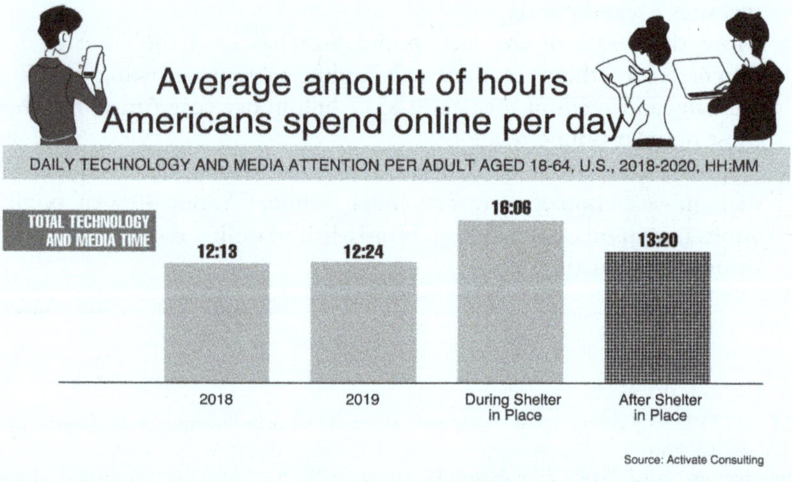

The start of an artificial intelligence (AI) revolution presents equal uncertainty and upheaval. Self-driving cars and medical advances should improve our lives, but experts fear that as AI advances it could eliminate many jobs or eventually eliminate humanity altogether. At the moment, it's largely unregulated. All of this tech has also taken a tremendous toll on the environment.

27 Wolf, Michael J., *How Covid-19 Has Transformed the Amount of Time We Spend Online*, Wall Street Journal, Aug. 7, 2020, https://blogs.wsj.com/experts/2020/08/07/how-covid-19-has-transformed-the-amount-of-time-we-spend-online/.

28 Miniwatts Marketing Group, *supra* note 18.

Though the Internet can significantly cut down on carbon emissions by allowing workers to telecommute, most activities we do online are not productive. The Internet's use of electricity now accounts for 10% of the world's carbon emissions, and it's expected to double through the 2020s as our technology takes on more advanced forms like AI and the developing 5G Network.[29]

As we reflect on the 50 years since the first computer message was sent, it's evident the Internet has completely changed the world. But more of the big changes that it will bring still lie ahead and its history has just begun.[30] "The way to think about where the Internet is going is not what's the future of the Internet, but what does the Internet mutate into and what are all the reaction products that go spinning off into different directions," said Paul Saffo, future studies chair at Stanford University. "And it's only just started."[31]

Whether these future developments make our lives easier and better or add complications and create new problems will depend largely on the regulations and norms we create to govern them. This book explores the law as it applies to the Internet now, and how these and new laws are likely to apply in the future.

CLOSING ARGUMENTS

The Internet was developed, in large part, as a result of the "Cold War" between the U.S. and the Soviet Union, which fostered technological innovation and led to the development of a resilient computer infrastructure that serves as the Internet's backbone. On the other hand, the Cold War also resulted in trillions of dollars of perhaps excessive military spending, and to American involvement in Korea, Vietnam and other foreign conflicts. Were the technological benefits of the Cold War worth the fear and uncertainty of those years?

29 Lozano, Kevin, *Can the Internet Survive Climate Change?*, New Republic, Dec. 18, 2019, https://newrepublic.com/article/155993/can-internet-survive-climate-change.

30 Blitz, Matt, *What Will the Internet Be Like in the Next 50 Years?*, Popular Mechanics, Nov. 1, 2019, https://www.popularmechanics.com/technology/infrastructure/a29666802/future-of-the-internet/.

31 The Internet Revolution and Digital Future Technology Documentary, *supra* note 2.

Additional Sources

Andrews, Evan, *Who Invented the Internet?*, History.com, Oct. 28, 2019, https://www.history.com/news/who-invented-the-internet.

Broom, Douglas, *Coronavirus Has Exposed the Digital Divide Like Never Before*, World Economic Forum, Apr. 22, 2020, https://www.weforum.org/agenda/2020/04/coronavirus-covid-19-pandemic-digital-divide-internet-data-broadband-mobbile/.

Buckley, Sean, *Vint Cerf and Bob Kahn, Co-Inventors of TCP/IP Protocol*, Fierce Telecom, Oct. 4, 2011, https://www.fiercetelecom.com/special-report/vint-cerf-and-bob-kahn-co-inventors-tcp-ip-protocol.

Chikhani, Riad, *The History of Gaming: An Evolving Community*, TechCrunch, Oct. 31, 2015, https://techcrunch.com/2015/10/31/the-history-of-gaming-an-evolving-community.

Computer History Museum, *Internet History of 1980s*, https://www.computerhistory.org/internethistory/1980s/.

Computer Innovations, Mar. 1, 2013, http://computinnovative.blogspot.com/2013/03/internet-and-its-works.html.

Craig, William, *The History of the Internet in a Nutshell*, WebFX, Nov. 14, 2019, https://www.webfx.com/blog/web-design/the-history-of-the-internet-in-a-nutshell/.

Dentzel, Zaryn, *How the Internet Has Changed Everyday Life*, Open Mind BBVA, 2014, https://www.bbvaopenmind.com/en/articles/internet-changed-everyday-life/.

Dewey, Caitlin, *36 Ways the Web has Changed Us*, Washington Post, Mar. 12, 2014, https://www.washingtonpost.com/news/arts-and-entertainment/wp/2014/03/12/36-ways-the-web-has-changed-us/.

FBI, *Operation Innocent Images*, https://www.fbi.gov/history/famous-cases/operation-innocent-images.

Giordano, Simon, *American Big Tech Will Not Protect You*, Brown Political Review, Nov. 20, 2019, https://brownpoliticalreview.org/2019/11/american-big-tech-will-not-protect-you/.

Graff, Garrett M., *Could Trump Win the War on Huawei — And Is TikTok Next?*, Wired, July 14, 2020, https://www.wired.com/story/could-trump-win-the-war-on-huawei-and-is-tiktok-next/.

History.com Editors, *The Invention of the Internet*, History.com, Oct. 28, 2019, https://www.history.com/topics/inventions/invention-of-the-internet.

Leigh, Peter, *The Nostalgia Nerd's Retro Tech: Computer, Consoles & Games* (2018).

Lester, Simon, *The End of American Internet Dominance*, Cato Institute, June 4, 2013, https://www.cato.org/publications/commentary/end-american-internet-dominance.

Marple, Liz, *Remember What Life Was Like Before the Internet*, It's Rosy, July 9, 2019, https://www.itsrosy.com/Life+Before+The+Internet.

Mujovic, Vuk, *Origin of Cyber Security: When Did Internet Privacy Become an Issue?*, Le VPN, Nov. 20, 2018, https://www.le-vpn.com/internet-privacy-cyber-security/.

NORSAR, *NORSAR Becomes the First Non-US Node on ARPANET, the Predecessor to Today's Internet*, https://www.norsar.no/about-us/history/arpanet.

Parker, Tom, *Twitter Locked Trump Campaign Account Until It Complied and Deleted a Tweet*, Reclaim The Net, Aug. 5, 2020, https://reclaimthenet.org/twitter-locks-president-trumps-campaign-account-prevents-tweeting/.

Parsons, Jeff, *What It Looked Like When TV Stations Would Go Off the Air* (Video), WJBQ. Apr. 17, 2015, https://wjbq.com/what-it-looked-like-when-tv-stations-would-go-off-the-air-overnight-video/.

Quodling, Andrew, *Doxxing, Swatting and the New Trends In Online Harassment*, The Conversation, Apr. 21, 2015, https://theconversation.com/doxxing-swatting-and-the-new-trends-in-online-harassment-40234.

Rathbone, Emma, *Before the Internet*, New Yorker, June 19, 2017, https://www.newyorker.com/magazine/2017/06/26/before-the-internet.

Williams, Weston, *How Friday's Cyberattack Shutdown Netflix, Twitter, and Spotify*, Christian Science Monitor, Oct. 23, 2016, https://www.csmonitor.com/Technology/2016/1023/How-Friday-s-cyberattack-shut-down-Netflix-Twitter-and-Spotify.

Zimmermann, Kim Ann and Emspak, Jesse, *Internet History Timeline: ARPANET to the World Wide Web*, Livestock Science, June 27, 2017, https://www.livescience.com/20727-internet-history.html.

2 Who Controls the Internet?

> The great risk is that digital nationalism will balkanize the Internet, breaking it up into a patchwork of incompatible and irreconcilable fiefs.
>
> — Akash Kapur

Who controls the Internet? It's complicated. In a sense, everyone does, and no one does. There are a variety of non-profit and for-profit entities working behind the scenes that control the basic operating procedures of the Internet — how information gets sent and received. But governments also have a role, through laws and regulations. If you're transmitting or downloading child pornography in the United States, the FBI will prosecute you. If you're a dissident living in Beijing and criticize the Chinese government on your blog, you could face legal troubles — or worse — there. However, there is no single regulatory unit that oversees the Internet globally and makes rules that everyone must abide by. After all, the Internet is a cross-border, international medium. Some people want to change that.

With so many entities and governments vying for control of the Internet, it can sometimes be confusing whose rules apply. For example, hate speech is protected by the First Amendment in the U.S., but it is illegal in many European countries. On the other hand, some countries have fewer restrictions on sexual content than the U.S., while others have more.

If we had one governing body that set rules for the entire Internet, we may be able to avoid such legal dilemmas and conflicts. In recent years, there has been a push to give the United Nations blanket authority over the Internet. But such a development is unlikely to occur given that there are nearly 200 countries that all have their own, often conflicting ideas of how to run the Internet. So, establishing global governance would require settling on shared standards and values, which may be impossible because of differing histories, social sensitivities and political realities. Think about it: would you want the U.N. or some other country to be in charge of the Internet if that meant you had to give up some of your rights as an American?

Internet Governance

The Internet has been referred to as the "Information Superhighway." Such a metaphor is useful in understanding how it's controlled. Just as governments establish driving laws on physical roads in the real world that prohibit activities such as speeding or drunk driving, so too can they create laws that regulate behavior in the virtual world.

Of course, before such laws can be made and enforced, actual roads need to be built. Civil engineers are responsible for deciding how to make these roads: things like where roads should be built, what type of material is used and where exits and on-ramps will be located. In the virtual world, several non-profit organizations — including the Internet Society, the Internet Architecture Board, the Internet Engineering Task Force and the World Wide Web Consortium — are tasked with developing the underlying architecture and protocols for the online world. They write the code that determines how people access the Internet, and how data and information is transmitted and shared.

Once a user is online, national governments may regulate how users in their country move about the Internet. Likewise, governments can also regulate content providers and telecommunications companies that do business with their citizens.

But no one country owns the Internet. Although the Internet was born in the U.S., it has now become a cross-border, international space. Content providers may have their physical offices in one country, conduct their business in another country, and store their content on servers in a third country. Whichever setup providers use for these purposes, their content can be readily accessible from anywhere in the world. Similarly, content may be transmitted through several nations on its way from a sender to a recipient. An e-mail sent from New York to New Zealand may pass through servers and networks in several countries before it reaches its destination. Content contained in that e-mail may be legal in one country but illegal in another. If a legal issue arises from the sending of that e-mail, which country should have jurisdiction? Invariably, disputes arise between countries over which country's laws should apply.

Internet Protocols

While each country makes rules for Internet use within its borders (and sometimes beyond, as you'll learn), the protocols — things like the code and architecture — for the Internet are essentially in no government's hands. As discussed in Chapter 1, the Internet grew out of the communications network survivability concerns of the U.S. Department of Defense during the Cold War era. As the Internet began its transition from a government defense tool to commercial resource, the U.S. government contracted the running of the

Internet first to the non-profit Internet Assigned Numbers Authority (IANA), and eventually to the Internet Corporation for Assigned Names and Numbers (ICANN), a nonprofit corporation formed by stakeholders of the Internet community that includes advisors from more than 100 countries.

ICANN currently handles various Internet protocols, including managing the system of domain names (web addresses) and maintaining the "root server" directory of domains. In simple terms: to reach another person on the Internet you have to give your computer a destination, usually entered as a name or number. That destination has to be unique, so computers know where to find each other. ICANN coordinates these unique identifiers across the world. Without that coordination we would not have one global Internet. Humans prefer to find desired web addresses and e-mail addresses by name (such as "whitehouse.gov" or "routledge.com") but computers know each other by numbers, or Internet Protocol (IP) addresses. ICANN manages the Domain Name System (DNS), often referred to as "the phone book of the Internet" because it matches domain names with appropriate IP address numbers. In short, ICANN is similar to a traffic cop directing traffic, but for the Internet. Until recently, the U.S. government had always controlled ICANN, because it essentially invented the Internet. But that changed in October 2016, when the U.S. agreed to relinquish sole oversight of Internet traffic. Now, the U.S. government equally shares governance of ICANN with foreign governments, tech companies and advocacy organizations.

The ICANN handover was controversial. For example, Senator Ted Cruz and then-presidential candidate Donald Trump preferred that the U.S. government maintain oversight of ICANN and took an "if it ain't broke, don't fix it" viewpoint. Some lawmakers even attempted, albeit unsuccessfully, to block the transfer through a lawsuit. Others supported ICANN's independence, but were concerned the transition plan was hasty and needed more fine-tuning. On the other hand, proponents insisted this power shift was necessary for various reasons. They argued that the Internet had become too American-centric. Since countries such as China and India have many more Internet users than the U.S., proponents reasoned it was no longer fair for one nation to control the world's communication tool. Moreover, the world no longer trusted the U.S. to oversee the Internet after the Edward Snowden surveillance scandal. There were also fears that some countries could form an alternate Internet rather than participate in our existing global and interconnected cyberspace.

There was more controversy in 2020 when ICANN proposed selling the ability to assign and control .org domain names to a private, for-profit entity, including fears of rising fees for .org domains and that a for-profit organization would have no commitment to the public interest. The sale was eventually rejected.

Governmental Regulation

While ICANN oversees the Internet's backbone — the domain-name system, IP address allocation and network protocol number assignments — individual governments still have a great deal of control over how the Internet operates in their individual countries. This means that each country can regulate which content its citizens can see and determine which content is illegal or censored in that nation.

Since the Internet became a global multi-communication medium in the 1990s, countries all over the world, including the U.S., have enacted laws aimed at regulating the segments of the Internet within their jurisdictions, or at least bringing those parts of the network within the ambit of their systems and legal jurisdictions. The result is a range of Internet regulatory models at the international and national levels that govern everything from Internet infrastructure to social networking sites like Facebook, Instagram and Twitter.

This multiplicity of regulatory approaches to the Internet essentially transforms cyberspace into a series of interconnected jurisdictions where each country attempts to apply its rules, regulations and culture to the networks and network traffic within its territorial jurisdiction. Internet law and regulation is further complicated because it arose at the same time that other media — information technology, telecommunications, print media, sound, still images and motion pictures — were converging, even though countries have traditionally regulated these media differently. This presented new questions about which media regulatory model should apply online.

Consequently, conflicts of laws invariably emerge. But, before we discuss those conflicts and how they're resolved, let's look at what regulations the international community agrees on.

International Regulations

Nations around the world have come to agreement on some elements of Internet regulation through a combination of international conventions, U.N. resolutions, declarations and plans of action. Areas of Internet content that are covered by international law include child pornography, data protection and intellectual property. Specifically:

Electronic Commerce: To help facilitate the global information economy we now live in, in which the flow of data is an essential component, a number of international agreements by members of the World Trade Organization have been made on issues including: the development and interconnection of satellites to facilitate such transfers; the elimination of tariffs on information technology products; the liberalization of telecommunications markets worldwide; and allowing the use of electronic signatures to facilitate e-commerce.

Child Pornography: Most countries have agreed to suppress child pornography on the Internet. As child pornography became prevalent on the Internet, the U.N. General Assembly adopted the Optional Protocol to the Convention on the Rights of the Child on the Sale of Children, Child Prostitution and Child Pornography. The U.N. called for worldwide criminalization of the production, distribution, exportation, transmission, importation, and intentional possession and advertising of child pornography. But it is up to individual countries to enact and enforce such laws, since there is no international body with the authority to prosecute such cases.

Intellectual Property: One of the most significant multilateral Internet agreements was carried out within the framework of the World Intellectual Property Organization (WIPO), an organization with a membership of 193 countries. When international disputes over issues such as whether copyright infringement has occurred, WIPO makes a determination based on internationally agreed standards of intellectual property protection on the Internet. The WIPO Copyright Treaty and the WIPO Performances and Phonograms Treaty of 1996 made international copyright law applicable to the Internet and laid the groundwork for a multilateral approach to the resolution of intellectual property disputes. One of the most important provisions of the treaty makes it a crime for hackers and cyber thieves to make illegal copies by circumventing digital anti-piracy measures that copyright holders embed in software programs, DVDs and other media that contains or is used to present copyrighted work.

Conflicts of Laws

Although international regulation has been established for a few elements of the Internet, there are no international agreements for many other areas. For example, in 2012, the U.N. organized a World Conference on International Telecommunications that sought to form consensus on how to regulate international phone calls made via the Internet. Eighty-nine nations agreed to a treaty, but the U.S. and 54 other countries refused.

There are many and varied reasons for these policy disagreements, including that different countries have differing ideas on Internet regulation; and that our existing remedies for resolving international conflicts of law, which are based primarily on physical locations, are inadequate for the Internet. With approximately 200 countries, there's no one-size-fits-all solution to these situations.

Models of Internet Regulation

Approaches to Internet regulation vary widely and include:

Self-Governance Model: The self-governance or self-regulation model insists that the Internet community is capable of regulating itself and that promulgation of domestic or international laws is both unnecessary and undesirable. In the early days of the Internet, this model initially flourished because the law invariably lags behind technology. Governments initially lacked an understanding of the workings of and an appreciation for the importance of the Internet, leaving Internet entrepreneurs and users to come up with their own norms and standards.

But this model is quickly becoming extinct worldwide. Lawmakers are starting to catch up with the times and most countries now regulate the Internet in some way, within the framework of their particular political, legal, moral and cultural values.

The Neo-Mercantilist Model: This model is based on the premise that the Internet is essentially a vehicle of commerce. The role of government, therefore, is to ensure the free flow of commerce online and to remove any impediments to such commerce. The American approach to Internet regulation generally falls in this category, based on the notion of a marketplace: of not only products and services, but also ideas. As such, except in the narrowest of circumstances, the government may not regulate speech on the basis of its content. These principles are the foundation of the U.S.'s neomercantilist Internet law regime.

This does not mean that the government has no involvement in the online world. The U.S. government has funded supercomputers and domestic networks and connectivity based on the premise that computer infrastructures were similar to the American interstate highway system, which provided the infrastructure for transportation and communication but allowed the free market to determine the flows of traffic on these systems.

In 1997, the Clinton Administration offered the world a framework for the expansion and regulation of electronic commerce that conceptualized the Internet as a global capitalist marketplace and appealed to governments to assume a minimalist regulatory posture toward e-commerce. The framework favored self-government, decentralization, public–private sector partnerships and the creation of international agreements as the values that should guide Internet regulation. It was aimed at creating a seamless global market economy with a fluid exchange of finance, goods, services and information. The plan essentially globalized America's libertarian principles: the marketplace of ideas, laissez-faire economics, free trade, and the free flow of information, goods and services.

The international Internet law regime promoted by the Clinton Administration led to the development of U.N. and WTO protocols that generally adhere to these principles.

The Culturalist Model: Many countries have the impression that their cultures are besieged by the globalization of American popular culture. Transformation of the Internet into an American-dominated commercial and multi-communication space, whose architecture closely mirrors America's socio-cultural and political logic, has prompted some countries to enact Internet laws that are designed to protect their national cultures.

France is an example of such a culturalist state. The French government has always defended what communication scholar Armand Mattelart calls "cultural sovereignty."[1] Under its ideology of *exception culturelle* (cultural exception), France does not want its culture subsumed within an undifferentiated "Western" culture. Since the 1970s, French law has classified the French language and the French media and telecommunications infrastructure as part of its cultural heritage that should be protected against Anglo-American domination.

This culturalist perspective has also been applied to the Internet. France views the Internet as a cultural rather than a commercial platform, and regulates it within its protectionist framework. In France, laws mandate that websites located in the country be in French and that Internet content accessible to French citizens on French territory abide by the country's laws on free speech. American companies such as Yahoo! have encountered legal problems for violating French Internet content laws. For example, in 2000 a French court held that sales of Nazi memorabilia on Yahoo!'s auction site violated French law, which bans such items.

In order to protect French national identity, language and culture on the Internet, new terminology spawned by technology is systematically replaced with French neologisms. For example, in 2003, the General Commission on Terminology and Neology officially approved replacement of the English word "e-mail" with the French equivalent, *courier éléctronique.*

Restricted: Some countries severely restrict Internet activities within their borders, either by having only a few data connections to the worldwide Internet, as in North Korea, or by blocking and censoring content that the government does not favor, as in China. In these nations, all Internet use, including e-mail, is monitored for subversive content. But there is often an elite of government officials and scholars who have broader access than most citizens.

Maintaining severe limitations on domestic Internet content and communications is increasingly difficult for nations such as China that are or seek to be involved in the system of global commerce. These governments face increasingly difficult challenges in maintaining internal restrictions while also fostering economic, academic and other international relationships. Another problem for these restrictive governments is the increasing availability and effectiveness of technologies that allow their citizens to bypass government controls.

Globalism: This model is based on multinational political, economic, technological and cultural cooperation in regulating the Internet, and it relies on treaties and international conventions to achieve that goal. There has been some progress in this direction, with the adoption of international rules regarding protection of intellectual property and prohibition of child pornography online. But there are still no international agreements resolving the multiple issues of Internet jurisdiction.

1 Mattelart, Armand, La Mondialisation de la Communication [Globalization of Communication] (3rd ed., 2002), 93.

While this is not an exhaustive list of the different models of Internet regulation, it illustrates a range of possible approaches. Given these differing models, conflicts between these philosophies and the countries that follow them invariably emerge.

Examples of Conflicting Laws

Ultimately, the disparate approaches towards Internet governance can be grouped into two camps: (1) a top-down approach where the government controls the Internet versus (2) a multi-stakeholder approach in which the private sector, civil society, academics, engineers and the government all have seats at the policymaking table.

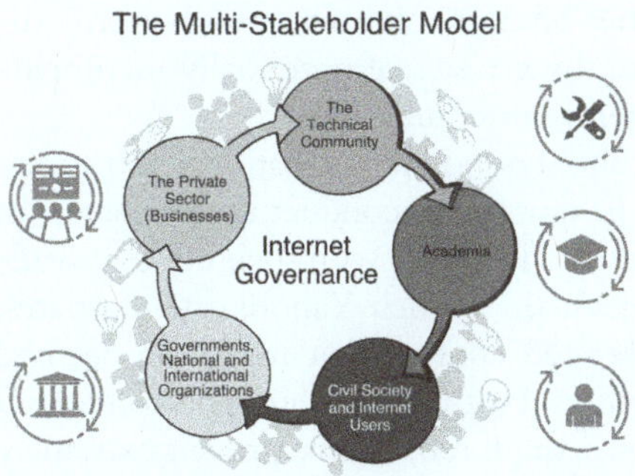

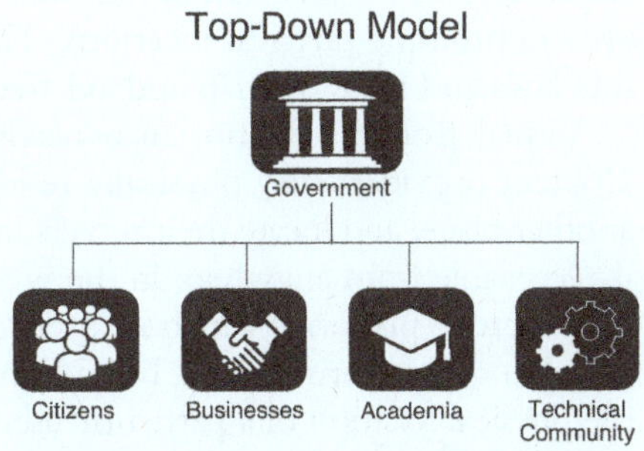

Both approaches have advantages and drawbacks. China and the U.S. provide a good contrast and comparison of these two approaches in practice. Both nations have a booming technology culture. Chinese companies such as Alibaba, Baidu and Tencent rival their American counterparts Amazon, Google and Facebook in terms of heft. But China has stringent limits on online content, while the U.S. favors giving its Internet users freedom of speech.

China's approach provides more security. China has been able to avoid controversies such as allegations regarding foreign interference in U.S. elections because its heavy-handed approach is effective in protecting against news of which the government does not approve, hacking and foreign meddling. Where Russia and other nations may have turned the Internet into a political weapon to use against rival countries, China has used it as a shield to guard against technology advancing quicker than the government can control it.

However, China's approach is incompatible with Western democratic ideals. China squelches online dissent and imprisons many of those who dare criticize the government. It blocks foreign news and information, including the websites of generally respected news sources such as *The New York Times*, and promotes homegrown technology companies that it can control while banning global services like Facebook and Twitter. Human rights observers frequently condemn China's Internet crackdown because it inhibits freedom of speech and thought.

Given these differences, it's easy to see how conflicts arise between the laws of various countries. Such conflicts are not uncommon in international law on a wide variety of subjects. But the Internet presents novel challenges for resolving them.

Why Existing Remedies are Inadequate

There's no disputing that a sovereign state may create and enforce laws concerning activities within its borders. In the physical world, it is relatively easy for courts to determine the geographical locations of the persons, objects and activities relevant to a particular case. Even international sea law, such as the U.N. Convention on the Law of the Sea, is based on territory. But the Internet is a cross-border space, and online activities often involve actors and intermediaries in multiple physical locations. Thus, diverse sets of potentially incompatible laws and rules overlap and are frequently in conflict.

Virtual frontiers do not map neatly into boundaries of national territories. Content providers may physically reside in one place, conduct their business in another place, and locate their servers in a third location, with their content readily accessible from anywhere in the world. As the French Yahoo! case illustrates, cross-border platforms can host user-generated content that might be deemed illegal in certain jurisdictions, but not in others. Furthermore, attempts to identify the physical location of a particular user over the Internet have proven extremely difficult, and many Internet users compound this problem by intentionally hiding their location. Traditional principles of international jurisdiction, particularly territoriality, are poorly suited for this sort of environment of geographic anonymity.

Courts around the world have struggled to develop a satisfactory solution, and no progress has been made toward a uniform global standard of Internet jurisdiction. This legal limbo has serious consequences. The economy suffers as businesses are less likely to invest and innovate due to legal uncertainties. Internet companies also waste valuable resources handling international legal disputes. And some users may find themselves facing legal claims abroad for activities that are legal in the users' country, while others must surf the web without any certainty that redress is available for harms they might suffer online. While U.S. courts routinely honor foreign court judgments as a matter of mutual respect among courts, a concept known as *comity*, there is an exception for defamation. Under the 2010 federal SPEECH Act, federal and state courts in the U.S. do not enforce foreign defamation judgments unless the U.S. court determines that the foreign court acted with due process and protects free speech similarly to the First Amendment.[2]

2 Barbour, Emily C., *The SPEECH Act: The Federal Response to "Libel Tourism,"* Congressional Research Service, Sept. 16, 2010, https://fas.org/sgp/crs/misc/R41417.pdf.

How to Resolve Conflicts of Law

Here are some common proposals for fixing the problem:

A Universal Regulatory Scheme: An international convention could lead to a treaty establishing substantive "universal standards" for what's legal and illegal. The treaty could also create an international body that would promulgate civil and criminal Internet regulations and jurisdictional rules. However, getting every nation around the world to agree on standards and then adopt them into their domestic legal codes seems daunting, if not impossible. Attempts to do this with outer space and the Moon haven't worked well: either few countries adopt the law or it's so vague as to be toothless. The creation of a global Internet law could also create new conflicts, between the common Internet law and individual nations' domestic laws.

A Global Standard for Determining Jurisdiction: A treaty could be signed by all nations that creates a single test for determining Internet jurisdiction. It could, for example, be an "effects" test. Under this principle, a nation may assert jurisdiction over conduct that has an effect in that nation, even if the conduct does not actually occur within its borders. For example, in 2001, Thailand prosecuted blog posts criticizing its king, even though the posts were written in the U.S., on the grounds that the impact — the "effect" — of the posts was in Thailand. As with the process of creating a global standard, reaching a consensus would be daunting.

Filtering and E-borders: Governments could regain control of their borders by placing blocking and tracking technologies at international access points or at the Internet service provider's (ISP's) servers to act as centurions. Many governments have already implemented such technologies to monitor and regulate Internet activities of their citizens. However, such filters can easily be circumvented and won't resolve issues such as determining which law applies in cases of defamation and copyright infringement. In addition, this could undermine the Internet's infrastructure and is antithetical to its founding purpose of being a tool to share information.

Choice of Law Provisions: Content providers and users could agree to resolve disputes in a particular forum by including choice of law provisions in Terms of Service contracts. But there would need to be an international consensus regarding the validity of such agreements. This seems unlikely given that it would limit governments' power and the European Union has been reluctant to allow such forum selection clauses. Also, there is the persistent issue of whether users are aware of such provisions, since most do not read the Terms of Service documents of the sites and services that they use.

Do Nothing: Not all of the issues of Internet regulation require solutions. We can allow the Internet community to regulate itself, as it originally did. But, of course, conflict will persist, and will often require litigation to be resolved.

Given that all of these proposals seem to have drawbacks, what is the solution? The best model for global Internet governance may be a hybrid that incorporates some elements from various models. Internet governance is a complex task requiring a complex set of regulatory mechanisms. As a result, the optimal system of governance may be a combination of regulation, with various stakeholders — government officials, tech companies and Internet users — involved in setting rules and making decisions. Admittedly, this solution may seem like a bit of a cop-out. But keep in mind, the reason for the deadlock concerning Internet jurisdiction is because each of the most common solutions has significant drawbacks. There is no silver bullet solution to this issue.

"Splinternet"

Clearly, it looks like the world won't reach any consensus on how to govern the Internet any time soon. Despite some goodwill gestures such as America's recent move to share oversight of ICANN with other nations, world powers have never been more divided over Internet governance.

Since the U.S. ceded control in 2016, ICANN has struggled to maintain its authority over the Internet. The EU has "started rejecting the organization's authority,"[3] while Brazilian officials told ICANN that only governments control the Internet. "ICANN lost 99% of its spine when the U.S. relinquished control over it. It now lost the remaining 1%," observed one industry analyst.[4] The EU is also asserting its power to force changes on how the Internet functions. Due to its perceived weakness, many critics now mockingly refer to ICANN as "ICANN'T."

ICANN could soon face a much greater existential threat. China, Russia and other nations remain concerned about possible external influence from the U.S. and Western nations. Consequently, the BRICS nations (Brazil, Russia, India, China and South Africa) announced in 2018 they plan to develop their own separate Internet. "We all know who the chief administrator of the global Internet is, and due to its volatility, we have to think about how to ensure our national security," stated the press secretary to Russian leader Vladimir Putin.[5]

Consequently, smaller nations could face a choice: join the BRICS Internet, which will be highly censored, or participate in the West's Internet, which enjoys great freedom of expression, but its content is primarily in English and caters to users located thousands of miles away. "The great risk is that digital

3 McCarthy, Kieren, *As GDPR Draws Close, ICANN Suggests 12 Conflicting Ways to Cure Domain Privacy Pains*, The Register, Feb. 9, 2018, https://www.theregister.co.uk/2018/02/09/icann_whois_gdpr.

4 Develegas, Theo, Comment to Andrew Allemann, I Just Fixed Whois and GDPR, Domain Name Wire, Apr. 13, 2018, 2:03 p.m., https://domainnamewire.com/2018/04/13/i-just-fixed-whois-and-gdpr/#comment-2249232.

5 Staedter, Tracy, *Why Russia Is Building its Own Internet*, IEEE Spectrum, Jan. 17, 2018, https://spectrum.ieee.org/tech-talk/telecom/internet/could-russia-really-build-its-own-alternate-internet

nationalism will balkanize the Internet, breaking it up into a patchwork of incompatible and irreconcilable fiefs," warns Akash Kapur, a senior fellow at the GovLab at New York University. "The prospect of a technical 'Splinternet' is no longer as inconceivable as it once was. In the decades ahead, we may look back wistfully to a time when data could move freely across the globe, without virtual customs or immigration checkpoints."[6]

CLOSING ARGUMENTS

At its best, the Internet is a global communication tool that allows people from around the world to share ideas, learn new things and crowdsource that knowledge to innovate. But the Internet is increasingly becoming balkanized. Is it possible to have a truly global Internet where everyone plays by the same rules? Or are we destined for a divided Information Superhighway? Who's at fault? Is the movement away from universal access online a good or bad thing?

Additional Sources

Bego, Katja, *The 'Splinternet' Is Coming: Why Countries Will Break Away from Today's Internet*, Qrius, Mar. 17, 2018, https://qrius.com/the-splInternet-is-coming-why-countries-will-break-away-from-todays-Internet.

Burnstein, Matthew, *Conflicts on the Net: Choice of Law in Transnational Cyberspace*, 29 Vanderbilt Journal of Transnational Law 75 (1996).

Eko, Lyombe S., *American Exceptionalism, the French Exception, and Digital Media Law* (reprint ed. 2017).

Gilbert, Ben, *Bernie Sanders Has a $150 Billion Plan to Turn the Internet into a Public Utility With Low Prices and Fast Speeds — Here's How His Plan Works*, Business Insider, Jan 22, 2020, https://www.businessinsider.com/bernie-sanders-internet-as-utility-plan-explainer-2019-12.

Grabowski, Mark, *Should the U.S. Reclaim Control of the Internet? Evaluating ICANN's Administrative Oversight Since the 2016 Handover*, Neb. L. Rev. Bull., Aug. 6, 2018, https://lawreview.unl.edu/Should-the-U.S.-Reclaim-Control-of-the-Internet%3F.

ICANN, *Frequently Asked Questions About the Transition*, Mar. 14, 2014, https://www.icann.org/en/system/files/files/functions-transfer-faqs-14mar14-en.pdf.

Keneally, Meghan, *Here's What the Internet Looks Like in North Korea*, ABC News, Dec. 23, 2014, https://abcnews.go.com/International/internet-north-korea/story?id=27789459.

McCarthy, Kieren, *Dot-Amazon Spat Latest: Brazil Tells ICANN to Go Fsck Itself, Only 'Govts Control the Internet'*, The Register, Sept. 27, 2017, https://www.theregister.co.uk/2017/09/27/brazil_dot_amazon_gtld.

6 Kapur, Akash, *The Rising Threat of Digital Nationalism*, Wall Street Journal, Nov. 1, 2009, https://www.wsj.com/articles/the-rising-threat-of-digital-nationalism-11572620577.

McCarthy, Kieren, *Whois? Whowas. So What's Next for ICANN and Its Vast Database of Domain-Name Owners*?, The Register, June 1, 2018, https://www.theregister.co.uk/2018/06/01/whats_next_for_.

Meehan, Kevin A., *The Continuing Conundrum of International Internet Jurisdiction*, 31 Boston College International and Comparative Law Review 345 (2008), http://lawdigitalcommons.bc.edu/iclr/vol31/iss2/8.

Peter, Peter et al., *Workshop 85: The Transboundary Internet: Jurisdiction, Control and Sovereignty* (video panel), Internet Governance Forum, Apr. 19, 2013, https://www.youtube.com/watch?v=utbG6znsO5c.

Reidenberg, Joel R., *Technology and Internet Jurisdiction*, 153 University of Pennsylvania Law Review 1951 (2005), https://papers.ssrn.com/sol3/papers.cfm?abstract_id=691501.

Solum, Lawrence B., *Models of Internet Governance*, in Internet Governance: Infrastructure and Institutions (L. Bygrave et al. eds., 2009), http://ssrn.com/abstract=1136825.

Stoltz, Mitch, *ICANN Needs to Ask More Questions About the Sale of* .ORG., Electronic Freedom Foundation, Jan. 17, 2020, https://www.eff.org/deeplinks/2020/01/icann-needs-ask-more-questions-about-sale-org.

Svantesson, Dan Jerker B., I*nternet & Jurisdiction Global Status Reporter*, Internet & Jurisdiction Policy Network, 2019, https://www.internetjurisdiction.net/uploads/pdfs/GSR2019/Internet-Jurisdiction-Global-Status-Report-2019_web.pdf.

Weise, Elizabeth, *U.S. Set to Hand Over Internet Address Book*, USA Today, Sept. 29, 2016, https://www.usatoday.com/story/tech/news/2016/09/29/icann-iana-internet-address-book-autonomous-department-of-commerce-ip-address-transition-internet-corporation-for-assigned-names-and-numbers/91281960.

Wyatt, Edward, *U.S. to Cede its Oversight of Addresses on the Internet*, The New York Times, Mar. 14, 2014, https://www.nytimes.com/2014/03/15/technology/us-to-give-up-role-in-internet-domain-names.html.

3 How Are Internet Regulations Made?

> Although we must not be overly optimistic about our freedom and our capacity for resisting infatuation with new technology, we must recognize that we do still have some degree of freedom in this world.
>
> — Professor Richard Spinello

While some question whether it is possible to regulate the Internet at all, the reality is that substantial regulations already exist in one form or another.

Laws — including constitutions, treaties, statutes and rules, as well as court rulings interpreting and applying them — are the most obvious form of regulation. As various nations and international organizations attempt to grapple with issues raised by the use of the Internet, they impose laws that are usually enforced through sanctions against violators. Such regulations govern areas like privacy, speech and fraud. But online behavior can be constrained in other ways, too.

In his highly influential book, *Codes and Other Laws of Cyberspace*, Harvard Law professor Lawrence Lessig argues that — in addition to law — architecture, norms and markets serve to regulate cyberspace.[1]

Architecture refers to how data can and cannot be transmitted across cyberspace. Users are physically and digitally restricted to the code the Internet and its applications are built on and can only work within its limits. Behavior can be limited by everything from filtering software, to passwords, to encryption programs, and even the very basic structure of Internet transmission protocols. In many ways, architecture is the most fundamental form of Internet regulation, and all users must relate to or rely upon it since it is, literally, how the Internet functions.

Norms refer to the generally accepted morals and ethics of a community. Most communities have a well-defined sense of acceptable behavior, based on custom, prevalent attitudes, public opinion and myriad other factors. Just as social norms govern what is acceptable behavior in the real world, norms also

1 Lessig, Lawrence, Code and Other Laws of Cyberspace (1999).

affect behavior online. When laws fail to regulate certain activities allowed by the architecture of the Internet, social norms may allow users to control such conduct. For example, posting racial epitaphs on social media isn't illegal in the United States, but it would likely result in criticism, content moderation and ostracism from many Americans. And platforms may decide, based on social norms, to restrict such posts. When a user is fired from work for an offensive tweet, that's a form of norm regulation. Like laws, such regulations may be perceived as just or unjust.

The final regulative force is market regulation. Patterns of conduct online may be governed by the traditional economic principle of supply and demand. If something is unpopular, it will lack demand and fail. But, if there is too much supply, businesses must find ways to differentiate themselves or they'll struggle to survive the competition. This helps to prevent predatory practices, fuel innovation, and forces businesses to self-regulate to keep customers and remain successful.

While all Internet users are constrained by market forces and code, laws and norms vary considerably across cyberspace. For example, citizens in China, Syria and Iran face blatant government censorship online whereas Americans enjoy a great deal of freedom of expression. Since the Internet is not geographically bound, national laws can not apply globally. Similarly, norms can also be quite different from culture to culture. And both have undergone transformation over time as the Internet continues to evolve. As this is a textbook focused on American cyber law and ethics, let's take a closer look at the laws and norms in the U.S.

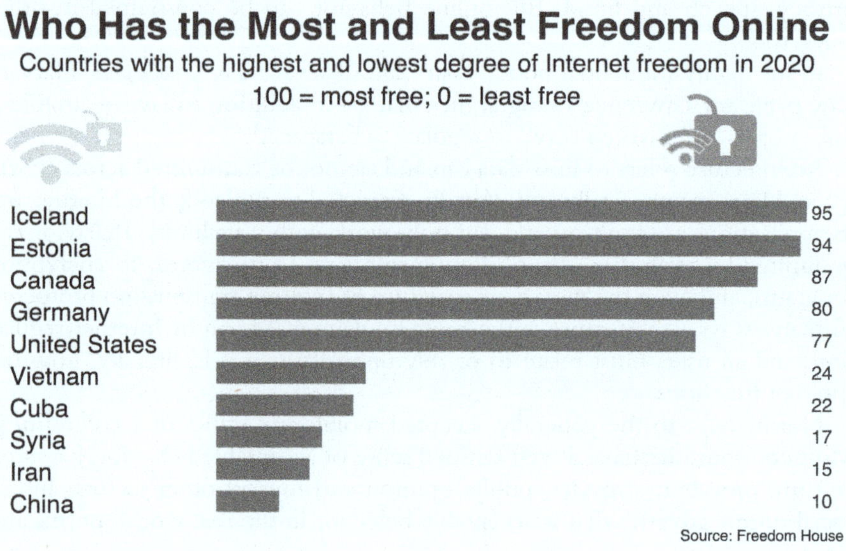

Cyber Lawmaking in America

In the U.S., Internet law, or cyber law as it is sometimes called, is arguably less a distinct field of law than a conglomeration of intellectual property law, contract law, privacy laws and many other fields, and how they pertain to the use of the Internet. In some cases, laws that apply to real space have been applied to cyberspace. In other cases, the ethereal nature of the medium has created novel issues requiring a unique set of laws. Laws come from five different sources: constitutional, statutory, administrative, executive and judicial.

All five types of law are distributed among federal, state and local governments. The federal government has exclusive control over some areas of law and covers many areas of law that affect multiple states. State governments, meanwhile, have broad control over law that applies within each state's boundaries, including most of the laws that we deal with on a daily basis, like criminal laws and traffic laws. Local governments have control over local issues, such as zoning and parking regulations. There is also a hierarchy of control, with federal law being the most important: no state law can conflict with a federal law. Similarly, a local law cannot conflict with state or federal law.

Constitutional law refers to the law that comes directly from the language of the U.S. Constitution and its amendments and the constitutions of the states. A variety of constitutional provisions apply to the Internet, including the First Amendment of the U.S. Constitution, which protects speech both online and offline. Every U.S. state also has its own constitution, which sometimes comes into play in Internet regulation.

Statutory law refers to laws made by the elected governmental bodies such as the U.S. Congress, state legislatures and community legislative bodies such as county commissions and city councils. The federal government has broad powers to regulate interstate commerce, so, congressional action can affect intellectual property rights, such as copyright. Congress also can make nationwide laws on how to regulate communications, including Internet service providers (ISPs) such as Comcast, Verizon and AT&T. And Congress establishes rules for competition between companies, including online advertising practices.

But the powers of Congress and the federal government generally are limited to national issues involving national concerns. State legislatures and state governments have broad powers to adopt laws and regulations in their states, as long as they do not interfere or conflict with the laws and regulations of the other states, or with federal laws or regulations, the U.S. constitution, or an international treaty that the U.S. has agreed to. States, for example, can enact laws regarding defamation and privacy, both online and offline, while the federal government cannot because it does not significantly involve interstate commerce. States can also impose sales taxes, including on e-commerce transactions, and other laws on a wide variety of subjects that can affect the Internet. City and county governments can pass local laws — often referred to as ordinances — that are limited in scope and regulate things such as where ISPs can construct and install Internet infrastructure such as cell towers.

One simplified explanation on the difference between constitutional law and statutory law is to say that constitutional law deals with large and abstract issues based in interpreting and applying the language of the constitution, while statutory laws are adopted to deal with matters that are more specific and concrete.

Administrative law refers to rules and regulations made by government agencies. These agencies are usually created by the legislative branch to focus on a particular issue, but after their creation the agencies are run by the executive branch of the federal, state or local government. After a legislative body passes a new statute, it's often up to a new or existing administrative agency to work out the details of how the law will be enforced. For example, if Congress were to pass a law requiring that new computers be manufactured with environmentally friendly parts, it would likely designate the Environmental Protection Agency to determine which materials are environmentally friendly and which are not. Thus, the agency would affect policy. At the federal level, agencies that have responsibilities in Internet law include the Federal Communications Commission (which oversees regulation of ISPs), the Federal Trade Commission (online advertising and marketing), the Federal Elections Commission (online political advertising), the U.S. Patent and Trademark Office (intellectual property) and the Department of Justice (investigates and prosecutes cybercrimes). State agencies, such as state public service commissions that oversee telecommunications services (known as common carriers) in their states, also may have responsibilities in Internet law.

Executive actions are those taken by government chief executives, such as the U.S. president, state governors, city mayors or county managers, and their assistants. Such actions usually have little direct effect on Internet law. For example, there are not many things that the president can do without congressional approval that would have a direct effect on the Internet: except, perhaps, in a grave national emergency such as a nuclear war. The president can set some policies by issuing executive orders, and in recent years presidents have issued presidential "signing statements" when approving legislation passed by Congress in order to explain the executive branch's understanding of the legislation and how it should be implemented. The president has an indirect effect on Internet law, however, through appointments of judges to federal courts (including the Supreme Court) and appointments to (and sometimes pressure on) administrative bodies, such as the FCC and FTC, that create and enforce administrative rules and regulations.

The judiciary — judges and the courts — can affect Internet law in many ways. Sometimes when Congress passes a new law it is challenged in court by individuals or organizations. A judge then decides whether the law is allowed or not allowed under the federal or state constitution. If the law is not allowed, it is "unconstitutional" and cannot be put into effect. Judges can also invalidate a law or regulation if it was not adopted properly in accordance with proper procedures.

For example, in the 1997 case *Reno v. American Civil Liberties Union*, the U.S. Supreme Court held that certain portions of the federal Communications Decency Act of 1996 that had been passed by Congress and signed by President Bill Clinton violated the U.S. Constitution because they placed restrictions on speech that is protected by the First Amendment. Since these provisions restricted too much protected speech, they were held by the court to be "overbroad."[2] Specifically, the court concluded that in trying to prevent minors from viewing certain sexual content via the Internet, the legislation interfered with adults' access to the content as well. This ruling also for the first time established that the First Amendment applies to speech on the Internet. Thus, the *Reno* decision is a "landmark" case, in which the U.S. Supreme Court set a precedent that is binding on future cases.

Because the U.S. Supreme Court is the highest court in the country, all state and federal courts are required to follow this precedent. As a result, any case trying to apply the provisions that were held unconstitutional — including cases brought by the government — must usually be dismissed. Oftentimes, statutes and regulations that are held invalid by a court are not formally repealed by the body that enacted them, even though the invalidated provision cannot legally be enforced. As a result, finding a statute "on the books" may not be the final declaration of the current law: additional research of the court cases regarding that provision is required.

Courts make these determinations by resolving cases that are brought before them. Sometimes, as in *Reno v. ACLU*, an individual, a group of individuals or an organization files a lawsuit against the federal, state or local government, alleging that a statute or administrative rule violates the individuals' or organizations' rights under the constitution. In other cases, people or organizations sue another party who they believe has violated their rights or harmed them. Such violations are referred to as torts. For example, people frequently sue bloggers for defamation when they believe they have published lies that hurt their reputation. Other cases involve individuals and organizations seeking to resolve legal disputes, such as contract disputes. These types of cases are known as civil cases, and they can result in having to pay money damages to the harmed party, and perhaps a court order restricting future behavior.

Criminal cases involve prosecution by the government of a person for an act that has been classified as a crime. In these cases, a local, state or federal prosecutor initiates the suit, often based on a police investigation and arrest. Persons convicted of a crime may be incarcerated, fined, or both. There are a number of crimes that can take place online, such as a federal law that bars hacking into computer systems without authorization.

2 *Reno v. American Civil Liberties Union*, 521 U.S. 844 (1997).

Both civil and criminal cases are resolved through the courts, which have adopted rules regarding various aspects of cases, including which court has power to hear a particular case ("jurisdiction"), what evidence can be presented and what procedure must be followed. A judge presides over each case and is responsible for shepherding the case to resolution while enforcing the applicable rules and laws. Many cases are dismissed early on, either because the legal claims are insufficient or because they are not supported by adequate evidence. In the end, for cases that survive early dismissal, the court holds a trial that results in a verdict; this verdict may be made by a judge alone or by a jury, depending on the type of case. (Criminal cases are more likely to have juries.) The verdict usually resolves a question of fact: for example, whether the defendant in a libel case actually published a statement or not. Judges may also make rulings regarding questions of law, such as whether someone suing for defamation (known as the plaintiff) has a claim that meets the basic legal requirements to have a case. Judges' rulings may be used as guidance by later courts, but only a decision by an appellate court is a precedent that is binding on all courts underneath that appeals court. All courts in the U.S. are bound by decisions of the U.S. Supreme Court.

Once a verdict is made, the losing party can usually appeal. Parties may also appeal rulings made by the trial judge in the course of the proceeding, including early dismissal of the case. While trials consist of evidence and witnesses in addition to lawyers' arguments, in appeals courts there are only oral and written arguments on points of law by the lawyers, who also answer questions from the judges in a proceeding known as "oral argument."

Every state has its own system of courts for appeals, ultimately ending in a highest court for the state. This court is usually called the state's Supreme Court. But some states give it different names: in New York State, for example, the highest court is the New York State Court of Appeals, while the New York State Supreme Court is the basic trial-level court.

In the federal courts, trial verdicts can be appealed to one of the 13 circuit courts of appeal, all but one of which are established for geographic regions of the country. Appeals of decisions by state supreme courts that involve a federal or U.S. constitutional issue or the decisions by the federal circuit courts may be brought to the U.S. Supreme Court. But that court gets to decide for itself which cases it will consider, a process known as granting or denying a petition for *certiorari*. In a typical year, more than 10,000 cases are appealed to the Court, but *certiorari* is granted and arguments are heard in fewer than 100.[3] The Supreme Court is more likely to accept cases if they involve important

3 FindLaw, *How Does the U.S. Supreme Court Decide Whether to Hear a Case?*, June 20, 2016, https://litigation.findlaw.com/legal-system/how-does-the-u-s-supreme-court-decide-whether-to-hear-a-case.html.

contemporary issues or issues on which lower courts have differed in their legal conclusions.

Geographic Boundaries

of United States Courts of Appeals and United Sates District Courts

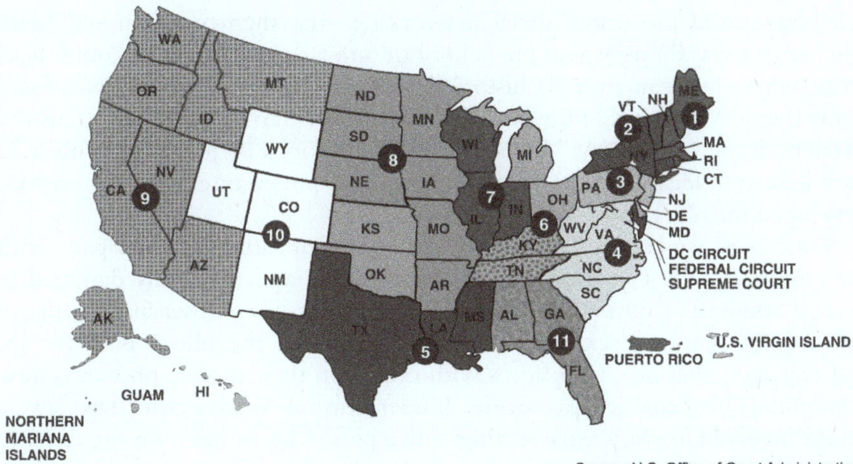

Source: U.S. Office of Court Administration

Whenever a judge — or, at appeals courts, a panel of judges — makes a ruling, either in the course of a case or as a final result, these court rulings are sometimes referred to as case law or "judge-made law." Such rulings by appeals courts are binding in future cases in lower courts within the appellate court's geographic area.

Internet law can be litigated in both civil and criminal cases, and at the federal, state and local levels. In certain categories of cyber law, the responsibility is shared.

Challenges to Internet Lawmaking

Developing Internet policies faces many challenges. Because technology is ever-evolving, cyber law is invariably playing catch up. Many judges lack the technological expertise necessary to make decisions on policies involving computers and the Internet. And most citizens lack a basic understanding of the law. Let's take a closer look at these obstacles.

Novel Issues

One major problem with trying to regulate the Internet is that the law invariably lags behind technology. A substantial amount of communications activity now occurs in environments that were not envisioned when our laws on privacy, defamation, obscenity and other areas were established. As a result, the legal principles governing conduct in cyberspace — including application of First Amendment principles to new forms of communication online — are still in a state of flux.

For instance, America's privacy laws haven't been substantially updated since 1986. Back then, there was no World Wide Web, nobody carried a cell phone, and the only "social networking" the then-two-year-old Mark Zuckerberg was doing was at pre-school or on playdates. Unlike in other legal areas, where we can turn to historical traditions to help settle disputes and guide the development of the law, the law of the Internet often has no history to fall back on. "Cyber law" is instead being developed by judges who must do their best to fit legal disputes on the Internet into preexisting legal frameworks, developed for older forms of technology.

Some of these laws are in desperate need of updating to keep pace with the Digital Age. For example, child pornography laws, originally designed to protect children against adult predators, also criminalize consensual sharing of sexual photographs ("sexting") when the person in the photo is under 18. But teenagers sharing such photos with others on their mobile phones is now common. The penalties are severe. Under current Washington state law, a minor involved in consensual sexting with a person his or her own age can face felony charges, which can result in up to five years in prison and mandatory sex offender registration. There have been several cases in which teens have been prosecuted under these laws. On the flip side, some states have slowly started easing penalties on such activities between teens, such as not requiring offenders who "sext" with a peer to register as sex offenders.

Another area in which states have been slow to adopt new laws is cell phone use while driving. While 48 states have laws banning texting while driving — Missouri only bans it for drivers aged 21 and under, and Montana has no law on the issue — less than half of all states have laws banning all cell phone use while driving.[4]

Lack of Expertise

Lawmakers, regulators and judges around the world are creating Internet law right now, a process that is both exciting and frightening to watch. Many of them lack the technological expertise necessary to craft laws related to the Internet. In particular, justices of the U.S. Supreme Court have come under fire for being averse to and unknowledgeable about the basic workings and culture surrounding new technology. Despite being viewed as some of the brightest and most accomplished people in the legal field, they have publicly admitted to being resistant to using technology in their own professional and

4 National Conference of State Legislatures, *Cellular Phone Use and Texting While Driving Laws* (current as of Oct. 5, 2020), https://www.ncsl.org/research/transportation/cellular-phone-use-and-texting-while-driving-laws.aspx.

personal lives, and have been ridiculed as woefully out of touch with the basic workings of technology that has been in common use for a decade or more.

With an average age of more than 60 years, no one expects the justices to be regular users of technology developed largely for the young, such as TikTok or Instagram. However, the perception that the members of the Supreme Court simply do not understand the basic workings or culture surrounding the use of technology has many observers worried about whether the highest court in the land is unprepared or unwilling to make truly informed rulings on today's pressing constitutional issues that are impacted by technology.

Consider some of these examples in recent years:

- During an oral argument in a case applying intellectual property law online, Chief Justice John Roberts, who reportedly drafts his opinions with pen and paper instead of a keyboard, said he doubted that anyone, other than drug dealers, carries more than one cell phone.[5]
- During oral argument of a case interpreting the privacy protections of the Fourth Amendment, Justice Anthony Kennedy (who retired in 2018) wondered what would happen if a text message were sent to someone at the same time he was communicating with someone else. "[Does] he ha[ve] a voicemail saying that 'Your call is very important to us; we'll get back to you'?" Kennedy asked, eliciting laughter from those in attendance.[6]
- In a candid interview, Justice Elena Kagan admitted she and her fellow Supreme Court justices aren't very tech-savvy and still communicate with each other with paper memos, the same way they did when she was a clerk at the court in 1987.[7]

The justices' tech-cluelessness is not just an irrelevant oops, but actually incredibly important in its decisions in cases involving technology. And it is part of the basis of the criticism that the Supreme Court is out of touch with ordinary people.

Of course, it is far better that justices ask dumb questions than just form an opinion without the answers. No one is an expert in everything. Most Americans would undoubtedly seem equally foolish if questioned about a constitutional law issue such as the Commerce Clause. However, technology touches virtually every aspect of our modern lives and is certainly affected by the law. The Supreme Court justices' lack of tech familiarity has legal scholars concerned and has the potential to be harmful to everyday citizens. With the president attempting to regulate social media, cyberbullying testing the limits

5 Transcript of Oral Argument at 34, *Bilski v. Kappos*, 561 U.S.593 (2010) (No. 08-964), https://www.supremecourt.gov/oral_arguments/argument_transcripts/2009/08-964.pdf.

6 Transcript of Oral Argument at 44, *City of Ontario v. Quon*, 560 U.S.746 (2010) (No. 08-1332), https://www.supremecourt.gov/oral_arguments/argument_transcripts/2009/08-1332.pdf.

7 Associated Press, *Elena Kagan: Supreme Court Hasn't "Gotten To" Email*, CBS News, Aug. 21, 2013, https://www.cbsnews.com/news/elena-kagan-supreme-court-hasnt-gotten-to-email/.

of free speech in schools, and bloggers seeking the same rights as journalists, the Supreme Court will invariably be called upon to make judgments that will help shape technology going forward.

It's crucial for our most important decision-makers to have at least a rudimentary understanding of technologies most Americans can't imagine living without. If the Court can't grasp how business inventions have changed since the Industrial Revolution, or how communication methods have changed since Alexander Graham Bell's time, then they might make decisions that misapply the law due to a misunderstanding of the facts about technology and hinder the development and growth of our increasing tech-based economy. If they do not understand that social media sites like Facebook make money primarily by selling advertising based on the demographic and other information that it collects from its users, they may not appreciate the privacy issues at stake. Or they might simply avoid hearing important cases on technology entirely.

Because the Supreme Court justices decide which cases to hear, unlike lower courts, cases involving technological issues may face the worst odds of being addressed by the current court. If the justices cannot appreciate why a particular case is important, they are even more unlikely to hear a case. Consequently, despite the fact that the legal questions such cases raise may be the most pressing given their novelty and the lack of precedents, these questions may remain unanswered.

In order to modernize the Supreme Court, a variety of measures could be taken. One idea is that future appointees should be vetted for their tech-savvy, but this may be impractical — if not pointless — given the rapid rate of technological change. Another proposal is to impose a mandatory retirement age on Supreme Court justices instead of allowing them to enjoy lifetime appointments. Or the U.S. could form a special court to address cases involving complicated technological matters. This has already been implemented in a limited way through the creation in 1982 of the U.S. Court of Appeals for the Federal Circuit, which handles appeals in patent, customs and claims against the federal government. Japan has gone further, establishing an Intellectual Property High Court in 2005 to deal with patent and intellectual property cases. An additional proposal comes from former federal judge Richard Posner, who suggested that the Supreme Court hire impartial experts agreed upon by both parties to advise the justices about the technology in complicated cases.

In the meantime, current Court members need to take the initiative to change themselves. While technology has forced workers in many industries to adapt or retire, justices can't be required to change since they enjoy lifelong tenure. Fortunately, many rely heavily on their law clerks to do everything from research to write their opinions. Clerks tend to be tech literate 20- and 30-somethings fresh out of law school, which may explain why the justices' bloopers occur in the off-the-cuff environment of oral arguments rather than in written opinions. But, ultimately, technology is best learned through hands-on usage, not from reading a legal memo.

In the absence of clear guidance from the Supreme Court and Congress, technology companies and their lawyers are essential in creating and establishing norms and rules for cyberspace. But should Mark Zuckerberg and his lawyers be kings of the virtual world?

Perhaps the Supreme Court justices can follow the lead of Justice Stephen Breyer, who said he learned about Twitter by sitting down with his son for a lesson. "Remember when we had that disturbance in Iran?" Breyer said at the congressional subcommittee meeting. "My son said, 'Go look at this.' And oh, my goodness. I mean, there were some Twitters, I called them, there were people there with photographs as it went on. And I sat there for two hours absolutely hypnotized. And I thought, 'My goodness, this is now, for better or for worse ... not the same world.' It's instant and people react instantly." Breyer, obviously, has some catching up to do on the Digital Age. But it's a start. And it's better than being complacent with being clueless. As Breyer noted about the Internet, "It's not something that's going to go away."[8]

The Supreme Court took a modest but historic step forward in 2020 when they held their first-ever oral arguments via a teleconference amidst a federal government lockdown during the COVID-19 pandemic.[9]

Uninformed Citizenry

As bad as Supreme Court justices' tech knowledge is, the average citizen's civics knowledge may be worse. The past few years have seen contention between Congress and the president over issues such as network neutrality, contested confirmation hearings for multiple Supreme Court justices, and impeachment proceedings related to whether Russia hacked the 2016 election. Despite all of this, Americans don't seem to know much about how their government functions, studies reveal. Consider that:

8 Fabian, Jordan, *Chairman to Justices: "Have Either of Y'all Ever Considered Tweeting or Twitting?,"* Hillicon Valley: The Hill's Tech. Blog, May 21, 2010, http://thehill.com/blogs/hillicon-valley /technology /99209-chairmanto-justices-have-either-of-yall-ever-considering-tweeting-or-twitting-.

9 Barnes, Robert, *Supreme Court Takes Modest But Historic Step with Teleconference Hearings,* Washington Post, May 4, 2020, https://www.washingtonpost.com/politics/courts_law/supreme-court-teleconference-hearings-bookingcom/2020/05/03/f5902bd6-8d76-11ea-a9c0-73b93422d691_story .html.

- 61% of Americans were unable to name all three branches of government and 22% could not name any.[10]
- 90% of likely voters agreed with the statement, "decisions made by the U.S. Supreme Court have an impact on my everyday life as a citizen," yet 57% couldn't name a single justice of the court.[11]
- Almost a tenth of college graduates thought Judith Sheindlin — better known as TV's "Judge Judy" — was a member of the Supreme Court.[12]
- 70% of Americans didn't know the Constitution is the supreme law of the land.[13]
- When it came to the First Amendment, 37% could not name any rights and only 1% could name all five rights.[14]
- Meanwhile, 12% of Americans thought that the Bill of Rights included the right to own a pet.[15]

Such findings might be humorous if not for the profound consequences that come with a public that is unfamiliar with its government and laws. Kathleen Hall Jamieson, director of the Annenberg Public Policy Center, called the lack of civics knowledge "dismal … The resilience of our system of government is best protected by an informed citizenry."[16] Lack of knowledge and interest in government can lead to an unscrutinized government abusing its power and violating the rights of its citizens.

Cyber Ethics

Perhaps it's understandable that Americans take their freedom for granted. Thanks to the U.S. Constitution and a vibrant marketplace, Americans can make a range of choices, both large and small, in their daily lives online

10 Rozansky, Michael, *Americans' Civics Knowledge Increases But Still Has a Long Way to Go*, Annenberg Public Policy Center, Sept. 12, 2019, https://www.annenbergpublicpolicycenter.org/americans-civics-knowledge-increases-2019-survey/.

11 Green, Robert and Rosenblatt, Adam, *Supreme Court Survey*, C-SPAN, 2017, https://static.c-span.org/assets/documents/scotusSurvey/CSPAN%20PSB%20Supreme%20Court%20Survey%20COMPREHENSIVE%20AGENDA%20sent%2003%2013%2017.pdf.

12 Gonch, William, *A Crisis in Civic Education,* American Council of Trustees and Alumni, Jan. 2016, https://www.goacta.org/wp-content/uploads/ee/download/A_Crisis_in_Civic_Education.pdf.

13 Shaw, Matthew, *Civic Illiteracy in America*, Harvard Political Review, May 25, 2017, https://harvardpolitics.com/culture/civic-illiteracy-in-america/.

14 Rozansky, Michael, *Americans Are Poorly Informed about Basic Constitutional Provisions*, Annenberg Public Policy Center, Sept. 12, 2017, https://www.annenbergpublicpolicycenter.org/americans-are-poorly-informed-about-basic-constitutional-provisions/.

15 Annenberg Public Policy Center, *Is There a Constitutional Right To Own a Home or a Pet?*, Sept. 16, 2015, https://www.annenbergpublicpolicycenter.org/is-there-a-constitutional-right-to-own-a-home-or-a-pet/.

16 Rozansky, *supra* note 10.

— unlike netizens living in most other countries. But why do Americans subscribe to certain news sites or block their children from viewing certain movies on Netflix? Why do they like certain controversial tweets but report others? Why do they donate to this online fundraiser or share that petition? That's where norms and ethics come into play.

AMERICANS' VIEWS ON INTERNET ETHICS:

- 83% believe the Internet should be considered a basic human right.[17]
- 74% say it's never OK to make oneself look younger on a dating profile,[18] but 64% admit they have manipulated a photo they posted online.[19]
- Only 16% said they were always honest when posting information about themselves online.[20]
- While nearly 80% consider shoplifting a "very serious offense," only 40% agreed that downloading copyrighted movies on the Internet without paying for them was wrong.[21]
- Only 43% of Americans say pornography is morally acceptable.[22] Yet, pornography is by far the most popular type of content online in the U.S.; 87% of men and 29% of women watch porn at least weekly.[23] Porn sites collectively get more visitors each month than Netflix, Amazon and Twitter combined.[24]

17 Hamilton, Valerie, *Survey: Internet Access a 'Basic Human Right'*, Government Technology, Nov. 25, 2014, https://www.govtech.com/network/Survey-Internet-Access-a-Basic-Human-Right.html.

18 Graham, Jennifer, *Americans Are Increasingly Comfortable with Many White Lies, New Poll Reveals*, Deseret News, Mar. 27, 2018, https://www.deseret.com/2018/3/28/20642361/americans-are-increasingly-comfortable-with-many-white-lies-new-poll-reveals.

19 Spector, Nicole, *So It's Fine if You Edit Your Selfies... But Not if Other People Edit Theirs?*, NBC News, May 30, 2017, https://www.nbcnews.com/business/consumer/so-it-s-fine-if-you-edit-your-selfies-not-n766186.

20 Drouin, Michelle et al., *Why Do People Lie Online? "Because Everyone Lies On The Internet"*, 64 Computers in Human Behavior (Nov. 2016), 134–142, https://doi.org/10.1016/j.chb.2016.06.052.

21 Vlessing, Etan, *Poll: Americans Think Downloading No Big Deal*, NBC News, Jan. 26, 2007, http://www.nbcnews.com/id/16828408/ns/technology_and_science-tech_and_gadgets/t/poll-americans-think-downloading-no-big-deal/.

22 Dugan, Andrew, *More Americans Say Pornography Is Morally Acceptable*, Gallup, June 5, 2018, https://news.gallup.com/poll/235280/americans-say-pornography-morally-acceptable.aspx.

23 Bucholz, Katharina, *How Much of the Internet Consists of Porn?*, Statista, Feb. 11, 2019, https://www.statista.com/chart/16959/share-of-the-Internet-that-is-porn/.

24 Moynihan, Ruqayyah, *Internet Users Access Porn Websites More Than Twitter, Wikipedia and Netflix*, Business Insider, Sept. 30, 2018, https://www.businessinsider.com/Internet-users-access-porn-more-than-twitter-wikipedia-and-netflix-2018-9.

- 62% think it's inappropriate to break up with a romantic partner via electronic communication.[25]
- Sex with a robot is considered cheating by about 50% of singles.[26]

In fact, the mere decision to embrace technology like the Internet may be considered an ethical choice. Some philosophers have long regarded technology as a dark and dehumanizing force. This technological pessimism posits that advances in science and technology do not lead to an improvement in the human condition, but instead lock us into a virtual but inescapable cage that menaces our individuality and authenticity. Its roots can be traced back to the Industrial Revolution with the Luddite movement. Luddites blamed the rise of industrial mills and advanced factory machinery for the loss of their jobs and set out to destroy them.

An infamous modern adherent is Theodore Kaczynski. Also known as the Unabomber, the former University of California-Berkeley math professor killed three people and injured 23 others in an attempt to start a revolution by conducting a nationwide bombing campaign targeting people involved with modern technology.[27] In the late 1990s, the reclusive terrorist was finally caught and sentenced to life in prison, following the longest and most expensive investigation in the history of the Federal Bureau of Investigation. In his 35,000-word manifesto, which was published in major newspapers, Kaczynski argued that his bombings were necessary to attract attention to the erosion of human freedom and dignity by modern technologies. Although they condemn his maniacal methods, many scholars consider the manifesto a "work of genius"[28] that "raises uneasy ethical questions."[29]

25 Moore, Peter, *Poll Results: Ghosting*, YouGov, Oct. 28, 2014, https://today.yougov.com/topics/lifestyle/articles-reports/2014/10/28/poll-results-ghosting.

26 Match.com, *Singles In America: Match Releases Largest Study on U.S. Single Population for Eighth Year*, Feb. 1, 2018, https://www.prnewswire.com/news-releases/singles-in-america-match-releases-largest-study-on-us-single-population-for-eighth-year-300591561.html.

27 MacFarquhar, Neil, *On the Unabomber's Track: The Victims; At the Places Where Bombs Killed, a Day for Memories and Nervous Optimism*, The New York Times, Apr. 4, 1996, https://www.nytimes.com/1996/04/04/us/unabomber-s-track-victims-places-where-bombs-killed-day-for-memories-nervous.html.

28 Hanrahan, Jake, *Inside the Unabomber's Odd and Furious Online Revival*, Wired, Aug. 1, 2018, https://www.wired.co.uk/article/unabomber-netflix-tv-series-ted-kaczynski.

29 Haven, Cynthia, *Unabomber's Writings Raise Uneasy Ethical Questions for Stanford Scholar*, Stanford News, Feb. 1, 2010, https://news.stanford.edu/news/2010/february1/unabomber-ethics-question-020110.html.

AN EXCERPT FROM THEODORE KACZYNSKI'S 1995 MANIFESTO, "INDUSTRIAL SOCIETY AND ITS FUTURE":

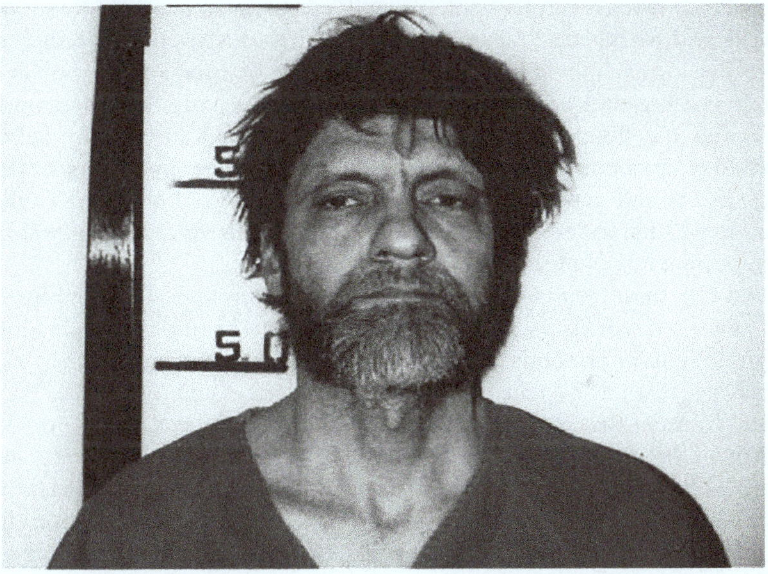

Ted Kaczynski. Credit: FBI.

> *The Industrial Revolution and its consequences have been a disaster for the human race. They have greatly increased the life-expectancy of those of us who live in "advanced" countries, but they have destabilized society, have made life unfulfilling, have subjected human beings to indignities, have led to widespread psychological suffering (in the Third World to physical suffering as well) and have inflicted severe damage on the natural world. The continued development of technology will worsen the situation. It will certainly subject human beings to greater indignities and inflict greater damage on the natural world, it will probably lead to greater social disruption and psychological suffering, and it may lead to increased physical suffering even in "advanced" countries.*[30]

In recent years, technological pessimism has grown among Americans, with a declining majority of adults saying the Internet has been good for society. A 2020 Pew Research Center poll found 21% of Americans said the Internet

30 Kaczynski, Theodore, *Industrial Society and Its Future*, Washington Post, Sept. 19, 1995, https://www.washingtonpost.com/wp-srv/national/longterm/unabomber/manifesto.text.htm.

was "bad for society,"[31] compared to 14% in 2018.[32] As artificial intelligence threatens to replace human workers, the Luddite movement could make a strong comeback.

In contrast to this bleak viewpoint is technological utopianism, a doctrine which holds that certain technologies will create an ideal world by improving lifestyles and workplaces. German philosopher Karl Marx believed that science and technology would help delegitimize the rule of kings and the power of the church and create a better, freer society. More recently, a techno-optimism movement has flourished in Silicon Valley, centered around the belief that technology, particularly the Internet, will improve communication, democratize society and make the market more efficient. But the negative effects of technology, such as increased isolation of individuals and limiting exposure to different people and ideas, are often ignored.

Between these two extreme positions is technological neutrality, which holds that technology is merely a tool that can be used for good or bad. Technology itself does not promote one type of behavior or another, neutralists believe. Rather, humans determine its objectives and outcomes. "Well it's not the Internet that is evil. It's human beings that are evil," explains Werner Herzog in his 2016 documentary, *Lo and Behold: Reveries of the Connected World*. "They only have a new, different instrument to make it manifest, but it's the same thing. Is the Internet good or evil? That's not a question that has any relevance. It's the same thing like, is electricity good or evil? You don't ask this question."[33]

Although living in the Digital Age may make resistance to technology futile — unless we hide out in a remote cabin in Montana like Theodore Kaczynski — we arguably have the capacity to control how it affects our lives. Boston University professor Richard Spinello explains in his book *CyberEthics: Morality and Law in Cyberspace*:

> We can still shape and dictate how certain technological innovations will be deployed and restrained, particularly when there is a conflict with the common good or core human goods … Although we must not be overly optimistic about our freedom and our capacity for resisting infatuation with new technology, we must recognize that we do still have some degree of freedom in this world.[34]

31 Vogels, Emily et al., *53% of Americans Say the Internet Has Been Essential during the COVID-19 Outbreak*, Pew Research Center, Apr. 30, 2020, https://www.pewresearch.org/internet/2020/04/30/53-of-americans-say-the-internet-has-been-essential-during-the-covid-19-outbreak/.

32 Smith, Aaron, *Declining Majority of Online Adults Say the Internet Has Been Good for Society*, Pew Research Center, Apr. 30, 2018, https://www.pewresearch.org/internet/2018/04/30/declining-majority-of-online-adults-say-the-internet-has-been-good-for-society/.

33 Lo and Behold, Reveries of the Connected World (Saville Productions, 2016).

34 Spinello, Richard A., Cyber Ethics: Morality and Law in Cyberspace (6th ed., 2016), 9.

For example, we can choose to implement laws and program code in ways that protect fundamental human rights such as autonomy and privacy. Charles Taylor, a Canadian philosopher known for his examination of the modern self, observes that throughout history there have been pockets of coordinated resistance against oppressive technologies that brought forth reforms. "We are not, indeed, locked in. But there is a slope, an incline in things that is all too easy to slide down," he writes in his book *The Ethics of Authenticity*.[35] We can avoid this fatal slide by developing sound ethical judgment on how to constrain behavior on the Internet through norms, laws, computer programming standards and market forces.

Behaving ethically may seem like a matter of common sense. But true ethical dilemmas often involve complicated situations that can't be easily solved through simple intuition or common sense. Ethics is not the same as feelings, either. Though feelings provide important information for our ethical choices, we may feel good even when doing something bad — or vice versa. Finally, ethics is not a matter of simply following the law. A good legal system incorporates ethical standards. But law can deviate from what is ethical, as some totalitarian regimes demonstrate, or it may be slow to address new problems, as many governments have been with issues raised by the Internet.

Ethical Frameworks

Several distinct types of ethical reasoning can help provide a moral compass in making judgments. These theories fall under two broad categories: teleological or deontological.

Teleological ethics, also called consequentialism, holds that whether an action is morally right or wrong depends on the consequences or end result of the action. This framework is also applied in context to determine whether an action in a given situation will produce a desired outcome. Consequentialism may justify certain actions that are otherwise considered unethical or morally wrong if they produce an otherwise positive outcome.

Deontological ethics, on the other hand, rely on whether an action is morally right in and of itself, rather than looking to the consequences or intentions of an action. In other words, there are absolute rules that do not change to fit different situations, but rather should be applied all the time.

For example, suppose that by killing an entirely innocent person we can save the lives of five other innocent people. A consequentialist would say that killing the innocent person is justified because it would result in only one person dying, rather than five people dying. A non-consequentialist would say it is inherently wrong to murder people and refuse to kill an innocent person, even though not killing that person leads to the death of four more people than killing just him.

35 Taylor, Charles, The Ethics of Authenticity (1992), 101.

More specifically, here are six major frameworks you should be aware of:

The Utilitarian Approach: British philosophers Jeremy Bentham and John Stuart Mill emphasized that the best action is the one that provides the most good or does the least harm for all affected individuals. In e-commerce, that means selecting the action that produces the greatest good and does the least harm for all stakeholders, such as customers, employees, shareholders, the community and the environment. Ethical cyberwarfare would balance the good achieved through a cyber attack with the harm done to all sides. Thus, the utilitarian approach calculates consequences to determine the ethical choice.

The Rights Approach: Other ethicists, such as German philosopher Immanuel Kant, suggest that the prudent action is the one that best respects and protects the moral rights of those affected. Moral rights are open to debate but may include the freedom of expression, a right to privacy and a right not to be harmed. This approach is predicated on the notion that humans have an inherent right to choose freely how to live their lives, and that they also have a moral duty to respect others in the same way. Kant believed that humans should be treated as ends and not merely as means to other ends. Some now argue that non-humans, including artificial intelligence, have rights, too.

The Fairness or Justice Approach: Greek philosopher Aristotle said that "equals should be treated equally and unequals unequally."[36] In other words, what is fair for one should be fair for all. Both favoritism and discrimination are unjust and wrong. That said, treating people equally may not mean treating them the same. For example, a company may hire one candidate over another based on who has more experience and say that is fair. But there is currently a debate over the lack of representation of women and minorities at tech companies, leading many to ask whether the huge disparity is based on a defensible standard or whether it is the result of discrimination and hence is unfair.

The Common Good Approach: The Greek philosophers also argued that ethical choices should benefit all members of the community. In order for a society to flourish, this philosophy holds, people must accept modest sacrifices for a common good rather than selfishly protecting their own interests. More recently, ethicist John Rawls defined the common good as "certain general conditions that are ... equally to everyone's advantage." An example of a common good approach would be providing Internet access to everyone, including rural communities, even though it might not be cost-effective and take resources away from city dwellers. This approach directly contrasts with a controversial philosophy known as ethical egoism, exemplified by *Atlas Shrugged* author Ayn Rand, who advocated looking out for oneself above all else.

36 Cohen, Ronald L., Justice: Views from the Social Sciences (1986), 15.

The Virtue Approach: A very ancient approach to ethics is that ethical actions ought to be consistent with certain ideal virtues that provide for the full development of our character. Developed by the Greeks and Chinese philosopher Confucius, this approach assumes that we acquire virtue through practice. By practicing being honest, brave, tolerant, and so on, people develop an honorable and moral character that helps them make the right choice when faced with ethical challenges. Virtue ethics asks of any action, "What kind of person will I become if I do this?" or "Is this action consistent with my character?" For example, a lawmaker might want to block constituents who criticize her on social media, but shouldn't she listen to her community's concerns?

The Religion Approach: Another ancient approach holds that ethics is ultimately based on the commands or character of God, and that the ethically right action is the one that God commands or requires. Under this divine command theory, being ethical is equivalent to doing whatever the Bible — or the Qur'an or some other sacred text or source of revelation — tells you to do. But this philosophy is premised, of course, on the existence of God, which is not universally accepted, and on interpretation and application of sacred texts.

While not exhaustive, this list represents a spectrum of some of the major theories on how to make an ethical decision. No philosophy is without its problems: we may not agree on what constitutes the common good, for example. We may not even agree on what is a good and what is a harm. But all of these frameworks deserve careful consideration and can be applied to many of the controversial issues we cover in this book. Although there's much debate among philosophers over whether ethics is relative to a particular society or if absolute truths exist, our purpose here is not to argue for one theory against another, but to get you thinking about why you see the world in a certain way, what other perspectives are out there, and what tools will be helpful in guiding your decisions as you forge ahead on the Information Superhighway. As we explore the law of cyberspace, it is useful to also keep these ethical approaches in mind and consider whether the law on a particular Internet issue is right or wrong, and whether it should be changed.

CLOSING ARGUMENTS

Most people think the Internet has had a positive role in society. But a noteworthy number disagree and believe the Internet hurts society. What do you think? Has the Internet been: Good for society? Bad for society? A mix of good and bad?

Additional Sources

Arulanantham, Rekha, *ECPA: Online Privacy Stuck in the '80s*, American Civil Liberties Union of Northern California, Oct. 17, 2017, https://www.aclunc.org/blog/ecpa-online-privacy-stuck-80s.

BBC, *About Consequentialism*, http://www.bbc.co.uk/ethics/introduction/consequentialism_1.shtml.

Bivens, Tom, Mixed Media: Moral Distinctions in Advertising, Public Relations, and Journalism (3rd. ed., 2018).

Bobbitt, Randy, Exploring Communications Law: A Socratic Approach (2nd ed., 2018), 8–17.

Chase, Alston, *Harvard and the Making of the Unabomber*, Atlantic, June 2000, https://www.theatlantic.com/magazine/archive/2000/06/harvard-and-the-making-of-the-unabomber/378239/.

de Waele, Rudy, *The Internet Is Not Evil (Interview with Werner Herzog)*, Technology vs. Humanity, Aug. 16, 2016, https://www.techvshuman.com/2016/08/16/the-internet-is-not-evil-interview-with-werner-herzog-new-film-lo-and-behold/.

Freedom Forum Institute, State of the First Amendment 2019, Aug. 2019, https://www.freedomforuminstitute.org/wp-content/uploads/2019/06/SOFAreport2019.pdf.

Governors Highway Safety Association, Distracted Driving, updated July 2020, https://www.ghsa.org/state-laws/issues/distracted%20driving.

Grabowski, Mark, *Are Technical Difficulties at the Supreme Court Causing a 'Disregard of Duty'*?, 3 Journal of Law, Technology & Internet 93 (2011), 93–112.

HG.org, *Internet Law - Guide to Cyberspace Law*, https://www.hg.org/internet-law.html.

Kilovaty, Ido, *Are Tech Companies Becoming the Primary Legislators in International Cyberspace?*, Lawfare, Mar. 28, 2019, https://www.lawfareblog.com/are-tech-companies-becoming-primary-legislators-international-cyberspace.

Kirkpatrick, Keith, *Technology Confounds the Courts*, 57 Communications of the ACM 5 (May 2014), 27–29.

Marcus, Adam, The Next Digital Decade: Essays on the Future of the Internet (2011).

Shahbaz, Adrian and Funk, Allie, *Freedom on The Net 2019*, Freedom House, 2019, https://freedomhouse.org/sites/default/files/2019-11/11042019_Report_FH_FOTN_2019_final_Public_Download.pdf.

Staff, *Pessimism v Progress*, The Economist, Dec. 18, 2019, https://www.economist.com/leaders/2019/12/18/pessimism-v-progress.

Thompson, Clive, *When Robots Take All of Our Jobs, Remember the Luddites*, Smithsonian Magazine, Jan. 2017, https://www.smithsonianmag.com/innovation/when-robots-take-jobs-remember-luddites-180961423/.

Transcript of Oral Argument at 49, *U.S. v. Wurie*, 573 U.S. 373 (2014) (13–212) (consolidated with *Riley v. California*, 573 U.S. 373 (2014)), https://www.supremecourt.gov/oral_arguments/argument_transcripts/2013/13-132_bp7c.pdf.

Velasquez, Manuel et al., *A Framework for Ethical Decision Making*, Markkula Center for Applied Ethics at Santa Clara University, May 2009, https://www.scu.edu/ethics/ethics-resources/ethical-decision-making/a-framework-for-ethical-decision-making/.

4 Freedom of Speech in an Online World

> One of the reasons we have the First Amendment is to protect speech that offends us. If it didn't offend, why would we need it?
>
> — Professor Ronald Collins

Freedom of speech is recognized as a fundamental human right by the United Nations, and around the world. Virtually every national government recognizes, at least formally, the value of free speech, even if the reality is that speech is routinely monitored and suppressed. (For example, article 67 of North Korea's constitution provides that "Citizens are guaranteed freedom of speech, of the press, of assembly, demonstration and association,"[1] even though the nation is an authoritarian country that is consistently rated as among the most severe restrictors of speech.) While many countries restrict speech, both online and offline, and ban certain websites, Americans enjoy a great deal of freedom when it comes to online speech thanks to the United States Constitution's Bill of Rights.

Online Speech in America

The Bill of Rights includes the First Amendment, which protects freedom of speech and of the press. The amendment also protects freedom of religion, the right to assemble and the right to petition the government about grievances. It was added to the U.S. Constitution in 1791. Back then, communication was much different, and our Founding Fathers likely had not conceived of anything like the Internet. The only forms of mass communication were books, pamphlets and newspapers. Other forms of media, such as the telegraph, telephone, movies, radio and TV, were more than a century away from becoming a reality. Each of these innovations has led some to call for limits on the use of the new technology. For example, it once was routine for cities and states to ban films that were judged to be overly salacious.

1 Elkins, Zachary, et al, *The Content of Authoritarian Constitutions*, in Constitutions in Authoritarian Regimes 141–64 (T. Ginsburg and A. Simpser eds., 2014).

Similarly, many lawmakers have called for tighter restrictions on online speech because of the Internet's unique qualities, such as its ability to spread potentially dangerous information quickly and widely, as well as its easy accessibility by children. But the Constitution still applies when it comes to regulating the Internet and, in the groundbreaking 1997 case *Reno v. American Civil Liberties Union*, the U.S. Supreme Court ruled that the Internet has First Amendment protection comparable to that enjoyed by the print media.[2]

The First Amendment is basically a promise by the U.S. government to respect the individual rights of its people, particularly expression in all its forms. But while it enables Americans to enjoy considerable freedom in speech — both online and in the real world — free speech rights are not unlimited. The Supreme Court often balances freedom of speech rights with other personal rights and societal interests such as the right to privacy, to protect reputation, to protect national security interests, and against obscenity — to name a few interests that are sometimes favored over First Amendment rights. Consequently, some types of expression, such as child pornography and death threats, are not protected by the First Amendment. But many types of controversial and offensive speech are protected, including hate speech, anonymous speech and adult pornography. "One of the reasons we have the First Amendment is to protect speech that offends us," said Ronald Collins, a law professor at the University of Washington. "If it didn't offend, why would we need [the First Amendment]?"[3]

Origins of the First Amendment

The concept of free speech is historically rooted in the Enlightenment, the era in the 17th to 19th centuries when Western European thinkers developed new ways of thinking based on scientific observation, questioning of authority and exaltation of self. On a practical level, this meant a government accountable to the people, freedom of thought, freedom of expression and general tolerance of the beliefs of others.

These ideas in large part formed the basis of the American Revolution, including aversion to monarchy and unrepresentative government. In fact, the original governing document for the new United States, the Articles of Confederation, exalted state governments and created only a weak national government with very limited powers. Dissatisfaction with this form of government led the participants in a convention of representatives from the states, which was originally convened to revise the Articles, to instead decide to create a whole new government structure with a stronger national government. The result of this convention became the U.S. Constitution.

2 *Reno v. ACLU*, 521 U.S. 844 (1997).

3 Benson, Thor, *Beyond the First Amendment: You're Probably Confused About Free Speech*, Salon, Aug. 31, 2016, https://www.salon.com/2016/08/31/beyond-the-first-amendment-youre-probably-confused-about-free-apeech/.

The drafting and ratification of the Constitution fostered robust debate over the nature and purposes of government. A major concern was that there was no explicit statement of individual rights that limited the powers of the expanded federal government in the proposed document. While proponents initially argued that such a statement was unnecessary because of the limited powers of the proposed national government, they eventually agreed to amend the Constitution shortly after ratification in order to protect such rights.

Congress proposed 12 amendments, which protected individual rights against encroachment of the new federal government. Ten of these amendments were eventually ratified by the states, including (after a renumbering) the First Amendment, which contains 45 words that protect five specific individual rights: "Congress shall make no law respecting an establishment of religion, or prohibiting the free exercise thereof; or abridging the freedom of speech, or of the press; or the right of the people peaceably to assemble, and to petition the Government for a redress of grievances."[4]

Meaning of the First Amendment

From its language, the First Amendment appears to give absolute protection: after all, the first words are "Congress shall make no law..." But First Amendment protections come with several caveats, and there are some types of speech that can be limited or prohibited despite the absolute language of the First Amendment.

The original version of the Bill of Rights approved by Congress, on display at the U.S. National Archives; Credit: U.S. National Archives.

4 U.S. Constitution, Amendment I.

First, the First Amendment applies only within the U.S. As Electronic Frontier Foundation founder John Perry Barlow famously said, "In Cyberspace, the First Amendment is a local ordinance,"[5] meaning it only applies to Internet users under the U.S.'s jurisdiction.

Beyond America's borders, Internet users in many nations can face severe governmental punishment for their speech online. In Myanmar, for example, Article 66(d) of Myanmar's Telecommunications Law allows anyone to file criminal charges against anyone else for publishing anything they don't like online. Such arbitrary use of the law to suppress and punish speech is not possible in the U.S. because of the First Amendment.

Since most media is now online, journalists are prime targets of Myanmar's law, including journalists working for news services outside of Myanmar. But, really, anyone who ever made a nasty comment on social media could be charged in Myanmar. The law could also be applied to authors of posts outside of Myanmar, but it would be difficult for the country to prosecute people outside its territory.

Second, the First Amendment prevents only the government from restricting and punishing speech. Courts have held it applies to not only the federal government, but also state and local government. This may come as a surprise to many Americans.

The First Amendment *does not* regulate the behavior of private individuals or organizations. So, a private social network, such as Facebook or Twitter, can block or remove content as it wishes. Also, freedom of speech does not give us freedom from the social consequences of our speech. In other words, the free speech provision of the First Amendment means that you will not go to jail for saying offensive or controversial things. But if what you say ticks people off, it could cause you to lose your job, customers or friends. For example, if you make a racist tweet or post a risqué (but not obscene) photo, the government cannot fine or arrest you. However, your employer may legally fire you for doing so if your online speech violates your employer's policies; you are not shielded from being fired by the First Amendment.

Public primary and secondary schools may also impose some limits on free speech rights in certain circumstances. If you attend a public school, the First Amendment protects your speech because public schools are operated by the government. But courts have ruled that K-12 school officials have some leeway to restrict speech if it interferes with the school's educational mission, including speech that occurs online and off-campus. So, courts have upheld punishments for high schoolers who were suspended for posting tweets, uploading videos and engaging in other online behavior that occurred off school grounds that school officials said had effects within the school. For example, a federal appeals court determined that public school officials could punish a student for

5 Barlow, John Perry, *Leaving the Physical World*, Electronic Frontier Foundation, https://www.eff.org/pages/leaving-physical-world.

a rap video he created off-campus and posted on Facebook and YouTube that referenced two teachers at the school who allegedly had engaged in sexually inappropriate behavior with female students.[6]

However, other courts have ruled that school administrators cannot discipline students for off-campus speech. Most recently, a public high school suspended a student for posting a photo of herself with the caption "f*** school f*** softball f*** cheer f*** everything" to Snapchat after she was cut from the varsity cheerleading team. She sued and in 2020 the U.S. Third Circuit Court of Appeals ruled in her favor. The court concluded that "a student's online speech" does not "substantially disrupt" the on-campus environment "simply because it involves the school, mentions teachers or administrators, is shared with or accessible to students, or reaches the school environment."[7] In 2021, the Supreme Court agreed to hear an appeal of this decision, which could determine how much public school administrators should be able to regulate students' speech on social media.[8]

If you attend a private school, you're completely out of luck, since the First Amendment doesn't apply. In recent years, Harvard University — a private institution — has rescinded admissions to several students after discovering they made offensive comments online. However, if a private school promises its students freedom of speech in its written policies or advertisements, such as its mission statement or admissions brochure, students could sue for breach of contract if school administrators attempt to restrict their speech. The Foundation for Individual Rights in Education — a non-partisan legal organization that's better known by its acronym FIRE and defends college students' speech rights — explains: "While private colleges and universities are not legally bound to uphold the First Amendment, when a private institution promises free debate and expression, the school is morally bound — and may be contractually bound, depending on the circumstances — to honor the free speech rights and academic freedom of its students and faculty."[9]

Third, the First Amendment differs from the broader concept of free speech, since it only defines the limitations *on the government* in restricting speech. The concept of free speech is broader than the constitutional provision. There are many ways that the concept of free speech can be violated and censorship can occur that do not involve the government. "Freedom of speech is a much bigger, bolder, braver idea," according to FIRE president

6 *Bell v. Itawamba County School Board*, 799 F.3d 379 (5th Cir. 2015), *cert. denied*, 136 S.Ct. 1166 (Mem.), 194 L.Ed.2d 240 (U.S. 2016).

7 *B.L. v. Mahanoy Area School District*, 964 F.3d 170, 180 (3d Cir. 2020).

8 *Mahanoy Area Sch. Dist. v. B. L.*, cert. granted, No. 20-255, 2021 WL 77251, 208 L. Ed. 2d 509 (U.S. Jan. 8, 2021).

9 Foundation for Individual Rights in Education, *Know Your School's Speech Code*, https://www.thefire.org/get-involved/student-network/defend-protect-your-rights/know-your-schools-speech-code/.

Greg Lukianoff. "It's much more expansive, and it's been around longer than the First Amendment."[10]

Greg Lukianoff is president of the Foundation for Individual Rights in Education (FIRE), one of several non-profit groups focused on protecting free speech rights in the U.S. The FIRE provides free legal assistance to college students and faculty who believe their speech rights have been violated. Credit: The FIRE.

Often people misequate these two things. When discussing censorship or free speech infringement, no First Amendment violation has occurred unless the action restricting speech is taken by the government. On the other hand, a social media site removing a user's posts or suspending a user's account is not a First Amendment violation. It's one example of the many ways that free speech can be violated and censorship can occur. But, because it does not involve the government, there is no legal remedy. As Lukianoff explains, "There's never been a Supreme Court case that said that there's a First Amendment violation when an entirely private entity regulates speech." Collins adds: while you can have a "denial of free speech that doesn't involve the government" or a "censorship that doesn't involve the government," you can't have a First Amendment violation that doesn't involve the government.[11]

But, with the Internet becoming our modern-day public square, some free speech activists say that needs to change. There is a push underway in the U.S. to prohibit popular online social media platforms from censoring speech

10 Benson, *supra* note 3.
11 *Id*.

on their sites, including reforms to the federal law that protects websites from liability for content posted by users.

Section 230

The reason why online platforms are able to moderate content as they see fit and avoid any legal repercussions is Section 230 of the Communications Decency Act, which has been a key legal shield for the tech industry and shaped today's online experience. It protects any "interactive computer service" (meaning website and app operators) from liability for the content users post on their platforms. It also allows operators to moderate content "in good faith" — which the courts have not precisely defined in this context — without incurring liability. In other words, social media networks like Facebook, information resources like Wikipedia and search engines like Google can't be sued because of what their users say or do on their sites. And courts have dismissed many lawsuits seeking to hold these companies liable for their users' activities.

YouTube's CEO Susan Wojcicki highlighted the importance of Section 230 to online businesses. "It's basically enabled the Internet as we know it," she said. "It's enabled us to have people upload content, not have every single comment be reviewed, not every single video be reviewed. And so, it has enabled new types of communication, new types of community, new types of content that we just wouldn't have had beforehand."[12]

Before the Internet era, both companies and individuals that produced content and redistributors of that content could be held liable for material that was libelous, invaded privacy or caused some other harm. This was known as the "republication rule": a person or entity that repeats harmful content could be held liable for the harm, along with the originator of the content. Thus, for example, both the author of a libelous letter to a newspaper editor and the newspaper that published the letter could be subject to a libel suit. But those who merely deliver or transmit material published by others — such as a newsstand or bookstore — generally could not be held liable for what they sold, unless they were able to know the material was illegal. (Similarly, courts have held that a website posting a link to harmful material does not constitute republication.)

These rules still apply to print and offline publications today. But these distinctions became antiquated and unmanageable with the advent of the Internet, with popular websites and apps such as YouTube and Instagram that feature user-generated content, which is generally considered too voluminous to be reviewed before it is posted.

In the early days of the commercial Internet, an online service called Prodigy offered its subscribers access to a broad range of networked services including

12 Farmer, Brit McCandless, *YouTube CEO Susan Wojcicki and the Debate Over Section 230*, CBS News, Dec. 1, 2019, https://www.cbsnews.com/news/youtube-ceo-susan-wojcicki-and-the-debate-over-section-230-60-minutes-2019-12-01/.

discussion boards, and it employed moderators to approve content and clean up foul language. But Prodigy's popularity meant that it was unable to guard against every harmful post, which led to a lawsuit over postings to a message board devoted to discussing the stock of a specific company. Because Prodigy actively moderated content on the message board, a court decided it had taken on a publisher's role, making its site like the newspaper in the letter-to-the-editor scenario discussed above.[13] Meanwhile, a competing online service at the time, CompuServe, decided not to regulate what its users posted. So, when it was sued for allowing harmful content on its site, CompuServe was found not liable because it was solely a distributor — like a newsstand or bookstore — having no say over what its users posted.[14]

Together, these two rulings set a precedent that online platforms could reduce their liability if they did not moderate users' words and images. But this created an undesirable situation. Wanting to prevent the Internet from turning into a cesspool where anything goes and instead empower online platforms to moderate content in "good faith" without risking liability, Congress enacted Section 230 as part of the larger Communications Decency Act of 1996. The provision, supported by a bipartisan group of lawmakers, states that "No provider or user of an interactive computer service shall be treated as the publisher or speaker of any information provided by another information content provider."[15] With few exceptions, the law provides sweeping immunity for online services — regardless of whether they allow users to post illegal content or remove content even if that speech is legal under the First Amendment.

The protection from liability provided by Section 230 applies only online. So, a writer and a newspaper are both still liable when the paper publishes in its physical paper a letter by the writer that is held to be defamatory. But the newspaper is not liable if the writer submits the same libelous content as a comment on the newspaper's website and it appears only there.

Also, Section 230 does not apply when a website effectively forces users to post illegal content. This issue arose with a roommate-finding website that had click-buttons that forced users to choose what personal characteristics they wanted in a roommate. The problem was that federal and state equal housing laws prohibit housing discrimination based on characteristics that were contained in some of the selections, such as race and sexual orientation. When the website was sued under these housing laws, it claimed that since the users chose which characteristics they desired, the website was not liable for these choices because of Section 230. However, a federal appeals court held that

13 *Stratton Oakmont, Inc. v. Prodigy Services Co.*, 1995 WL 323710, 1995 N.Y. Misc. LEXIS 229, 23 Media L. Rep. 1794 (N.Y. Sup. Ct., May 24, 1995), *rearg. denied*, 1995 WL 805178, 1995 N.Y. Misc. LEXIS 712, 24 Media L. Rep. 1126 (N.Y. Sup. Ct., Dec. 11, 1995).

14 *Cubby, Inc. v. CompuServe Inc.*, 776 F.Supp. 135 (S.D.N.Y. 1991).

15 47 U.S.C. § 230 [as discussed above, most of the "decency" provisions of this law were held unconstitutional by the U.S. Supreme Court].

Section 230 did not protect the website from possible liability, because the website required users to make these choices.[16]

The enactment of Section 230 is credited with spurring innovation in online businesses and services and fostering robust online speech and communities. But it has also created problems. For example, Section 230 has faced criticism for creating open forums that terrorist organizations and hate groups use to spread their ideologies. Citing the immunity provided by Section 230, judges have dismissed lawsuits against online platforms brought by the families of victims killed by these groups and those inspired by them, who planned or were inspired by online posts. "Section 230 provides the strongest protection for user content on online platforms in the world," said Jeff Kosseff, a law professor at the U.S. Naval Academy and author of a book on Section 230, "so it is not a surprise that so many of the most successful platforms are based in the United States." But, he adds, "As platforms have grown to play an increasingly central role in our lives, the platforms' use of this responsibility and power is under unprecedented scrutiny."[17]

Section 230 is now under siege as lawmakers seek to hold tech giants accountable. Many Democrats and Republicans on Capitol Hill agree that Section 230 has got to change, but they can't agree on why or how. As technology journalist Issie Lapowsky explains: "Depending on which side of the aisle politicians sit on, Section 230 is either the reason social platforms don't moderate enough, or moderate too much. Democrats blame it for why Facebook can keep false political ads or doctored videos on the site, and Republicans point to it as the reason why social media sites can silence conservative commentators in their crackdown on hate speech and fake news."[18]

In mid-2020, President Donald Trump weighed in with an Executive Order that sought to lay the groundwork for the federal Department of Justice, the Federal Communications Commission and the Federal Trade Commission to take administrative actions to limit the protection that Section 230 provides to online providers.[19] Although Trump is no longer president, the law remains on shaky ground. Trump's successor, President Joe Biden, told *The New York Times* during his campaign that Section 230 "immediately should be revoked." However, Biden and others argue that more social media censorship is actually needed due to the pervasiveness of harassment, violent videos and fake news online.

16 *Fair Housing Council of San Fernando Valley v. Roommates.com*, LLC, 521 F.3d 1157 (9th Cir. 2008), *later proceeding*, 666 F.3d 1216, (9th Cir. 2012).

17 Kosseff, Jeff, *The 26 Words That Guard the Open Internet and Open-Source Intelligence*, War on the Rocks, Mar. 14, 2019, https://warontherocks.com/2019/03/the-26-words-that-guard-the-open-internet-and-open-source-intelligence/.

18 Lapowsky, Issie, *Section 230 Under Siege: A Guide to All the Ways the Law Could Be Gutted*, Protocol, Feb. 15, 2020, https://www.protocol.com/section-230-guide-under-siege.

19 An Executive Order is a statement issued by the president that directs federal agencies to interpret and apply a federal statute or a court decision in a particular way.

With elected officials of all political stripes urging changes or outright repeal, it seems likely that the protection provided by Section 230 will change or perhaps even disappear in the near future.

A Right to Social Media?

A big part of the debate over Section 230 centers around how much freedom users should have to express themselves on social media.

For many people, social media has become an essential component of their daily lives. And it is clear that social media posts are protected by the First Amendment to the same extent as statements in other media, with only a few limitations such as defamation, invasion of privacy and obscenity. So, the government can't place many limitations on what people post on social media.

But can the government limit access to social media itself? In a 2017 case, the U.S. Supreme Court unanimously struck down a North Carolina law barring sex offenders from accessing social media platforms, with the court repeatedly and strongly emphasizing that social media is now a crucial instrument of public discussion and debate.[20]

Limitations imposed by social media platforms themselves are a different matter, since the First Amendment applies only to government actions. As private companies, social media sites are free to limit expression on their sites in any way they choose. These sites are effectively "acting as quasi-states to reshape political speech," according to Casey Newton, Silicon Valley editor for tech news site The Verge.[21]

Various groups and organizations, including the LGBT community, cryptocurrency companies and even major news outlets, have complained that their content has been removed from social media platforms without explanation or that they're banned from advertising on them. Conservatives have argued that their posts receive limited exposure because of bias by tech giants. A 2018 analysis by *Vice News* found that prominent conservatives were being "shadowbanned" by Twitter, or having their content secretly blocked from being viewed by other users, while a Hill.TV American Barometer survey that year found that 58% of registered voters — including 83% of Republicans — think that social networks are unfair to conservatives.[22] In some cases, promi-

20 *Packingham v. North Carolina*, 582 U.S. ___, 137 S. Ct. 1730, 198 L. Ed. 2d 273 (2017).

21 Newton, Casey, *Why Activists Get Frustrated with Facebook*, The Verge, Jan. 14, 2020, https://www.theverge.com/interface/2020/1/14/21063887/activists-facebook-iran-free-speech-authoritarianism.

22 Collins, Eliza, *Report: Prominent Republicans See Their Influence Limited on Twitter, Democrats Don't*, USA Today, July 25, 2018, https://www.usatoday.com/story/news/politics/onpolitics/2018/07/25/report-some-gopers-shadow-banned-twitter/836734002/; and Sheffield, Matthew, *Majority Thinks Tech Giants are Biased Against Conservatives, Poll Shows*, The Hill, Dec. 13, 2018, https://thehill.com/hilltv/what-americas-thinking/421238-poll-majority-of-americans-think-social-media-companies-are.

nent Republicans, including President Trump, have even had their social media accounts permanently banned — a practice known as "deplatforming." And when conservatives have attempted to create their own platforms, they've sometimes been denied web hosting services and had their apps delisted on popular distribution platforms such as The App Store.[23]

CHECK IF AN ACCOUNT IS "SHADOWBANNED"

A free app, available at https://shadowban.eu/, purports to be able to determine whether Twitter is limiting the availability and reach of a user's account.

While it's not a violation of the First Amendment, some free speech advocates contend that Twitter, Facebook or YouTube censoring or limiting certain content or kicking people off of their platforms is concerning. In response to Twitter banning President Trump over concerns he might incite violence over his 2020 election defeat, German Chancellor Angela Merkel said it's "problematic" for social media management to have the power to essentially evict world leaders from cyberspace's public square.[24] But courts have rejected efforts to stop sites from enacting these policies, even when the sites' Terms of Service purport to allow freedom of speech.

Nearly 70% of U.S. adults use Facebook.[25] Twitter now has more than 300 million users and plays a critical gatekeeper and distribution role in the high-speed promulgation of content and news.[26] And Google has 90% of total U.S. search engine market share, and its corporate sibling YouTube is similarly dominant in video.[27] Given their monopolistic positions, these companies control a substantial share of the information that Americans consume and therefore provide a public benefit. Even Mark Zuckerberg for many years described Facebook as "a social utility" and "more like a government than a traditional company."[28] Some legal experts argue that giant social networks

23 Parker, Tom, *Parler Sues Amazon for Antitrust Violations, Requests Temporary Restraining Order*, Reclaim The Net, Jan. 11, 2021, https://reclaimthenet.org/parler-sues-amazon-aws-antitrust/.

24 Staff, *Germany's Merkel: Trump's Twitter Eviction "Problematic,"* Associated Press, Jan. 11, 2021, https://apnews.com/article/merkel-trump-twitter-problematic-dc9732268493a8ac337e03159f0dc1c9.

25 Gramlich, John, *10 Facts About Americans and Facebook*, Pew Research Center, May 16, 2019, https://www.pewresearch.org/fact-tank/2019/05/16/facts-about-americans-and-facebook/.

26 Lin, Ying, *10 Twitter Statistics Every Marketer Should Know in 2020*, Oberlo, Nov. 30, 2019, https://www.oberlo.com/blog/twitter-statistics.

27 Ahern, Pat, *25 Mind-Bottling SEO Stats for 2020 (+ Beyond)*, Junto, Jan. 10, 2020, https://junto.digital/blog/seo-stats/.

28 Carl, Jeremy, *How to Break Silicon Valley's Anti-Free-Speech Monopoly*, National Review, Aug. 15, 2017, https://www.nationalreview.com/2017/08/silicon-valleys-anti-conservative-bias-solution-treat-major-tech-companies-utilities/.

should be required to operate in a politically impartial fashion — not moderate posts on the basis of political ideology — because they are essentially public utilities. Therefore, shouldn't they be required to deliver their services in a neutral manner, without discrimination, as telephone companies and electric companies do?

But others contend that social media sites allow too much speech, and do not do enough moderation of posts. They blame Facebook, Twitter and other sites for exacerbating problems such as online harassment, fake news and more, and want lawmakers to impose more restrictions on the platforms. "For every story … about an activist's post wrongly (and often temporarily) being removed, there are three more about the consequences of a post that was left up: a piece of viral misinformation, a terrorist recruitment video, a financial scam, and so on," according to Newton of The Verge.[29]

Each year, the Simon Wiesenthal Center issues an online report card on how well or poorly various social media sites deal with hate speech. Most sites get grades of C or D, although in 2020 Twitter received a B, while Facebook and Google/YouTube each received a B−. In releasing the center's 2019 report card, Rabbi Abraham Cooper, associate dean and director of global social action of the center, said, "The idea of online hate and terror posing a danger is not an abstraction." He added that the report card "proves that social media giants can and must do more to degrade the capabilities of racists, anti-Semites and terrorists."[30]

Anonymity

One reason why harmful speech flourishes online is anonymity. The majority of online trolling and hate speech attacks come from pseudonymous accounts. But, given that even seemingly innocuous online comments sometimes cause trouble, there can also be good reasons to conceal one's identity online. Moreover, journalists, activists and whistleblowers frequently utilize anonymity to expose injustices. Whatever the reasons a user may have, anonymous speech is a staple of the Internet.

In fact, there's a famous *New Yorker* cartoon showing a dog at a computer, talking to another dog, with the caption, "On the Internet, nobody knows you're a dog."[31] This is true, to the extent that people — and dogs, apparently — can operate online using a false or hidden identity. But Internet websites and services often are able to collect identification information from their users, even those who take elaborate efforts to hide their true identities online.

29 Newton, *supra* note 20.

30 Simon Wiesenthal Center, *Simon Wiesenthal Center Releases 2019 Digital Terrorism and Hate Report Card*, Mar. 14, 2019, http://www.wiesenthal.com/about/news/2019-digital-report-card.html.

31 The cartoon can be viewed at https://bit.ly/2U1zc5t.

As a legal matter, courts have generally recognized that anonymous speech is protected by the First Amendment. If you operate a website and the police or another government official wants information to determine who posted comments on your site, you don't need to reveal anything unless they first obtain a court order or a subpoena. But a court may still issue such a court order or subpoena to compel a website or app operator to reveal identity information of users — including but not limited to the user's IP address, which can identify the device or Internet connection point used — to identify the source of online speech that is defamatory, threatening or otherwise illegal.

In 2007, two Yale law students used litigation to determine the identities of several anonymous authors who the students said defamed and threatened them by posting malicious falsehoods on an Internet message board.[32] They were able to identify some of the posters, and eventually reached settlements with them.

But in 2001 a New Jersey appellate court held that a company seeking the identity of an anonymous poster on an online bulletin board could not obtain the poster's identity because the company had not shown that the post was harmful.[33]

So, tell your dog to be mindful of what he posts online. He may not be as anonymous as he thinks.

CLOSING ARGUMENTS

Unlike in the U.S., hate speech is illegal in many European countries. Does America need to change its free-speech laws in the era of instant global communications, and make hate speech illegal here too? And how would you define hate speech? Or does the right to free speech, even if we don't agree with it, outweigh concerns over hate speech?

32 *Doe v. Ciolli*, No. 307CV00909 CFD (D. Conn. Nov. 8, 2007).

33 *Dendrite International, Inc. v. Doe No. 3*, 342 N.J. Super. 134, 775 A. 2d 756 (N.J. App. Div. 2001).

Additional Sources

Associated Press, *Missing Myanmar Blogger Seen Detained*, Fox News, Feb. 4, 2008, https://www.foxnews.com/printer_friendly_wires/2008Feb04/0,4675,MyanmarMissingBlogger,00.html.

Citron, Danielle K., *Law's Expressive Value in Combating Cyber Gender Harassment*, 108 Michigan Law Review 373 (2009), https://repository.law.umich.edu/mlr/vol108/iss3/3.

Force v. Facebook, 934 F.3d 53 (2d Cir. 2019), *cert. denied*, 140 S.Ct. 2761, 206 L. Ed. 2d 936 (May 18, 2020).

Gitlow v. New York, 268 U.S. 652, 666 (1925).

Greenwald, Glenn, *Facebook and Twitter Cross a Line Far More Dangerous Than What They Censor*, The Intercept, Oct. 15, 2020, https://theintercept.com/2020/10/15/facebook-and-twitter-cross-a-line-far-more-dangerous-than-what-they-censor/.

Guardian Staff, *Thai King Pardons American Convicted of Insulting Monarchy*, The Guardian, July 10, 2012, https://www.theguardian.com/world/2012/jul/11/thai-king-pardons-american-insulting.

Human Rights Watch, *North Korea*, https://www.hrw.org/asia/north-korea.

In re Philadelphia Newspapers, LLC, 690 F.3d 161, 175 (3d Cir. 2012), cert. dismissed sub. nom. *Gureghian v. Philadelphia Newspapers, LLC*, 568 U.S. 1151 (2013).

Levenson, Eric, *Harvard Rescinded Admission for Racist Comments. It Wasn't the First Time*, CNN, June 18, 2019, https://www.cnn.com/2019/06/18/us/harvard-rescind-admission/index.htm.

North Korea Constitution, English translation. https://www.kfausa.org/dprk-constitution/.

Prager University v. Google LLC, 951 F.3d 991 (9th Cir. 2020).

Seager, Ilana, *Law Graduates Settle Suit*, Yale Daily News, Oct. 23, 2009, https://yaledailynews.com/blog/2009/10/23/law-graduates-settle-suit/.

Simon, Joel, *A New Candidate for World's Worst Media Law*, Columbia Journalism Review, June 30, 2017, https://www.cjr.org/opinion/media-myanmar-law-journalism.php.

Simon Weisenthal Center, *2020 Digital Terrorism + Hate Report Card*, 2020, http://www.digitalhate.net/inicio.php.

Stromberg v. California, 283 U.S. 359, 368 (1931).

Twitter v. Super, Ct. ex. rel. Taylor, No, A154173 (Cal. App., 1st Dist. Aug. 17, 2018).

United Nations, International Covenant on Civil and Political Rights, Article 19, enacted 1976.

United Nations Universal Declaration of Human Rights, Article 19.

Wilson, Bradley, *Scholastic Journalism Law: A New Case*, 54 Communication: Journalism Education Today 2 (2020), 34–39.

Zeran v. America Online, Inc., 129 F.3d 327 (4th Cir. 1997), *cert. denied*, 524 U.S. 937 (1998).

5 Limitations on Online Speech

> [B]ullying, stalking and other forms of harassment are serious problems in our society.
>
> — Minnesota Supreme Court

As explained in the previous chapter, the right of free speech protected by the First Amendment is not absolute: there are a few, limited exceptions. If online speech falls within one of these exceptions, it can be declared to be illegal, and whoever posts such material can be legally penalized. In most circumstances, the penalties are limited to civil damages: money required to be paid to someone to compensate them for the damage done by the speech. But in limited circumstances, there may be criminal penalties — fines and perhaps even jail time — for particular types of illegal speech.

This chapter explores speech restrictions in cyberspace. Both statutory law and common law have determined that Internet users, and not service providers, are responsible for violations of the law in the material they post online. Social media sites such as Facebook and Twitter may further restrict speech on their platforms through their Terms of Use.

Restricted Speech Online

While the language of the First Amendment to the United States Constitution provides that "Congress shall make no law … abridging the freedom of speech, or of the press;" in fact the law does allow some limitations on free speech. The restrictions on speech that apply online are detailed in this chapter.

Defamation

Defamation, also sometimes referred to as slander for oral statements or libel for written statements, is the dissemination of a false statement of fact that seriously harms someone's reputation.

While the Internet and social media enable us to quickly and widely publish statements online, these statements are still subject to defamation laws.

Given the increasing number of lawsuits involving defamation on social media platforms such as Twitter, online statements should be made thoughtfully. In one such lawsuit, musician Courtney Love had to pay a $430,000 settlement to fashion designer Dawn Simorangkir in 2011 as the result of Love's tweets, MySpace posts and commentary on other social media sites that expressed negative and false accusations about the designer.[1]

To provide a hypothetical to illustrate libel: if you post a tweet that says, "Professor Johnson stole a computer from the university," you'd better be right or you could end up in legal trouble like Courtney Love. If you're wrong, you have probably seriously harmed — defamed — Professor Johnson's reputation and could be sued for a significant amount of money. But whether Professor Johnson will win depends on a number of factors.

The Plaintiff's Case

There are five things that a person suing traditionally had to show before he could successfully sue for libel. And the U.S. Supreme Court added one more. The requirements for a defamation lawsuit are explained in this section, followed by a summary in the box below.

The first thing the person suing must show is that the defamatory statement has been disseminated to at least one person other than the speaker or the person being spoken about. (This is referred to as "publication," regardless of the medium used.) Posting a statement online would qualify as dissemination, even if it is posted to a site or page where access is limited to only a few people. Thus, defamatory statements can appear on news and other websites, blogs, tweets, Yelp reviews, YouTube videos, podcasts, wikis, online discussion boards and elsewhere online. Even if the statement is quickly deleted or only one other person sees the statement, it could be considered published.

Second, a person suing for defamation must also show that he has been individually identified. If there is no "identification," a person cannot successfully sue for libel even if he believes that he is the one being targeted by a false accusation.

Because of this requirement, a group of people cannot sue for harm to their individual reputations when statements are made about the group as a whole; however, an organization may be able to sue for harm to its reputation.

In many cases, it's pretty easy to determine whether a statement is about an individual or not. If a person is named, he will almost certainly meet this "identification" requirement. But in other cases, it's not so clear. If you do not explicitly name the person but provide enough specific details that there can be no confusion over whom you're referring to, the identification standard is met. So, if you defame the "government executive who makes his home

1 *Simorangkir v. Cobain*, B254895 (Cal. Ct. App. Feb. 26, 2015).

at 1600 Pennsylvania Avenue," it is still reasonably identifiable as the U.S. president.

Third, the person suing must show that the defamatory statement is an assertion of an alleged fact, not a statement of opinion. If a statement contains only opinion, it cannot be libelous.

Unfortunately, it is sometimes difficult to tell one from the other. For example, the statement "Professor Johnson stole a computer from the lab" is clearly an assertion of fact. For one thing, facts are objective; they are either true or false. Either he unlawfully took a computer or he didn't. Compare that with the statement, "Professor Johnson is awful." This statement can't really be proven true or false, so it would be considered purely opinion. Such a statement is fully protected in a defamation lawsuit, and a lawsuit would likely be dismissed.

This requirement that a statement must assert a fact in order for it to be libel is one of the reasons that cyberbullying and Internet trolling are so difficult to regulate. Most cyberbullying and trolling consist of insults and name-calling that can seriously harm someone's feelings but are not defamatory because they do not assert facts. Statements such as "You stink," and "Your life is not worth living," while hurtful, do not assert facts that can be proven or disproven, and thus do not meet the requirements for proving libel.

Some statements can contain both opinion and fact. For example, "I think Professor Johnson is awful because he is a thief" is a mixed statement that might support a libel claim. The first assertion in the statement, that Professor Johnson is "awful," is a statement of opinion. But the second assertion, that he is "a thief," is provably true or false and can be the basis of a libel claim if it can be proven to be untrue. Note that starting the sentence with "I think" does not make the statement that Professor Johnson is "a thief" a statement of opinion; it is still asserting a fact.

A close cousin of opinion is satire and humor, which are statements that appear to assert facts but are made in a way or context which clarifies that the statement is not to be understood as a truthful statement. The publication of April Fools' e-mails, spoof articles on websites like *The Babylon Bee* and other humorous or satirical online content occasionally prompts threats of defamation or other lawsuits by individuals who find themselves the target of ridicule. Generally, it is not a defense to a defamation suit to claim that you were "just trying to be funny" or meant it "only as a joke." Humor is not necessarily the same as "opinion," and does not enjoy blanket protection from lawsuits. However, if a statement cannot reasonably be interpreted by readers to be one of express or implied fact, it cannot be defamatory. A federal appeals court explained that "a satire or parody must be assessed in the appropriate context; it is not actionable if it 'cannot reasonably be interpreted as stating actual facts about an individual.'"[2] In other words, as long as most readers would

2 *Farah v. Esquire Magazine*, 736 F.3d 528 (D.C. Cir. 2013), *reh'g en banc denied* (D.C. Cir. Jan. 23, 2014).

understand that a joke or cartoon is not meant to be taken seriously, its subject cannot successfully sue for defamation. Subtle humor can be dangerous, though. For example, posting a photo to Instagram of a coach and an athlete standing together and writing a joking comment that the two are having an affair might be funny to those who know it's a joke, but it might also be fairly believable to those who don't; and possibly harm reputations. To be safe, if you intend something as a joke, be sure to make it clear that everyone should recognize it as such.

Fourth, only false statements of fact can be defamatory. Truth is an absolute defense to a charge of defamation: if something is true, it is the fact itself that hurts reputation, not the statement of that truth. But proving you're telling the truth may be difficult. For example, even though you know that Professor Johnson stole a computer, do you have sufficient, reliable evidence — verifiable documents, police reports, photographs, trustworthy and unbiased witnesses, etc. — to back your claim if Professor Johnson denies it? If you don't, you may not be able to rely on the truth to get you out of a defamation lawsuit. On the other hand, if you make a statement saying something that you know is true — and you can prove that it is true — you can never be successfully sued for online defamation for that statement, no matter how much it might damage a person's reputation or how angry he might be.

Fifth, in order to successfully sue for online defamation, the person suing must also show that the false statement about him caused serious harm to his reputation. Being mildly offended or embarrassed is not enough. That said, some statements about a person — if false — will almost always be sufficiently harmful to a person's reputation to support a defamation claim. For example, if you publish a statement that accuses a person of having committed a crime — such as stealing school property — your facts must be accurate because such accusations will almost always seriously harm a person's reputation among the general public. On the other hand, if you tweet that Professor Johnson gave you a dirty look in class today, he can't sue you for defamation even if you're lying. Even if such a statement would hurt his reputation among students, it's the perception of him by the general public in the community — not just students — that matters.

The sixth requirement for a defamation lawsuit was added by the U.S. Supreme Court in the 1964 decision *New York Times v. Sullivan* and subsequent cases. In these cases, the Supreme Court said that in order to successfully sue for defamation, the First Amendment requires that in addition to the other requirements, the person suing must also show — at a minimum — that the defendant messed up, that he or she was somehow at fault. In this context, "messing up" means either doing something that a reasonable person would not have done or failing to do something that a reasonable person should have done.

The level of fault required depends on the nature of the person suing and the subject of the statement that is said to be defamatory. If the person who claims that she has been libeled is a public official or a public figure, she may have to show that the person who made the statement about her knew that the statement was false or acted with reckless disregard for the truth, meaning the person who made the statement should have checked out whether it was true or not but did not do so. In *New York Times v. Sullivan*, the U.S. Supreme Court called this "actual malice."[3] This term should not be confused with "malice," which in both legal and non-legal contexts means an animus or ill-will towards a person or organization.

"Actual malice" is a very high standard to meet. Showing that the person who made the statement made a mistake, or relied on a source that was in error, is not enough. Also, showing that the speaker/writer made a false statement is insufficient, without also showing that the defendant knew that the statement was false or that the statement was so outrageous that he should have verified it. For example, a judge won $2 million from a Boston newspaper that reported that he had said that a 14-year-old rape victim should "get over it," without verifying whether the judge actually made the statement with anyone who was present when and where he allegedly said it.[4] On the other hand, tabloids and gossip websites that cover celebrity news are able to avoid many lawsuits by not thoroughly investigating information they receive, so they can claim that they did not know whether the information was actually true or not.

Some people, including President Donald Trump and U.S. Supreme Court justices Antonin Scalia (now deceased) and Clarence Thomas, have criticized the "actual malice" standard as being too difficult to prove, claiming that it allows for irresponsible reporting about people who willingly or unwillingly become known to the public. But changing the law would require a ruling by the U.S. Supreme Court overturning the *New York Times v. Sullivan* precedent, which is very unlikely because that case is the foundation of multiple court decisions over the more than 50 years since that ruling.

People aren't the only ones who can be defamed. Business defamation, also known as business disparagement, is another potential pitfall relating to online speech. It involves belittling someone's business, goods or services with a remark that is false or misleading but not necessarily defamatory. To succeed in a business disparagement case, the plaintiff must prove that (1) the defendant made the disparaging remark, (2) the defendant intended to injure the business, (3) the statement resulted in financial damages to the plaintiff's business, and (4) the defendant speaker knew the statement was false, or recklessly disregarded whether it was true (acted with "actual malice"). It is very difficult for businesses to win such cases, though, because of the high "actual malice" requirement. As a result, courts will impose liability for business disparagement only in the most egregious cases.

3 *New York Times v. Sullivan*, 376 U.S. 254 (1964).

4 *Murphy v. Boston Herald, Inc.*, 449 Mass. 42, 865 N.E.2d 746 (2007).

REQUIREMENTS OF A DEFAMATION LAWSUIT

To win a defamation lawsuit, a plaintiff must show the following "elements":

1. **Publication:** Defendant published statement to a third party.
2. **Identification:** Statement was about ("of and concerning") the plaintiff.
3. **Factual Statement:** Statement asserts or implies a provable fact.
4. **Falsity:**
   - If the plaintiff is a public figure or the statement involves a public issue, the plaintiff must show that statement was false.
   - If the plaintiff is a private figure and the statement involves a private issue, falsity is presumed but the defendant may show that statement is true.
5. **Defamation/Harm:** Statement harmed the plaintiff's reputation; the plaintiff may also be required to show actual financial harm, depending on the type of plaintiff and type of issue.
   - If the plaintiff is a public figure and the statement involves a public issue, damages may be presumed for inherently libelous statements (known as "libel per se"). But for other statements (known as "libel per quod"), the plaintiff must prove actual damages.
   - If the plaintiff is a public figure and the statement involves a private issue, damages may be presumed, but the plaintiff must show actual malice to be awarded money to punish the defendant for making the harmful statement ("punitive damages").
   - If the plaintiff is a private figure and the statement involves a public issue, the plaintiff must prove actual damages, and must show actual malice to be awarded punitive damages.
   - If the plaintiff is a private figure and the statement involves a private issue, damages may be presumed, and punitive damages may be awarded without the plaintiff having to show actual malice.
6. **Fault:** The plaintiff must show that the defendant acted with some level of fault, with the level of fault depending on the type of plaintiff and issue.
   - If the plaintiff is a public figure, the plaintiff must show "actual malice."
     - This applies whenever the plaintiff is a public figure, regardless of whether the statement involves a public or private issue.
   - If the plaintiff is a private figure and the statement involves a public issue:
     - To receive money to compensate for the harm caused by a defamatory statement (known as "compensatory damages"),

> the plaintiff must meet the standard set by the state in which the lawsuit is heard (and, the Supreme Court has held, that standard must be at least negligence).
> - To receive punitive damages, the plaintiff must show "actual malice."
>
> - If the plaintiff is a private figure and the statement involves a private issue, the plaintiff must meet the standard set by the state in which the lawsuit is heard (that standard cannot be strict liability).

The Defendant's Case

Once a plaintiff sues for defamation, it is important to note that the defendant must respond. Failure to respond will likely result in the court issuing a default judgment for the plaintiff and against the defendant. This will mean that the defendant will have to pay the amount of money sought by the plaintiff.

But aside from failing to respond, the individual or organization sued has a number of ways to react to being sued. Normally, the defendant — or, most commonly, their lawyers — will assert one or more "procedural defenses" to argue that the plaintiff has not met the procedural and similar requirements, and that the case should be dismissed for not meeting these requirements.

Some of the most commonly used arguments for dismissal of defamation lawsuits are the following.

Time Limits

Those who sue for defamation must do so fairly soon after the defamatory statement is made. In most states, the statute of limitations for filing a libel suit is one or two years, with the time period to sue for slander often shorter than the period to sue for libel. Many courts have adopted the so-called "Single Publication Rule," which provides this time period begins at first publication of the material, despite later reposts or continued availability online of the same material.

SLAPP Lawsuits

Sometimes businesses or individuals will file defamation lawsuits as a way to censor valid criticism. The plaintiff knows there is no chance of winning the lawsuit, but merely wants to intimidate customers, rivals and others from expressing negative opinions about them. This practice is known as a "strategic lawsuit against public participation" (SLAPP). In response, many states have passed anti-SLAPP laws to allow early dismissal of such lawsuits. Congress has enacted a limited provision, the Consumer Review Freedom Act, which allows for dismissal of such lawsuits brought over consumer reviews of businesses. But these laws do not eliminate the problem entirely, since it's still a headache for defendants to have to respond to such lawsuits — usually including hiring a lawyer — in order to get them dismissed.

Section 230 Immunity

The interactivity of the modern Internet raises a new, interesting legal issue for online defamation: can website operators get sued for defamatory comments that people post on their sites? The short answer is generally no. If you operate a blog, discussion board or other website that allows users to comment or post material, you are not legally responsible for libelous comments made by outsiders. This covers both personal blogs and websites, and large social media sites and services such as Facebook and WhatsApp.

In short, sites cannot be sued for material posted by users, with only a few, limited exceptions. The exceptions are if the material violates federal law or facilitates sex trafficking. But this protection only applies to the sites: the authors of such comments can and do get sued regularly. So, in the Courtney Love case discussed earlier, she could be sued for what she posted on Twitter and other sites, but the sites themselves were protected from lawsuits.

The source of this protection from liability is Section 230 of the federal Communications Decency Act. This law was passed in the early days of the Internet in 1996, because Congress did not want to stifle web development by placing an enormous burden on website owners to screen every comment posted by users for libel and other issues. Without such a law, massive online discussion boards such as Reddit and 4chan, and group chat apps such as Telegram and Discord would likely not be possible. While most of the Communications Decency Act was held unconstitutional by the U.S. Supreme Court in *Reno v. American Civil Liberties Union*, Section 230 remains.

Section 230 provides that a site operator can retain legal immunity even if it voluntarily screens profane or libelous comments. But if the site starts rewriting comments to "improve" them, then it may become responsible as a creator of the post. For example, the operators of conspiracy websites were held to not be immune under Section 230 when they added their own commentary and headlines to materials posted by users.[5] Also, sites are not immune from liability for posts that violate federal law or promote sex trafficking. Section 230 is discussed in more detail in Chapter 4.

Finally, Section 230 does not protect website operators or bloggers who republish defamatory statements. If you write your own blog post that quotes someone else making a defamatory statement, it could land you in legal hot

5 *Gilmore v. Jones*, 370 F.Supp. 3d 630 (W.D.Va. 2019), *appeal denied*, No. 19-381 (4th Cir., Nov. 6, 2019).

water just the same as if you had said or written the defamatory statement yourself.

Other Defenses

In addition to the arguments above, defendants sued for defamation over online content can also use various defenses that were developed for older forms of media. These defenses, along with the Internet-specific ones, are summarized in the box below.

RESPONSES TO A DEFAMATION LAWSUIT

The following can be used to dismiss a lawsuit shortly after it is filed, without the need to gather any evidence:

1. **Failure to State a Claim:** Defendant shows that the plaintiff has not shown the required elements of defamation that are listed above, including "actual malice," if it is applicable.
2. **Retraction Statute:** In many states, before suing for defamation the plaintiff must first demand that the person or entity who made an allegedly defamatory statement retract the statement. Failure to make this demand is a ground for dismissing the case.
3. **Anti-SLAPP Statute:** Defendant shows that the primary aim of the defamation lawsuit is to limit discussion of a legitimate public issue or controversy. (See above.)
4. **Jurisdiction:** If the court in which the lawsuit is brought does not have the authority to hear the case, it will be dismissed.
   - A court's jurisdiction is generally limited to a specific geographic area: the defendant must reside or do business within that area, or the incident leading to the lawsuit must have occurred there.
   - Courts struggled a bit with jurisdiction over Internet cases when the web was new, but have generally settled on the notion that if a website has impact with a court's geographic area, it has jurisdiction.
5. **Statute of Limitations:** Cases must be filed within a certain time period. (See above.)
6. **Section 230 of the Communications Decency Act:** A website operator is not liable for material posted by someone else, without the provider's involvement. (See above.)
7. **Other Defenses:** Two additional defenses that are very rare are consent, which is when the plaintiff consented to the defendant making the defamatory statement; and the archaic "right of reply"

principle, in which the victim of a defamatory statement has the right to respond with a defamatory statement against the original speaker, and cannot be sued for it.

The following can be used to dismiss a lawsuit after some evidence has been gathered in a process known as pre-trial "discovery." The arguments above can also be used at this stage.

1. **Truth:** Evidence shows that the statement is true or that there are only minor, inconsequential errors ("substantial truth").
2. **Privilege:** The statement at issue under one of several recognized legal privileges. Privileges are either absolute (complete protection) or conditional (must meet certain criteria).
   - **Absolute Privileges:**
     - **Speech and Debate Clause:** Members of Congress have full immunity for statements during congressional debates ONLY. This does not extend to their other statements, including online and on social media.
     - **Public Proceeding ("record libel"):** Immunity for statements during public government proceedings, including videos and transcripts posted online. This does not extend to statements outside such meetings, including online and on social media.
     - **Official Duties:** Government employees have immunity for statements made in the course of their official duties, including on official websites or social media accounts.
     - **Other:** Other absolute privileges that apply primarily outside the online context are statements in the context of an employer–employee relationship, an employer's evaluation of an employee to another employer and credit bureau rating reports.
   - **Qualified Privileges:** These vary by state.
     - **Fair Report:** A report of an official government proceeding or document is privileged if it is shown to be an accurate and fair account of the proceeding. This privilege is recognized in virtually all states.
     - **Neutral Reportage:** A fair report of a statement made by a responsible and preeminent source is privilege. This is recognized by a few states.
     - **Wire Service Defense:** Repeating a statement from a credible wire or news service is privileged in a few states.
3. **Opinion:** Statements of opinion can't be defamatory, but facts contained or assumed in a statement of opinion can be. (See above.)

- Specific types of statements covered by the opinion defense are:
  - **Fair Comment and Criticism:** Opinions about an individual or organization (for example, restaurant and movie reviews).
  - **Rhetorical Hyperbole:** Overstatement to make a point that is not meant to be taken as literally true (for example, a restaurant's boast that it has the "best coffee in town").
  - **Sarcasm/Parody:** An explicitly or implicitly false statement, made to ridicule, based on the context.

Foreign Law and the SPEECH Act

U.S. law is generally very protective of speech and imposes high standards for defamation claims. But most other countries do not provide such vigorous protection of speech under their laws, and courts in these countries routinely impose large fines or even criminal prison sentences on those who defame others. In some of these nations, making a disparaging statement about a high government official is a major crime, regardless of whether the statement is true or false.

The global nature of modern media means that content published in the U.S. for an American audience is now likely to be available worldwide, and to be viewed differently by authorities in other countries. This led some celebrities and wealthy individuals to sue U.S.-based media entities or individuals for defamation in countries that are not as protective of free speech as American courts. They would then obtain large monetary judgments and would then turn to the American courts to enforce the foreign judgments.

Some courts resisted this, ruling that enforcing such judgments would violate the First Amendment. Then several states passed laws barring their courts from enforcing such judgments. Finally, in 2010 Congress passed and President Barack Obama signed the "Securing the Protection of our Enduring and Established Constitutional Heritage" (SPEECH) Act, which bars all American courts from enforcing defamation judgments from countries that do not provide protections to speech similar to those in the U.S. So far, American courts have not found any country — even Great Britain and Australia — that meets this standard.

It is important to note that the SPEECH Act applies only to defamation claims. It does not apply to other claims, such as copyright.

Obscenity

Material deemed "obscene" is not protected by the First Amendment, the U.S. Supreme Court has ruled.[6] The problem comes in defining what mate-

6 *Roth v. U.S.*, 354 U.S. 476 (1957).

rial is "obscene," and can be banned, and what is merely "indecent," which cannot. In order to determine what content qualifies as obscene, in 1973 the Supreme Court developed what's known as "the *Miller* Test," named for *Miller v. California*, the case in which the court announced the current standard. Under this test, content is obscene only if three conditions are met: (1) "the average person, applying contemporary community standards, would find that the [content], taken as a whole, appeals to the 'prurient interest'" (defined as "a shameful and morbid interest in nudity, sex, or excretion"[7]), (2) "the work depicts or describes, in a patently offensive way, sexual conduct or excretory functions specifically defined by applicable state law," and (3) "the work, taken as a whole, lacks serious literary, artistic, political, or scientific value."[8]

The first and second parts of this test are based on local standards in a particular community, while the third is meant to be based on a nationwide standard. This presents a particular dilemma online, where material is available in a variety of places that may have different standards. What may be readily accepted in Manhattan, New York may be considered illicit in Manhattan, Kansas. This test for obscenity has also been criticized by legal scholars as being too vague, since it does not identify criteria for determining "community standards," and overly broad, since it does not specify what types of materials can be banned by the test.

Nevertheless, there is not much online that is, legally speaking, considered obscene. As a result, there are not many federal obscenity prosecutions these days. But research by scholar Jennifer Kinsley shows that such prosecutions continue at the state level.[9]

The only type of content that the Supreme Court has consistently ruled is obscene is child pornography. It is illegal for anyone to purchase, own, view or distribute sexually explicit content showing minors under the age of 18. Just merely viewing such a photo or video is illegal.

But even this sensible restriction has led to unintended consequences, since the restrictions also apply to the children themselves. The result is that "sexting" — minors taking and sharing sexual photos of themselves — is considered illegal child pornography. For example, if a 16-year-old sends a sexually explicit photo of himself to his 16-year-old girlfriend, either the sender or the recipient could be charged with a felony: one for transmission of child pornography, the other for possession. In some cases, teens have been convicted and required to register as sexual offenders. As a result, some states have changed their laws to ease penalties for teen sexting. But other states have imprisoned teens for these kinds of offenses.

7 *Miller v. California*, 413 U.S. 15, 18, n.1 (1973) (citing Cal. Penal Code § 311(1969)); Model Penal Code § 251.4 (1962 draft)).

8 *Id.*, 413 U.S. at 24.

9 Kinsley, Jennifer, *The Myth of Obsolete Obscenity*, 33 Cardozo Arts & Entertainment Law Journal 607 (2015), https://ssrn.com/abstract=2600017.

Congress attempted to outlaw digitally created images of children generated by computer that appear to be of real minors by passing the Child Pornography Prevention Act of 1996. But the U.S. Supreme Court questioned the supposed link between computer-generated pornography and the abuse of actual children and overturned the law, ruling it was overly broad.[10]

Sexual material that does not meet the *Miller* test for obscenity may be "indecent." Indecent material is generally protected by the First Amendment and cannot be banned or punished by the government. The sole exception is on broadcast radio and TV: the U.S. Supreme Court has upheld Federal Communications Commission (FCC) rules barring indecent broadcasts between 6 a.m. and 10 p.m., when children are likely to be in the audience, but has also held that the FCC cannot enforce these rules without consistent standards.[11]

In 1996, Congress attempted to impose a similar ban on obscene or indecent material online that was accessible to children. But the following year the Supreme Court held that the restrictions were unconstitutional for three reasons: because the inclusion of "indecent" material made the ban too broad; because the restrictions were so extensive that they would limit adults' access to such materials; and because there was no reason that material on the Internet should be more restricted than print material.[12]

The upshot is that adult pornography is generally legal online. But the U.S. Supreme Court allowed the federal government to require libraries and schools to install filters blocking such material to minors on their computers as a condition for receiving federal aid.[13]

Many other types of content, which reasonable people would probably agree are disturbing or disgusting, are also legal. For example, the Supreme Court struck down a law banning videos of animal abuse.[14] To be clear: it is still illegal to abuse an animal and doing so could result in a prison sentence. But posting or watching an online video of an animal being abused is not illegal. As absurd as this seems, there are reasons why courts have kept it that way: PETA and other animal rights groups wouldn't be able to show their commercials or educational videos if animal abuse videos were banned.

Outside the U.S., the bar for obscene material is lower. New Zealand authorities, for example, deemed a 2019 video of a mosque shooting that killed 51 along with a manifesto published by the gunman to be "objectionable and restricted material" and threatened to imprison anyone who shared it online. In fact, one violator was sentenced to 21 months in prison.[15]

10 *Ashcroft v. Free Speech Coal.*, 535 U.S. 234 (2002).

11 *F.C.C. v. Pacifica Foundation*, 438 U.S. 726 (1978).

12 *Reno v. American Civil Liberties Union*, 521 U.S. 844 (1997).

13 *U.S. v. American Library Association*, 539 U.S. 194 (2003).

14 *U.S. v. Stevens*, 559 U.S. 460 (2010).

15 Hollingsworth, Julia, *Man Who Shared New Zealand Mosque Shooting Video Online Jailed For 21 Months*, CNN, June 18, 2019, https://www.cnn.com/2019/06/18/asia/christchurch-livestream-sentence-nz-intl-hnk/index.html.

Threats and Incitement

Other types of speech that are not protected by the First Amendment include "true threats" and speech threatening "imminent lawless action." For example, sending an e-mail to someone that threatens to physically harm them would be considered a true threat. Similarly, inciting others to imminent lawless action is illegal. For instance, tweeting to agitated students that they should vandalize the college president's office over her proposal to raise tuition, in a situation where it was likely to happen, could qualify as such speech.

In a controversial 2002 decision, the U.S. Court of Appeals for the Ninth Circuit ruled that an anti-abortion group's website listing "Wanted" posters along with the names and addresses of abortion doctors constituted a true threat that was not protected by the First Amendment.

However, the U.S. Supreme Court has held that threats may not be punished if a reasonable person would understand them as obvious hyperbole. Threats of social ostracism and of politically motivated boycotts are also constitutionally protected.[16]

Comedian Kathy Griffin illustrates both of these exceptions. In 2017, after a graphic photo of her holding aloft the bloody severed head of a dummy made to look like President Trump went viral on social media, she was not arrested by the U.S. Secret Service. "People are allowed to wish the president dead," Stanford University law professor Nathaniel Persily explained.[17] But Griffin is not immune from the consequences of her post. People are allowed to be outraged over what they consider a joke done in bad taste, and to express that outrage, as long as they do not make a "true threat" against Griffin. And, following a public outcry and advertising boycott over the post, CNN dropped Griffin as host of its popular New Year's Eve program.

Saying things that are so provocative that they are likely to incite someone who hears it to act violently against the speaker is also illegal. Under the U.S. Supreme Court's "fighting words" doctrine, "insulting or 'fighting words' — those that by their very utterance inflict injury or tend to incite an immediate breach of the peace" — are not protected by the First Amendment.[18] For example, a violation might occur if a speaker hurls insulting language directly at another person, intending to instigate a violent reaction. However, the Supreme Court has not upheld any fighting words conviction since its original 1942 case on the issue.

Legal scholars question whether fighting words are even possible online: "In *Chaplinsky*, the 'fighting words' were uttered directly into the face of the victim," says the Cato Institute's John Samples. "On Twitter such abuse is shared

16 *N.A.A.C.P. v. Claiborne Hardware, Inc.*, 458 U.S. 886, 913 (1982).

17 Cummings, William, *Did Kathy Griffin Break the Law with Her Photo of a Decapitated Trump?*, USA Today, May 30, 2017, https://www.usatoday.com/story/news/nation/2017/05/31/did-kathy-griffin-break-law-her-photo-decapitated-trump/356840001/.

18 *Chaplinsky v. New Hampshire*, 315 U.S. 568 (1942).

among strangers separated by space and time ... While some social media feuds may in some sense spur real world violence, the delay between online provocation and terrestrial reaction is more than sufficient to foreclose fighting words designations based on threats of imminent violence."[19]

Fighting words — direct personal insults made against a specific person or persons in their presence — are commonly confused with hate speech, which is hostile, but non-violent, speech aimed at a group of people (not specific individuals) based on race, religion, ethnicity, gender, sexual orientation or other characteristics. Hate speech is not illegal. As explained by scholar Eugene Volokh, "Hateful ideas (whatever exactly that might mean) are just as protected under the First Amendment as other ideas. One is as free to condemn Islam — or Muslims, or Jews, or blacks, or whites, or illegal aliens, or native-born citizens — as one is to condemn capitalism or socialism or Democrats or Republicans."[20]

Texting and Driving

The government may ban texting — along with operating all electronic devices — while driving, and it is not considered a violation of the First Amendment. The U.S. Supreme Court has said that "laws regulating the time, place or manner of speech stand on a different footing than laws prohibiting speech altogether."[21] Such restrictions on speech are constitutional if: (1) they do not treat speech differently based on content (are "content neutral"); (2) they are narrowly tailored to serve a governmental interest; and (3) they leave open ample alternative means of expression. In the case of banning texting while driving, the restriction is constitutional because the limitation is content neutral (it doesn't matter whom you text or what you say; it's all banned); there are alternatives (people can text when they are not driving); and banning texting while driving serves the governmental interest of keeping the roads safe.

As of 2018, nearly all states had banned text messaging for all drivers. In addition, almost 40 states at least ban novice or teen drivers from using cell phones while driving. About one-third of states prohibit any use of cell phones while driving for all drivers. However, while studies show that texting and driving is as dangerous as drunk driving, most states only punish texting drivers with relatively minor penalties. As more and more accidents and deaths are caused by texting while driving, some lawmakers have begun pushing for much tougher penalties to deter the practice.

19 Samples, John, *Fighting Words and Free Speech*, Cato Institute, June 25, 2018, https://www.cato.org/blog/fighting-words-free-speech.

20 Volokh, Eugene, *The Volokh Conspiracy: No, There's No "Hate Speech" Exception to the First Amendment*, Washington Post, May 7, 2015, https://www.washingtonpost.com/news/volokh-conspiracy/wp/2015/05/07/no-theres-no-hate-speech-exception-to-the-first-amendment/.

21 *Linmark Associates, Inc. v. Township of Willingboro*, 431 U.S. 85, 93 (1977).

Other Restrictions

Beyond the speech restrictions above, there are some other forms of online speech and expression that are legally prohibited, including: blackmail (threatening a harmful action if a demand is not met — e.g., "If you don't pay me $100, I'll e-mail the professor and let him know you cheated."), perjury (lying under oath in an official proceeding, such as a court trial or a legislative hearing), and solicitations to commit crimes (e.g. posting an ad for a hitman on Craigslist). In addition, judges may restrict online and offline speech by trial participants, including jurors, during trials in order to uphold the right to a fair trial, which is protected by the Sixth Amendment. Also, a judge may prohibit jurors from using social media or watching TV news during a trial so that media coverage of a case won't sway their opinion.

Advertising — what the law refers to as "commercial speech" — is entitled to somewhat less protection under the First Amendment than the protection given to other forms of speech. As discussed in Chapter 8, false advertising (e.g., making false statements about the advertising product or service such as posting fake photos of rental apartments on a website such as AirBnB) and spamming (sending unsolicited commercial e-mail messages) are examples of online advertising that are illegal.

Political advertising is different, and enjoys much greater First Amendment protection than other forms of advertising. On broadcast media, stations must offer political candidates their most favorable advertising rates, must offer ad time to all candidates equally, and cannot edit ads for truthfulness (and are also not liable for falsehoods in such ads). Furthermore, the U.S. Supreme Court has also held that the First Amendment gives some protection to campaign fundraising and spending since that's what pays for political speech, which is protected by the First Amendment. As a result, several attempts to limit campaign fundraising and spending have been held unconstitutional. That said, the Federal Election Commission is considering placing new requirements on political ads to guard against foreign propaganda in future elections. Meanwhile, online platforms are becoming an increasingly important outlet for political ads. Unlike broadcast media, however, online platforms are free to reject ads they don't like.

Finally, speech that violates privacy or copyright law is not protected by the First Amendment and may also be punished. We address each of these areas in depth in other chapters.

Grey Areas

While it is clear that certain types of speech can be limited without running afoul of the First Amendment, there are some types of speech where the boundary between free speech and harmful speech that can be limited or punished is unclear. The courts continue to struggle with limitations on these types of speech.

Cyberbullying

Cyberbullying is the use of e-mail, instant messaging, social media posts, chat rooms, cell phones or other forms of information technology to deliberately harass, threaten or intimidate someone. A 2017 survey found that roughly 40% of Americans have personally experienced online harassment, and 62% consider it a major problem.[22]

Some forms of cyberbullying are patently illegal. If a statement is a true threat, as described above, it's not protected by the First Amendment, such as when a Harvard student, seeking to avoid taking an exam, e-mailed university officials claiming that bombs had been placed in two buildings on campus. Or if the statement is defamatory, as described above, or an invasion of privacy (as explained in Chapter 6) it's also not protected. These forms of cyberbullying are illegal and similar statements were illegal long before the Internet became a thing.

One of the most high-profile cases occurred in 2012, when Rutgers University student Dharun Ravi was accused of directly causing his roommate, Tyler Clementi, to commit suicide due to Ravi's cyberbullying. Ravi was ultimately sentenced to prison after he was convicted of invading Clementi's privacy by using his webcam to secretly film him kissing a man and then tweeting about it.[23]

However, the illegality of other types of cyberbullying is less clear. For example, online insults about things like someone's physical appearance, intelligence, friends, etc. — insults like "Sam is dumb," "Jamal is fat" or "Pedro is ugly" — may violate student conduct codes and lead to school discipline, but isn't illegal per se. Such statements are simply opinions, albeit mean opinions, and therefore protected by the First Amendment. But this kind of cyberbullying has also traumatized some children and teens to the point of committing suicide.

Consequently, many states have passed or are considering laws that would criminalize this kind of cyberbullying. But court rulings have been mixed. In 2014 and 2016, respectively, New York and North Carolina courts struck down state laws that would have criminalized cyberbullying on the grounds that the laws were overly broad and would have restricted protected speech.[24] In 2014, a Massachusetts court convicted a 17-year-old girl of involuntary manslaughter after it determined she had encouraged her 18-year-old boyfriend to commit suicide through a series of text messages. The judge rejected her First Amendment defense, saying that she

22 Duggan, Maeve, *Online Harassment 2017*, Pew Research Center, July 11, 2017, https://www.pewresearch.org/internet/2017/07/11/online-harassment-2017/.

23 Waldman, Ari Ezra, *State v. Dharun Ravi: What Happened?*, PrawfsBlawg, Sept. 12, 2016, https://prawfsblawg.blogs.com/prawfsblawg/2016/09/state-v-dharun-ravi-what-happened.html.

24 *People v. Marquan M.*, 24 N.Y. 3d 1, 19 N.E. 3d 480 (2014) and *State v. Bishop*, 368 N.C. 869, 787 S.E. 2d 814 (2016).

was guilty of inciting the boy to commit suicide, and her conviction was affirmed on appeal.[25] In 2019, Minnesota's Supreme Court, citing the First Amendment, overturned the conviction of a high school student who used homophobic language against a schoolmate, suggested he kill himself by drinking bleach and mocked his autism on Twitter. While acknowledging that "bullying, stalking and other forms of harassment are serious problems in our society," a judge explained that enforcing the state's cyberbullying law in the case could "prohibit and chill protected expression" because "essentially all of the tweets … contained cruel and egregious insults."[26] In 2019, a man was convicted of aggravated assault for tweeting a flashing image to a journalist that induced an eight-minute epileptic seizure. The image read: "You deserve a seizure for your post."[27] Another common form of cyberbullying is revenge porn, which is often illegal and covered in Chapter 10.

Social Media Blocking

One remedy for dealing with cyberbullies and online critics is to block them. Many social media networks, including Facebook, Instagram and Twitter, have privacy features that allow users to block other users for any reason. Elected U.S. government officials may not be able to use that option, however. In a 2019 case, the U.S. Court of Appeals for the Second Circuit affirmed the district court's holding that President Trump's practice of blocking critics from viewing his Twitter account violated the First Amendment. The court found that by using the account to conduct government business and announce government policies, Trump had made his Twitter account a "public forum," and he could not exclude specific Americans from reading his posts — and engaging in conversations in the replies to them — because he does not like their views.[28] Thus the court ordered Trump to unblock his critics. Lawsuits against other elected government officials have led to similar court rulings and settlements to stop blocking critics.

25 *Commonwealth v. Carter*, 481 Mass. 352, 115 N.E.3d 559 (2019), *cert. denied sub nom. Carter v. Massachusetts*, 140 S. Ct. 910, 205 L. Ed. 2d 456 (2020).

26 *Matter of Welfare of A. J. B.*, 929 N.W.2d 840, 846 (Minn. 2019).

27 Thebault, Reis, *A Tweet Gave A Journalist A Seizure. His Case Brings New Meaning to the Idea of 'Online Assault.'*, Washington Post, Dec. 16, 2019, https://www.washingtonpost.com/health/2019/12/16/eichenwald-strobe-gif-seizure-case/.

28 *Knight Institute v. Trump*, 928 F. 3d 226 (2d Cir. 2019), *reh'g en banc denied*, 953 F.3d 216 (2d Cir. 2020), *vacated as moot*, No. 20–197, 2021 WL 1240931 (U.S. Apr. 5, 2021).

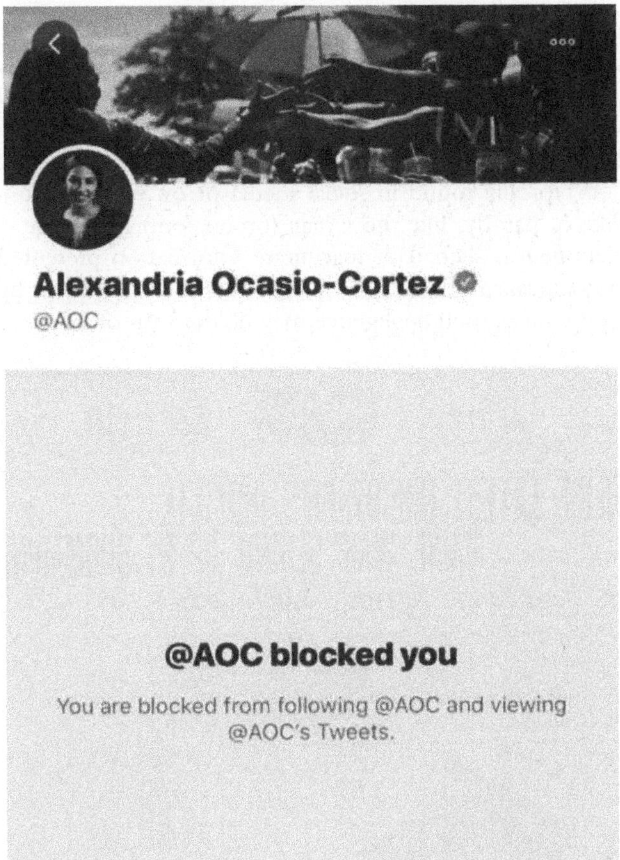

Congresswoman Alexandria Ocasio-Cortez in 2019 apologized and agreed to stop blocking critics on Twitter following two federal lawsuits. Credit: U.S. District Court, E.D.N.Y.

Catfishing

Catfishing is an Internet scam or hoax in which someone pretends to be someone else online and fools an unsuspecting victim. Currently there is no general law that makes catfishing illegal, but elements of the activity could be covered by different parts of the law. If the catfishing is done with the intent to engage in illegal activities — such as harming, threatening, defrauding or kidnapping the victim — the perpetrator could be prosecuted for fraud along with the underlying crime. In addition, someone using a fake profile of another person to post offensive messages or doctored images designed to humiliate the person they're pretending to be could also face a civil lawsuit for defamation or false light. But many other types of common catfishing practices, such as posting old, photoshopped or misrepresentative photos of oneself on a dating app, are not illegal. If that were against the law, many people on dating apps like Tinder would probably be in trouble.

Fake News

Fake news commonly refers to fabricated news — information that is completely made up but presented as being factually accurate and shared through media — although some people use the term to allege that factually accurate information that they dislike or refuse to accept is not actually true. Using the first definition, "fake news" is typically found in social media or on websites, some of which are clearly fake or parody, like the *Onion* (onion.com), but some of which are not easily identified as such. But inaccurate information presented as "news" sometimes also appears in traditional media, either intentionally or by negligence or mistake. (Of course, such negligence may be the basis of a defamation case.)

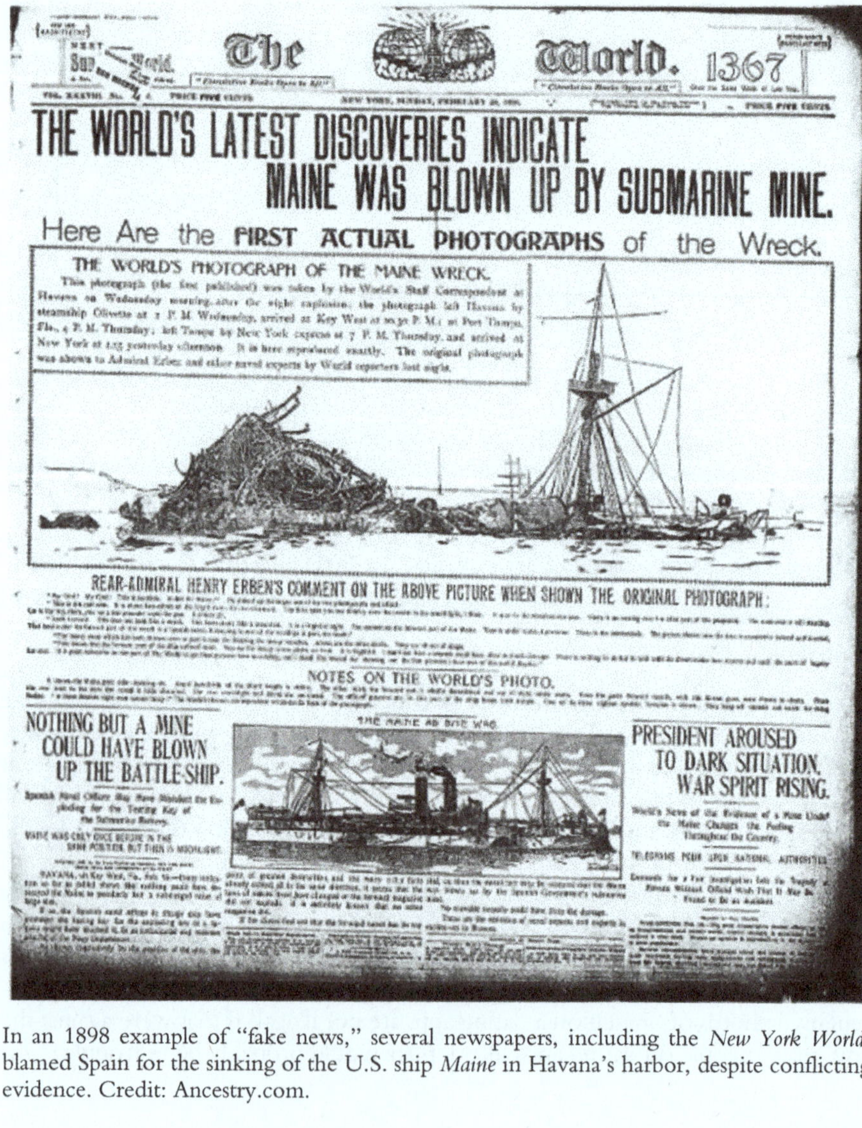

The World. 1367

THE WORLD'S LATEST DISCOVERIES INDICATE MAINE WAS BLOWN UP BY SUBMARINE MINE.

Here Are the FIRST ACTUAL PHOTOGRAPHS of the Wreck.

THE WORLD'S PHOTOGRAPH OF THE MAINE WRECK.

This photograph (the first published) was taken by the World's Staff Correspondent at Havana on Wednesday morning after the night explosion; the photograph left Havana by steamship Olivette at 1 P. M. Wednesday, arrived at Key West at 10.30 P. M.; at Port Tampa, Fla., 4 P. M. Thursday; left Tampa by New York express at 7 P. M. Thursday, and arrived at New York at 4.15 yesterday afternoon. It is here reproduced exactly. The original photograph was shown to Admiral Erben and other naval experts by World reporters last night.

REAR-ADMIRAL HENRY ERBEN'S COMMENT ON THE ABOVE PICTURE WHEN SHOWN THE ORIGINAL PHOTOGRAPH:

NOTES ON THE WORLD'S PHOTO.

NOTHING BUT A MINE COULD HAVE BLOWN UP THE BATTLE-SHIP.

PRESIDENT AROUSED TO DARK SITUATION, WAR SPIRIT RISING.

In an 1898 example of "fake news," several newspapers, including the *New York World*, blamed Spain for the sinking of the U.S. ship *Maine* in Havana's harbor, despite conflicting evidence. Credit: Ancestry.com.

Fake news is not a new phenomenon. In fact, historians believe it may have led to the Spanish–American War of 1898, when leading American newspapers blamed Spain for the sinking of an American ship based on inconclusive evidence. But the claims of "fake news" reached epidemic proportions during the 2016 presidential election. Modern technology has allowed fabulists to create content that looks real and spread it rapidly. A 2019 survey found that Americans view made-up news and disinformation as a bigger problem than other critical issues, including terrorism, immigration, climate change and racism.[29]

Some governments actively engage in disinformation campaigns as a way to control the media narrative inside their countries or create distrust in other countries. During the worldwide coronavirus outbreak, for example, Chinese officials and state-run media spread false reports that China was successfully dealing with the pandemic and even accused the U.S. Army of engineering and unleashing the virus.

Some nations, such as Germany, are beginning to crack down on fake news by imposing steep fines on fabulists along with others who spread their phony stories. But because of the U.S.'s liberal free speech protections and press freedoms, Americans are more limited in their ability to seek redress for false news reports. That said, there are a couple of options for people and companies who have been wronged by fake news.

First, individuals and organizations that have had their reputation seriously harmed by a fake news story can sue for defamation. But litigating such cases can be costly and winning them is not easy. Second, another legal recourse may be copyright or trademark infringement (which is discussed in detail in Chapter 7), since many of these fake news sites closely mimic real news sites, including use of trademarks and copyrighted work. The notorious fake news site abcnews.com.co, for instance, utilized a URL and a logo nearly identical to the actual website for ABC News, a respected TV news outlet. So, ABC News might be able to sue on intellectual property grounds. But keep in mind, many of these fake news sites operate overseas, outside of the jurisdiction of U.S. laws. They may be here one day and gone the next. So, trying to haul a fake news operator into court and collecting damages may prove to be an impossible task.

29 Mitchell, Amy et al., *Many Americans Say Made-Up News Is a Critical Problem That Needs to Be Fixed*, Pew Research Center, June 5, 2019, https://www.journalism.org/2019/06/05/many-americans-say-made-up-news-is-a-critical-problem-that-needs-to-be-fixed/.

The notorious fake news site abcnews.com.co popped up during the 2016 U.S. election and utilized a URL and logo nearly identical to the actual website for ABC News, a respected TV news outlet. It has since vanished from the web. Credit: Times of San Diego.

Although the government's ability to fight fake news is limited, social media platforms are run by private companies that are not inhibited from censoring fake news or labeling material from suspicious sites. Facebook, Google and Twitter have increasingly introduced programs to clearly label content that's considered fake news after coming under fire for hosting content from Russian operatives aimed at stoking social and political unrest in the 2016 presidential race. However, some watchdog groups worry that the tech giants' proposed remedies are fraught with problems. For example, Facebook considered asking its community to help rate news producers' credibility. But studies show that many Facebook users have difficulty judging the credibility of news sources. In addition, partisan Facebook users with a high interest in promoting "their" media could bias the results.

Media Leaks

The past several years have seen a number of high-profile media leaks in which U.S. government employees have secretly shared information with journalists. They may leak out of concern about the public's right to know, to get a monetary reward, to promote a political agenda or to embarrass someone or some group. Sometimes leaks are illegal and other times they're not. But while the leakers may face prosecution, depending on the circumstances, the journalists who receive and publish the information do not.

It's generally a crime to disclose information related to national security or about spying methods. It's also a crime to steal or sell any "record, voucher, money or thing of value" owned by the U.S. government.[30] However, there are exceptions. Under the Whistleblower Protection Act, leakers who disclose information about a government agency violating the law, wasting money or abusing its authority may be protected from being punished by the agencies they work for.

In one of the most scandalous recent leaks, CIA subcontractor Edward Snowden in 2013 shared more than a million classified documents with journalist Glenn Greenwald, detailing a massive program by the National Security Agency (NSA) of collecting information on all phone calls by American citizens. Although Snowden was charged with violating the Espionage Act, he fled the U.S. before authorities could arrest and prosecute him. Another well-known illegal leak involved Chelsea Manning, a U.S. Army soldier (formerly known as Bradley Manning before sex reassignment surgery) who was convicted in 2013 of violating the 1917 Espionage Act and other offenses, after disclosing to WikiLeaks nearly 750,000 classified or sensitive military and diplomatic documents, including material regarding ongoing foreign military and intelligence operations. Manning was sentenced to 35 years in prison, but President Barack Obama commuted the sentence and Manning was released in 2017. Julian Assange, the head of the Wikileaks.com website that published the material, received asylum in the embassy of Ecuador in London for nine years, after which he was removed from the embassy to face charges in the United Kingdom and possibly the U.S.

But journalists and news outlets that published the leaked information were not charged with crimes. According to Lata Nott, executive director of the First Amendment Center: "There's no official standard for when it's a crime for a journalist to publish leaked information, because the government has never prosecuted such a case … Also, a journalist can't be punished for publishing info that was obtained illegally, as long as the journalist didn't do anything illegal."[31]

Assange's supporters claim he should be protected as a journalist as well. "Any prosecution by the United States of Mr. Assange for Wikileaks' publishing operations would be unprecedented and unconstitutional, and would open the door to criminal investigations of other news organizations," warned the American Civil Liberties Union after Assange's arrest.[32] The U.S. government, however, maintains that the prosecution of Assange is for hacking, because he allegedly tried to crack a password that would have helped Manning cover her tracks.

30 18 U.S.C. § 641.

31 Nott, Lata, *Leaks and the Media*, Freedom Forum Institute, May 2019, https://www.freedomforuminstitute.org/first-amendment-center/primers/leaks-and-the-media/.

32 Robertson, Adi, *The Case Against Julian Assange Is Serious — But Smaller and Shakier Than Some People Feared*, The Verge, Apr. 11, 2019, https://www.theverge.com/2019/4/11/18306327/julian-assange-wikileaks-cfaa-indictment-first-amendment-explainer.

In the past, the government has sought to prevent leaked information from being published by seeking court injunctions ordering journalists not to publish the information. But courts have rejected this as a violation of the First Amendment. The most famous example was in 1971 when the U.S. Supreme Court rejected the government's attempt to stop publication of a history of the Vietnam War that government officials claimed would threaten the then-ongoing conflict.[33] Now, in an era where news can be disseminated as fast as it takes to compose a tweet, a news organization can publish before the government even knows what happened. The *Dallas Morning News* did just that in 1997. Fearing the government was seeking to prevent it from publishing in tomorrow's newspaper that suspect Timothy McVeigh had confessed to the bombing of a federal office building in Oklahoma City, editors decided to break the story immediately on the newspaper's website.

CLOSING ARGUMENTS

In 2019, a white supremacist live-streamed on Facebook his shooting rampage at two New Zealand mosques. Government officials there subsequently banned sharing the video and imprisoned violators. Should the U.S. adopt similar laws? Following the tragic events at a Parkland, Florida high school in which a student shot and killed 17 classmates, some media outlets showed videos from the shooting that survivors took with their smartphones. Media outlets contend they should air these videos because they are newsworthy and they show the public how big of a problem gun violence is. Should it be illegal for the U.S. media to show these kinds of graphic videos? Should such a ban be an exception under the First Amendment? Or is this more of an ethical issue?

33 *New York Times v. U.S.*, 403 U.S. 713 (1971).

Additional Sources

CNN Staff, *Harvard Student Eldo Kim Charged in Final-Exam Bomb Hoax*, CNN, Dec. 18, 2013, https://www.cnn.com/2013/12/17/justice/massachusetts-harvard-hoax/index.html.

Dennis, Alan et al., *Facebook's Bad Idea: Crowdsourced Ratings Work for Toasters, But Not News*, Buzzfeed, Jan. 20, 2018, https://www.buzzfeednews.com/article/alandennis/facebooks-bad-idea-crowsourced-ratings-work-for-toasters.

F.C.C. v. Fox Television Stations, Inc., 567 U.S. 239 (2012).

Finnegan, Conor, *False Claims about Sources of Coronavirus Cause Spat Between the US, China*, ABC News, Mar. 13, 2020, https://abcnews.go.com/Politics/false-claims-sources-coronavirus-spat-us-china/story?id=69580990.

New York Times v. U.S., 403 U.S. 713 (1971).

Planned Parenthood of the Columbia/Willamette, *Inc. v. American Coalition of Life Activists*, 290 F. 3d 1058 (9th Cir. 2002), *cert. denied*, 539 U.S. 958 (2003).

Pope v. Illinois, 481 U.S. 497 (1987).

Watts v. U.S, 394 U.S. 705 (1969).

6 Digital Privacy

> U.S. privacy laws are so far behind the rest of the world that it … falls short of the requirements of international human rights norms.
>
> —Jeremy Malcolm

The term "online privacy" may seem like a contradiction. With free online maps at our fingertips that can zoom in for a view of anyone's address, the apparent ability of both government and private companies to track individual cell phones' locations, and constant media reports of corporate data breaches and online identity theft, it may seem like there's no such thing as privacy in our modern technological world.

Believe it or not, there are laws that protect people's privacy online. But they make a distinction between public and private places, and many courts have determined that websites and online services are inherently public spaces.

Moreover, United States privacy laws haven't been substantively updated since 1986. Back then, almost no one had a cell phone and the only drones flying above were bees. The only "social networking" the then-two-year-old Mark Zuckerberg may have been doing was at pre-school or on playdates. If you did something embarrassing, people eventually forgot about it or, if worse came to worst, you could change your name and move away. No one in your new community would know who you are because you'd have no online history. In a digital world, however, every move and action can be tracked, collected, archived and analyzed.

This new era of Net nosiness can't sit well with Americans, who say in surveys that they overwhelmingly favor strong privacy protections. But while Americans say that they support strong privacy protections, they also routinely click "I agree" to complex Terms of Service and privacy policies without reading them. Usually, these documents contain broad language which gives websites and services broad rights to do almost whatever they like with users' data.

More than 80% of Americans are concerned about the amount of personal information social media sites and advertisers know about them

% who say they are concerned a lot or a little about how much personal information _______ might know about them

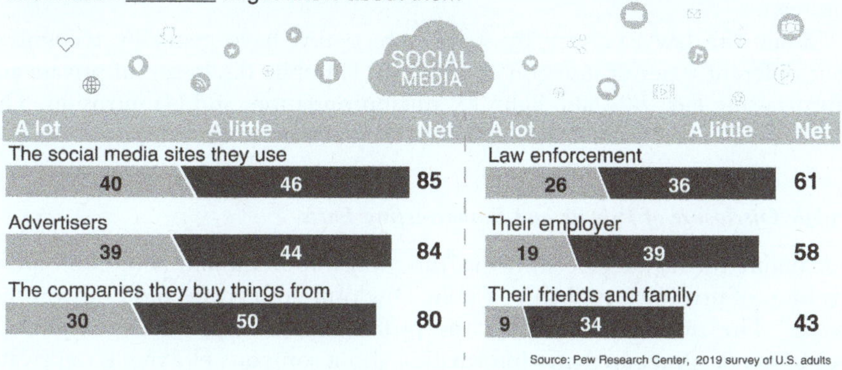

Civil liberties advocates such as the American Civil Liberties Union and Electronic Frontier Foundation (EFF) say that America's privacy laws are in dire need of updating by lawmakers and clarification by courts. Until that happens, your cell phone carrier, your Internet service provider, the websites you visit and the apps you use will be able to collect all kinds of information about you that you consider private. They may also give or sell the information to others. Employers will be allowed to "Google stalk" you and perhaps even require you to tell them your social media passwords. And one silly mistake you made years ago could be recorded online permanently and forever tarnish your reputation. "U.S. privacy laws are so far behind the rest of the world that it … falls short of the requirements of international human rights norms," said Jeremy Malcolm, an analyst at EFF, a San Francisco-based digital rights group.[1]

Privacy Protections

Let's begin with the good news first. There are some privacy laws in the U.S. that protect you in both the virtual and non-virtual worlds. Everyone has — under certain circumstances — a legal right to simply be left alone. The law recognizes that there are certain information, actions and places that

1 Grabowski, Mark, *It's Time to Update National Digital Privacy Laws*, Times of San Diego, Apr. 21, 2016, https://timesofsandiego.com/opinion/2016/04/21/its-time-to-update-national-digital-privacy-laws/.

are nobody else's business. However, the law also recognizes that there are limits to a person's right to privacy. For example, many things that people do significantly affect others; and people may have a right or a need to know about them. Such information is said to be "newsworthy" or of "public interest." Privacy law attempts to balance these two sometimes competing interests.

While the law can vary by state, U.S. courts have generally recognized four different types of invasion of privacy: (1) public disclosure of private and embarrassing facts, (2) false light, (3) misappropriation, and (4) intrusion. This chapter will cover each briefly and how they pertain to the Internet.

Public Disclosure of Private and Embarrassing Facts

For online media and social media, the most important and common type of invasion of privacy is probably "Public Disclosure of Private and Embarrassing Facts." The title aptly describes the problem. This type of privacy breach occurs when someone shares information about someone else that is so private, so intimate and so embarrassing that a reasonable person would be shocked that it was actually published. In order to successfully make this claim, the information must actually be true, since that's what makes the revelation of it embarrassing. (An untrue statement may meet the requirements of a defamation claim, which is discussed in Chapter 5.) It is illegal simply because a line was crossed by conveying it to others, by posting it online or by some other means.

Fortunately, this usually involves the type of information that should raise some red flags prior to posting online. For example, providing graphic details about a person's private sex life, disclosing that a person has a health condition that they've not publicly revealed or sharing detailed information about a person's grades without a legitimate or "newsworthy" reason would be examples of this type of invasion of privacy. On the other hand, it's likely not public disclosure of private and embarrassing facts if the information shared is just mildly embarrassing — such as a revelation that a plaintiff ate insects — or if it is already well known.

The primary defense to this kind of invasion of privacy claim is "newsworthiness" or "public interest." If information is truly "newsworthy" or in the "public's interest" to know, it will not be considered public disclosure of private and embarrassing facts. Also, if a person gives permission to someone to publish otherwise private information about them, they generally cannot later claim their privacy has been invaded. In addition, if a person posts information about themself online, including on their own website or social media account, they probably cannot sue for invasion of privacy when someone else shares it, unless it is used in a context or manner that the original poster could not have anticipated. The nature of social media leads courts to determine that online posts are public, even if a user utilizes a site's controls to limit access to the material. So, for example, someone's post on their Instagram account that is restricted to viewing by only their friends could still be interpreted as public by the courts simply because it was posted on social media.

To illustrate these legal principles in action, consider two cases. In 2017, then-New York Giants defensive end Jason Pierre-Paul settled a privacy lawsuit against ESPN after a reporter for the network tweeted a photo of Pierre-Paul's medical records from an incident in which a July 4 firework exploded in Pierre-Paul's hand.[2] The reporter apparently obtained a photo of the electronic records from two hospital workers who were fired over the incident. By contrast, in another case a court ruled that car accident photos a defendant posted on Facebook were not private and could be used as evidence in a personal injury case stemming from the accident. The court noted there were ways the defendant could have kept the posted photos from others' view by changing his Facebook privacy settings and, because he did not change these settings, the photos were public. Public information "posted on a public medium, and available to anyone with access to the Internet" is not private, the court ruled.[3] But many courts have held that any information that is voluntarily shared online is not private, regardless of any privacy settings placed on the information.

When it comes to exposing our private lives, we can often be our own worst enemy. Although the Internet seems to offer perfect anonymity, users should not behave as if they cannot be seen. Warnings about revealing personal information online may seem obvious, but they often go unheeded.

Spend a few minutes searching online and you'll find posts from Internet users in health forums who are shocked to discover their supposedly private discussions about colon cancer are now full-text searchable online. In fact, according to a 2016 study by Pew Research Center, 36% of Internet users have sought online support for health, family and mental health issues, and 24% of those have logged in with their real name and e-mail address.[4] Every question they've asked and every statement they've made is now stored on a server somewhere.

In recent years, the controversial practice of "doxing" has raised privacy concerns. Doxing (sometimes spelled "doxxing") is an Internet-based practice of researching and sharing private, embarrassing or identifiable information about a person so that others can target them with malicious attacks.

2 *Pierre-Paul v. ESPN Inc.*, No. 16-21156-CIV, 2016 WL 4530884 (S.D. Fla. Aug. 29, 2016) (partially granting and partially denying defendants' motion to dismiss).

3 *Womack v. Yeoman*, 83 Va. Cir. 401 (2011).

4 Pew Research Center, *Health Online 2013*, Jan. 15, 2013, https://www.pewresearch.org/internet/2013/01/15/health-online-2013/.

In 2019, Texas Congressman Joaquin Castro tweeted a list of individuals from San Antonio who had donated the maximum to President Donald Trump's reelection campaign, along with their employers. "Sad to see so many San Antonians as 2019 maximum donors to Donald Trump …," Castro wrote in the tweet. "Their contributions are fueling a campaign of hate that labels Hispanic immigrants as 'invaders.'"[5] Republicans said that Castro's list was doxing, and the hashtag #ImpeachJoaquinCastro began to trend on Twitter. But, as Castro and others pointed out, the names and occupations of political donors are publicly available information.

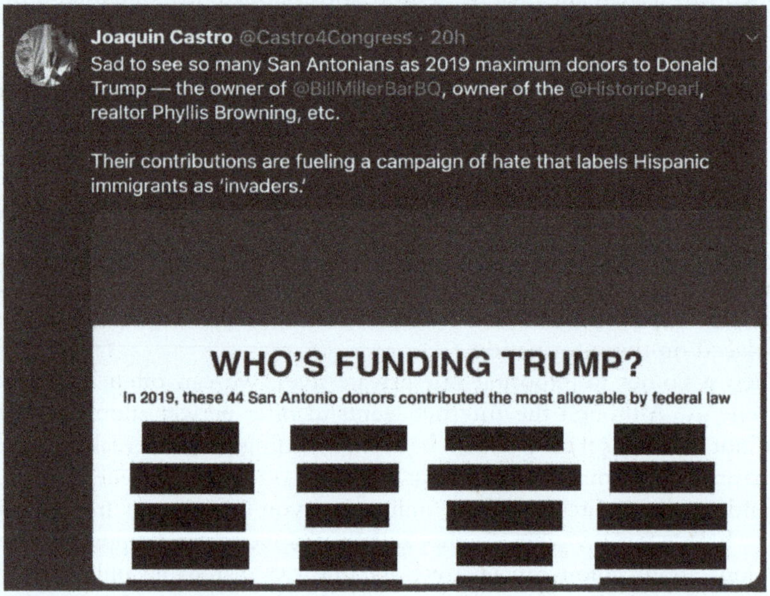

A screenshot of Congressman Joaquin Castro's controversial tweet that's been edited to redact the names of local residents he publicized because of their political activity. Credit: Republican Party of Texas.

Another widely publicized example resulted from the violent 2017 rally in Charlottesville which attracted white supremacists and resulted in a counter-protester dying. Images of those who participated in the march were shared and spread on social media by activists and ordinary citizens alike in an effort to identify the marchers. Captions read, "Is this racist your neighbor?" and

5 Castro, Joaquin (@Castro4Congress), Twitter (Aug. 5, 2019 11:13 PM), https://twitter.com/castro4congress/status/1158576680182718464.

"Does this Nazi work for you?"[6] Their aim was to identify rally participants in order to publicly shame them and pressure their schools to expel them or their employers to fire them. In some cases, the pressure worked, especially because private employers and schools in many states can fire or expel employees or students "at will."

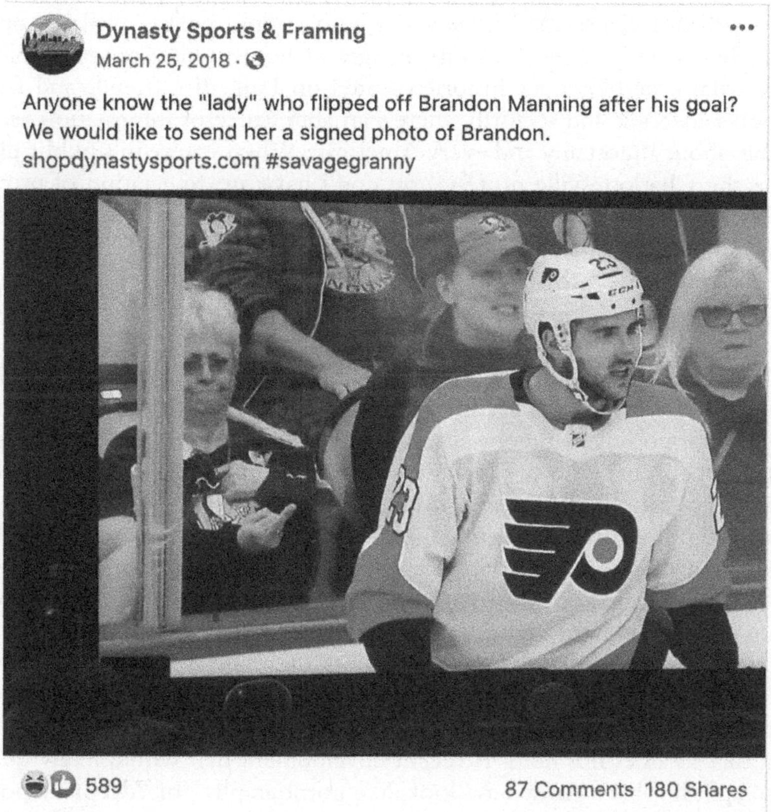

Doxing on social media, such as the example shown, can lead to the target being harassed and threatened. In some cases, the target's family members and friends have also been harassed or the wrong person has been identified. Credit: Dynasty Sports & Framing.

While many view doxing as completely justified and even virtuous, there's also been increasing backlash against the practice. Some critics question whether it's ethical to dox people who aren't public figures and aren't breaking

6 Fetzer, Mary, *Charlottesville: Is "Doxing" Rally Participants Legal?*, Avvo, Aug. 28, 2017, https://stories.avvo.com/rights/privacy/charlottesville-doxing-rally-participants-legal.html.

any laws simply because they hold a controversial opinion. The spotlight can lead to social media shaming and calls for the offender to be fired from their job or expelled from their school: a phenomenon known as "cancel culture." Oftentimes, the doxed person receives death threats and friends and family get harassed, as well.

But so long as the information gathered and shared is from publicly available sources, it's not illegal. And, nowadays, with voting records available online (if someone voted, not for whom), images of home addresses searchable on Google Maps, employment histories posted on LinkedIn, friends and family listed on Facebook and so forth, there's an abundance of information readily available about almost any and every American. When you're in a public place, such as the Charlottesville protest, you don't have an expectation of privacy. If someone snaps a photo of you marching out in the open, posts it on social media and others connect the dots and identify you, that's perfectly legal.

False Light

Another category of invasion of privacy claims is known as "false light," which is the publication of truthful words or images in such a way that it gives a false impression or portrays someone as something they are not. Not all states recognize this type of invasion of privacy because it is similar to a defamation claim in that it is based on a false impression.

One example would be posting a photo on Facebook or Instagram with an extremely misleading photo caption. For instance, a Chicago plastic surgeon was sued by and apparently paid a settlement to a former patient after allegedly posting before-and-after pictures of her nose surgery on his website and labeling them "cocaine nose," when that was not the cause of the patient's condition.[7] Another example of false light would be posing as someone else online and posting "fake" comments on Reddit that attribute opinions to an individual that he does not hold. A recent development that would likely qualify as false light is what's known as "lookalike pornography" or "deepfake porn," in which artificial intelligence technology is used to swap celebrities' faces into porn videos. Victims might claim misappropriation (discussed below) as well.

The false information doesn't necessarily have to be negative. In one case, a former star baseball player won money in a false light case over a biography that falsely stated that he had won a war medal.[8] But unlike a defamation claim, in which the statement at issue must be false, false light can also result from placing true information in a context that would cast a different light on the information that is published. For example, in a 2006 case a Florida jury awarded a businessman $18 million after a newspaper reported at the beginning

7 The Smoking Gun, *Woman Sues Doc Over "Cocaine Nose" Photos*, July 30, 2014, http://www.thesmokinggun.com/documents/doctor-sued-over-cocaine-nose-photos-687321.

8 *Spahn v. Julian Messner, Inc.*, 18 N.Y.2d 324 (N.Y. 1966).

of an article that he had killed his wife but did not report until much later in the article that it was a hunting accident, not a murder. The verdict was reversed on appeal.[9]

Misappropriation

The third type of invasion of privacy is also the easiest to spot and avoid. You can get sued for misappropriation — also sometimes referred to as a violation of the victim's "right of publicity," or ironically, as "appropriation" — if you use another person's name, voice, image or other likeness to help sell something without first obtaining their permission. The main trouble spot is usually advertising and commercial endorsements. If you want to use a photo of someone — or anything else that is identified with them — in an ad to help sell something, you must first get their permission.

Unauthorized product celebrity endorsements are common with the proliferation of websites and new media. For example, after the dietary supplement Resveratrol garnered attention on *The Oprah Winfrey Show*, many websites popped up that made unproven health claims and used false celebrity product endorsements for anti-aging and weight-loss pills made from the supplement. In response to the misappropriation of their names, Oprah Winfrey and her guest medical expert, Dr. Mehmet Oz, publicly denounced the websites, said they did not endorse the products and filed a lawsuit. Several of the companies behind the websites eventually settled.[10]

In addition to a person's name or image, successful misappropriation lawsuits have been based on impersonations of an individual's image, voice or persona for a commercial purpose. TV game-show hostess Vanna White successfully sued Samsung for $400,000 over an ad that showed a glamorously dressed robot ready to turn a letter as White famously did on *Wheel of Fortune*.[11] In another case, actress Katherine Heigl sued a New York drug store chain that tweeted a photo of her leaving one of their stores and added wording implying that she was endorsing the store. The case was settled.[12]

9 *Anderson v. Gannett Co., Inc.* 947 So.2d 1 (Fla. App. 2006) (reversing jury verdict), *aff'd*, 994 So.2d 1048 (Fla. 2008).

10 James, Susan Donaldson, *Oprah Winfrey and Dr. Mehmet Oz Settle in Acai Lawsuit*, ABC News (May 5, 2010), https://abcnews.go.com/Health/oprah-dr-mehmet-oz-settle-monavie-image-acai/story?id=10561547.

11 *White v. Samsung Electronics America, Inc.*, 971 F.2d 1395 (9th Cir.1992), as amended (Aug. 19, 1992), *reh'g denied*, 989 F.2d 1512 (9th Cir. 1993), *cert. denied*, 508 U.S. 951 (1993).

12 *Heigl v. Duane Reade, Inc.*, Civil No. 14-2501, 2014 WL 1383558 (S.D.N.Y settled Aug. 27, 2014).

Ms. C3PO?

Wheel of Fortune co-host Vanna White successfully argued that this photo of a robot in a VCR ad was a use of her image and persona. Credit: Ninth Circuit Court of Appeals.

In several states, misappropriation claims can even be made after death: a boot manufacturer settled a lawsuit brought by the estate of actor John Wayne over an advertisement that showed a photo of him getting fitted for that brand of boots.

However, it doesn't matter whether the misappropriated person is famous or not. Everyone has the right of publicity: the right to decide how their likeness is used when it comes to advertising and endorsements. For example, Facebook settled a class action lawsuit on behalf of its users after it used profile pictures in ads on the site based only on users' "liking" a particular brand's Facebook page. Tiktok settled a similar case.

Website operators should be particularly careful in their use of user-submitted photos, including user profile photos, by advertisers on the site. In order to avoid lawsuits, the best practice is to obtain signed permission before producing any ad that includes pictures of identifiable people. (You must also be cognizant of copyright issues, as described in Chapter 7.) If the person is a minor and money is involved, you should also get permission from the minor's parent or guardian. If you publish or broadcast an ad that was produced by a third party, you should have them sign an agreement stating that valid permission has been obtained and that they will be responsible for reimbursing you for any legal claims that might result if a problem arises. If you ever manage a website or social media accounts for an organization, before posting photos of employees or clients online, you should have them sign a release form in order to avoid legal issues.

Note that both the advertiser and the advertising agency that created an ad can be held liable for misappropriation claims.

Intrusion

Unlike the other categories, intrusion claims are not based on what is published, but rather on how the information was obtained in the first place. The law provides that there are certain private places that are off limits to others unless a person gives others permission to be there. In the real world, homes, bathrooms and private offices are common examples of a private place where a person could be found to have invaded someone's privacy if they entered without permission or if they planted a secret listening device or camera to spy.

Intrusion is considered a personal harm to the individual whose privacy is harmed because of the apprehension and disturbance it is presumed to cause. The legal claim of trespassing is slightly different, since the harm is to the individual's ability to control access to and use of their property and possessions. Trespassing can also be a criminal offense.

Just as disturbing someone's private physical spaces can lead to legal action, snooping around a person's computer or accessing their cell phone text messages or e-mail account without their permission would be considered intrusion. Even investigative journalists are required to obey the law just like everyone else and do not have special license to sneak or trespass into private areas when gathering the news.

On the other hand, other places in the real world are clearly public — a street or sidewalk, a park, a courthouse, a stadium — and you generally have the right to observe, photograph or shoot video and post online anything that happens in such spaces. Some places may fall in a grey area and it may be left to a court to decide how public or private the space is. The key question in such cases is: does the person suing for intrusion have a "reasonable expectation of privacy" in the particular location? If not, there can be no successful claim.

A 1998 case pointed out this distinction. A woman who was involved in a car accident alongside a highway was rescued by paramedics who took her to the hospital in a helicopter. She was not aware that a camera crew for the TV show *On Scene: Emergency Response* had accompanied the paramedics and had recorded video and audio of her rescue, and her treatment in the helicopter. When she sued for intrusion, the courts held that she had a valid claim for the material recorded in the helicopter, where she had a reasonable expectation of privacy, but not on the roadside, which was public space.[13] In 2016, a celebrity won a large jury award against a website that posted excerpts from a video of him having sex.[14] Although the case was later settled for less than the jury award, it still led to the website's bankruptcy.

Google's Street View and other sites that allow a person to search for street-level images have led to a number of privacy concerns, including legal actions in Europe. In Pennsylvania, residents on a private road brought an action against Google asserting a claim for invasion of privacy arising from the presence of images of their residence as part of an online map. A federal court ruled that Google had intruded against the residents by entering and photographing from their privately owned road, but awarded only $2 because the intrusion was minimal.[15] In California, a celebrity lost her case over photos of the coast posted online by an environmental organization that showed her home because the photos were taken from a helicopter, and her home was readily visible from the air.[16]

But even if the place intruded is determined to be private, there's still a possibility that the access may not be ruled unlawful. Consent is usually the primary defense to an intrusion claim, though any permission to enter a private space must be given by someone with the authority to grant such consent. It's also important not to lie or misrepresent oneself to get permission.

"Newsworthiness/public interest" may also be a defense in appropriate cases. For example, a federal appeals court held that a TV program's use of hidden cameras in a private medical laboratory was justified because of the public interest in medical testing errors.[17]

Other Privacy Laws

Keep in mind that the aforementioned laws are general privacy laws. In addition, certain professions have additional privacy standards that must be followed by people working in that profession. For example, doctors, nurses and other healthcare professionals must abide by the Health Insurance Portability and Accountability Act of 1996 (HIPAA), which protects patient privacy by limiting what information medical professionals can share about patients with family, friends and the public. HIPAA covers electronic health records and electronic communications as well. In education, school officials and teachers must follow the Family Educational Rights and Privacy Act of 1974 (FERPA). This federal law protects students' privacy. Under this law, professors, for

13 *Shulman v. Grp. W Prods., Inc.*, 18 Cal. 4th 200, 210, 955 P.2d 469, 475 (Cal. 1998), *as modified on denial of reh'g* (July 29, 1998).

14 *Gawker Media, LLC v. Bollea*, 129 So.3d 1196 (Fla. 2d DCA 2014); 170 So.3d 125 (Fla. 2d DCA 2015).

15 *Boring v. Google*, 362 Fed. Appx. 273 (3d Cir. 2010), *cert. denied*, 562 U.S. 836 (2010).

16 *Streisand v. Adelman*, No. SC 077 257 (Cal. Super. 2003).

17 *Medical Laboratory Management Consultants v. ABC, Inc.*, 306 F.3d 806 (9th Cir. 2002).

example, cannot discuss a student's grades or class performance with her parents unless she gives the professor permission to do so, even if her parents pay her tuition.

Note that while these laws apply to specific professions or individuals, they generally cannot be used to stop online or offline media from reporting such information if it is obtained by the media entity legally, even if the original source violated the law. So, in the Jason Pierre-Paul case discussed earlier in this chapter, Pierre-Paul sued ESPN for public disclosure of private and embarrassing facts, which ended in a settlement. But his legal claims against ESPN under Florida's equivalent of HIPAA were dismissed.

Privacy Problems

Here's the bad news: since 1986, technology has advanced at a breakneck speed while electronic privacy law has remained at a standstill, making privacy laws grossly outdated and out of touch with how people use, store and share information nowadays. Fear of another terrorist attack similar to September 11 has also provided law enforcement with incredible surveillance powers to closely monitor citizens' activity online that arguably undermines civil liberties. Let's take a closer look at some existing loopholes in U.S. privacy law, along with how it compares to other nations.

Outdated Laws

In 1986, Congress enacted the Electronic Communications Privacy Act (ECPA). The ECPA generally protects the privacy of peoples' oral, telephone and electronic communications from unlawful wiretapping, eavesdropping, and other forms of unauthorized access and disclosure by others. The law, originally intended to cover telephone communications, has been expanded so that it now also prohibits unauthorized access to computer communications. Violation of the ECPA is both a civil infraction and a federal crime.

However, courts have held that some information related to electronic communications, such as the time and duration of the communication — but not the content of the communication itself — is not private because it is necessarily shared with the communications provider — a "third party," since it is not the originator or recipient of the message — for billing and other purposes. The U.S. Supreme Court held in 2018 that this "Third-Party Doctrine," which applied to wired telephone communications, did not extend to cell phone location records.[18] But it is unclear whether this means that other forms of electronic communications are now exempt from the doctrine.

Another problem with the ECPA is the distinction it makes between communications when they are "in transit," moving between the sender and the

18 *Carpenter v. U.S.*, 585 U.S. ___, 138 S. Ct. 2206, 201 L. Ed. 2d 507 (2018).

recipient, and "in storage," stored somewhere for any length of time before, after or during its transmission. The ECPA bans interception of communications when they are "in transit," but not when they are "in storage." When the ECPA was first passed, e-mails were stored on a third party's server for only a short period of time: just long enough to facilitate transfer of e-mail to the consumer's e-mail client, which was usually located on their personal or work computer. Now, with popular online e-mail services such as Gmail, users are more likely to store e-mails online indefinitely, accessing them only through their online virtual inbox. If an e-mail comes into the virtual inbox of a Gmail user, is it in storage or is it in transit until the user logs in and accesses it? What if the recipient gets an alert of the incoming e-mail on their cell phone? Is a message in "the cloud" in storage, in transit, or both?

Another problem with the ECPA is when it does and does not require government police agencies to obtain warrants to access online materials. In order to obtain a warrant, law enforcement must prove to a judge that they have "probable cause": a reasonable basis that evidence of a crime will be discovered. Under the ECPA, police agencies must obtain a warrant to access electronic communications such as e-mails, text messages and chats only if they are less than six months old. If it's older than six months, no warrant is necessary. Draft e-mails, web browsing history and files stored in the cloud are available without a warrant regardless of how old they are.

Government Surveillance

In addition to the ECPA, government surveillance of electronic communications and data is also constrained by the Fourth Amendment, which prohibits "unreasonable" searches and seizures by the government, and by the generalized right of privacy that the U.S. Supreme Court has determined to be embedded in the U.S. Constitution. But new technology and its ubiquitous usage raise several issues, such as the federal government's battles with Apple and Microsoft to access customers' data, and the question of whether the government may track individuals through their cell phones' geolocation functions.

Although law enforcement officials typically need a warrant to search people's home computers, read their postal mail, eavesdrop on their phone conversations or even to see which library books they borrowed, they often don't need one when creeping into Americans' virtual lives.

After the terrorist attacks of September 11, 2001, national security laws were adopted and interpreted broadly to allow the National Security Agency (NSA) to collect and retain information about phone calls and e-mails nationwide, although usually not the actual contents of these communications. After disclosure of this practice caused a public uproar, the law was changed so that communications companies had to retain this information and provide it to the government in specific cases upon request.

While the U.S. Supreme Court never ruled on the NSA data collection, in recent years the nation's highest court has ruled in a number of cases whether law enforcement must obtain warrants before accessing certain types of electronic data, in addition to the warrant requirements of the ECPA. The Court has held that a warrant is required to put a tracking device on a criminal suspect's car, search the contents of an arrestee's cell phone, and to track someone using their cell phone's geolocation capabilities.[19] But lower courts have also held that border and immigration agents need only "reasonable suspicion" to search cell phones upon entry into the U.S.[20]

Private Surveillance

The government isn't the only one taking advantage of America's outdated privacy laws: private companies do it too. Prying eyes are everywhere. Data-mining is defined in many different ways but generally involves a series of techniques used to extract intelligence from vast stores of digital information. For example, if you use Google, the search engine can see not only what you search for and which sites you visit, but track your subsequent movements, record the data and analyze it to find patterns. This may be beneficial, such as when the data is used to track infections such as the COVID-19 virus. But uses can also be more intrusive, such as the possible use of Facebook and Alexa data to predict when couples are about to break up. In one widely publicized incident, Target determined that a teenage girl was pregnant based on her purchases. These practices raise serious privacy issues that have not been fully explored and debated.

Cell phone carriers, Internet service providers, websites and apps can mine all kinds of personal information about their users and often sell it to the highest bidder. Based on such intel, advertisers may be able to target and tempt us into buying particular products or supporting certain causes. That's why users often see ads that mirror the content of their messages or see similar ads on different websites. In 2018, Facebook came under fire after it was exposed for allowing its users' data to be shared with political campaigns. In 2019, the U.S. Army announced that it was examining whether collection of personal data by TikTok, which is owned by a Chinese company, posed a security threat. The Army and Navy later banned the app from government phones. In 2020, President Trump declared that TikTok would be banned from the U.S., unless the Chinese company that owned it sold the app. However, a federal judge rebuffed Trump, ruling that the president overstepped his authority in using his emergency economic powers.[21]

19 Grabowski, *supra* note 1.

20 Fisher, Keith, *Update on Border Searches of Electronic Devices*, Business Law Today, Mar. 26, 2020, https://www.americanbar.org/groups/business_law/publications/blt/2020/04/border-searches/.

21 Allyn, Bobby, U.S. Judge Halts Trump's TikTok Ban, the 2nd Court to Fully Block The Action, NPR, Dec. 7, 2020, https://www.npr.org/2020/12/07/944039053/u-s-judge-halts-trumps-tiktok-ban-the-2nd-court-to-fully-block-the-action.

The law does give some privacy protection to children. The federal Children's Online Privacy Protection Act of 1998 (COPPA) requires that websites and online services directed to children obtain parental consent before collecting personal information from users under the age of 13. For this reason, many sites such as Facebook and Instagram state that users must be 13 or above. But nevertheless, children often use these sites. In 2019 TikTok paid a record $5.7 million fine for knowingly collecting information from children under 13.[22]

In addition, most websites post privacy policies on their sites that detail what information they collect from users and how they use it, and a few states require the posting of such policies. But few consumers bother to read these disclosures. Fewer understand them. And even fewer are willing to abandon their favorite sites and apps to protect their privacy.

TEST YOUR ONLINE PRIVACY

Try these online privacy tests:

1. http://mybrowserinfo.com/detail.asp
2. https://panopticlick.eff.org

The first website offers an interactive tool that shows you all of the information about your own computer that is made available to every website you visit. The second website lets you know if you're being tracked. Look through the list of info collected about your computer and reflect on which pieces of info were surprising, why this info is available, how servers might collect and use this info, and what impact this may have on your privacy. The second site includes information on tools to limit this information.

Under the current rules, schools and employers can still "Google stalk" applicants without their knowledge. A person can be rejected for a job or from a college because of a scandalous photo a friend posted of him on Facebook years ago, and never know the reason for the rejection. Some schools and employers have gone so far as requiring applicants to reveal social media passwords, a practice that is currently prohibited in only about half of the states. Once hired for a job or enrolled in a university, your boss or school administrators may

22 Federal Trade Commission, *supra* note 21.

also monitor all of your Internet activity. In fact, one survey found that one out of every three IT employees admits to taking a peek at coworkers' data including private files, wage data and personal e-mails.[23] Courts have ruled that employees and students have no reasonable expectation of privacy when using an organization's computer, as long as the employer/school notifies employees/students of the policy. And while schools and employers may not generally search students' or employees' personally owned computers without permission, they may monitor Internet usage when the school's or employer's Internet connection is used.

Yes, your university certainly has such a policy, but you may not be aware of it unless you read the fine print when you log on or when you enroll.

Even Americans who manage to avoid the Internet altogether are not immune from privacy concerns. For example, MyLife.com is one of many sites that provide details on almost any person, including age, address, assets, marital status, political party affiliation, relatives' names and more. This information was publicly available pre-Internet from various sources, but technology has made it much easier to quickly dig up information about anyone. That can be useful, but it's also made stalking, identity theft and blackmail easier than ever, too.

An online industry has developed around the controversial practice of posting mugshots of people who were arrested, including mere jaywalkers and juvenile offenders. This is the modern incarnation of a practice that some newspapers and TV stations have done for years. While the sites are based entirely on information already publicly available from police, they usually do not specify who was ultimately convicted of a crime or those who had the charges against them dropped. The sites cannot generally be sued because the information they are posting is true: the person depicted was arrested. Some opportunistic websites charge hundreds of dollars to remove the arrest information. In response, some police departments are limiting access to mugshots, and several states have passed laws banning the practice. In addition, as the zeitgeist on criminal justice has shifted in recent years, expedited by national protests over the 2020 police killing of George Floyd, some newsrooms are beginning to reevaluate their mugshot galleries. As Laura Hazard Owen, deputy editor of Harvard University's Nieman Journalism Lab, put it: "The old American newspaper standard is: never change anything that's true; news values come first. But [today], it's clear that standard isn't exactly working; a brief item on Page A17 in one day's print newspaper doesn't have the same sort of impact

23 Kearns, Dave, *Survey: IT Pros Admit to Peeking Inside Confidential Data Files*, Network World, June 13, 2007, https://www.networkworld.com/article/2291014/survey--it-pros-admit-to-peeking-inside-confidential-data-files.html.

as a permanent digital record."[24] A few news organizations have even adopted policies allowing for removal of some archived material.

Unlike people, the Internet never forgets. Now, that information lives online forever — unless you live in the European Union, where "right to be forgotten" laws allow individuals to request that search engines remove search results for their name under certain conditions. California has passed a similar law, but allowing removal only of social media posts by children under age 18.

Can these privacy loopholes be fixed? Yes. But it won't be easy. In 2012, the U.S. House of Representatives rejected a proposed federal law that would have prevented employers from demanding Facebook and other social media passwords. Meanwhile, the U.S. Supreme Court has been reluctant to address these issues and make broad declarations on how ECPA should be interpreted in the Internet Age. For example, can the police search your e-mail messages without a search warrant? Can Facebook track what you do on their site and which sites you visit after you leave their site? Congress and the courts have so far declined to address many of these issues on a national level.

Tired of waiting for the federal government to act, some states have implemented their own laws aimed at protecting digital privacy.

California has been a trailblazer on this front. Its online privacy laws include: criminalizing "revenge porn" and the publication of identifiable nude photos online without the subject's permission; banning employers and schools from asking for applicants' passwords; requiring police to get a warrant for any online data; prohibiting paparazzi from flying drones above private property to record any activity; and giving children the right to erase social media posts. Many more pieces of legislation aimed at expanding Californians' digital privacy rights are under consideration. Most recently, the state's Consumer Privacy Act went into effect in 2020 and gives consumers the right to opt out of the selling of their personal information, and it requires companies that collect such data to make individual users' information available to those users. Because of the size of its market, California's law may become a de facto national standard in the U.S. Other states have recently adopted their own, generally more limited online privacy laws.

While all of these new requirements help, no state can fully remedy privacy concerns on its own, as civil rights advocates point out. "The Internet goes through every state and outside of the country and, if we're really going to be serious about protecting privacy, we need a national approach to that," said Ari Rosmarin, an attorney with the American Civil Liberties Union.[25] While

24 Owen, Laura Hazard, *Fewer Mugshots, Less Naming and Shaming: How Editors in Cleveland Are Trying to Build a More Compassionate Newsroom*, NiemanLab, Oct. 18, 2018, https://www.niemanlab.org/2018/10/fewer-mugshots-less-naming-and-shaming-how-editors-in-cleveland-are-trying-to-build-a-more-compassionate-newsroom/.

25 Grabowski, *supra* note 1.

support for such a federal law is growing, until that happens Americans may have to choose between new technology and privacy.

PROTECTING YOUR PRIVACY ONLINE

Protecting your privacy requires a lot of vigilance to avoid the many ways that Internet service providers (ISPs), web browsers, online apps and websites collect personal information. Using a virtual private network (VPN) to access cyberspace can prevent ISPs from monitoring users' activities. Browsers such as Tor are built around protecting user privacy, while add-ons such as the EFF's "Privacy Badger" offer some protection for users of more common browsers. Some of these require some technical understanding, but online resources are available to help.

Comparative Law

As limited as privacy may seem living in the Digital Age in the U.S., the situation is far more dire in countries such as China, where the government uses facial recognition and big data to control and monitor its citizens. These data collection policies may also apply to data about non-Chinese citizens that is held by Chinese-owned companies, which led to concerns about Chinese-owned TikTok.

In 2020, China fully rolled out its controversial social credit score system to closely monitor citizens' everyday behavior and punish or reward them according to certain standards of appropriate conduct. Under this intrusive surveillance system, both financial behaviors like "frivolous spending" and bad behaviors like lighting up in smoke-free zones can result in penalties including loss of employment, educational opportunities and travel privileges. Those with high scores get perks, like discounts on utility bills and faster application processes to travel abroad.

On the other end of the privacy spectrum is the European Union, where much greater online privacy protections exist than in the U.S. For example, Germany, Finland and other countries ban employers from conducting Google searches of job applicants. Most countries prohibit employers from asking applicants for social media passwords. In 2014, the European Court of Justice ruled that Google and other search sites could be forced by individuals in the E.U.'s member nations to remove links to embarrassing and outdated information.[26] European courts have even ruled that criminals may order search sites to remove links to stories about their convictions.

26 Lynskey, Orla, *Control over Personal Data in a Digital Age: Google Spain v AEPD and Mario Costeja Gonzalez*, 78 Modern Law Review 3 (May 2015), 522–534, doi:10.1111/1468-2230.12126.

While these European laws allow for the removal of links in search results, the information itself may remain online, unless it was published illegally. However, deleting the links on popular search engines such as Google will make it harder to find.

In addition, in 2018 the E.U. implemented its General Data Protection Regulation, which imposes strict data privacy regulations on European companies and empowers individuals to protect their information online. These regulations require companies to notify users of all data collected about them and require that users be permitted to opt out of such collection, to view the data collected about them, and to request the removal of specific information.

Currently, these policies apply only in E.U. member countries. But some European government officials argue that in order for these protections to be effective, they must apply to websites worldwide, including those based and aimed at users in the U.S.

Some free speech advocates decry such privacy policies because they worry it could lead to censorship of embarrassing truths. On the other hand, with the advent of the Internet, individuals risk being branded negatively forever because of one stupid mistake they made years ago. Or, in the case of mugshot galleries, an individual's reputation may suffer as a result of a false accusation or arrest that is never prosecuted. As *The New York Times* observed in a story about people hurt by negative online data, "The Web is like an elephant — it never forgets, and if let loose it can cause a lot of trouble."[27] Many say that our privacy laws should change to keep pace with the times.

The Price of Privacy

While our desire for more privacy is certainly understandable, it may also be a case of "be careful what you wish for." Less intrusion may come with unexpected costs. In the Information Age, surrendering privacy and sharing our personal information can have major benefits for us as individuals and collectively as a society. Enacting stringent privacy protections may impair those benefits.

First, the current setup provides a plethora of entertaining and informative online content for free. Facebook, Twitter, Google and other popular apps are free because they use users' information to draw all kinds of insights and sell that data to third parties such as advertisers, marketers and political campaigns. The revenue they generate pays for the staff and equipment necessary to operate their platforms.

Second, sharing our information provides convenience. Individuals can access all kinds of data at their fingertips that improves their own lives. For instance, health researchers can use streams of data from patients' Internet

27 Sullivan, Paul, *Negative Online Data Can Be Challenged, At a Price*, The New York Times, June 10, 2011, https://www.nytimes.com/2011/06/11/your-money/11wealth.html.

searches to reveal signals for possible drug side effects or to identify other health concerns. That was the case in South Korea, where the government's heavy use of surveillance technology was cited as a reason for its successful containment of the outbreak and spread of the coronavirus disease COVID-19. By utilizing CCTV and tracking bank card and mobile phone usage, officials were able to identify who to initially test for the virus. On a personal note, one of your textbook authors was able to recover his wallet after accidentally dropping it in a taxi in Taiwan thanks to local police having cameras everywhere and reviewing the footage to help him identify the taxi's license plate. These are just a couple of countless examples. As described by *The Atlantic*, "Throughout the day, in any number of potential transactions, people are navigating the space between convenience and surveillance."[28]

Third, fewer privacy hurdles can help improve safety and security overall. In 2018, for example, lax digital privacy laws enabled law enforcement to track down a dangerous serial killer who used bombs to kill several people in Austin, Texas. Police caught the suspect by using a variety of resources, including Google search history, online shopping purchases and cell phone information. Without access to such data, the killer might still be on the loose. As described earlier, because this data was shared with "third parties" — cell phone companies — the police were able to request the information from the companies without first obtaining a warrant.

So, while the latest Facebook scandal may have everyone talking about privacy, we need to ask ourselves a difficult question: how many of us would be willing to give up such conveniences in exchange for more privacy? Many of us probably wouldn't even consider deleting our favorite apps or paying for them. It doesn't make Google and Facebook's intrusions right, but it partially explains why we don't have stronger laws limiting the collection and use of our private data.

CLOSING ARGUMENTS

In recent years, the controversial practice of "doxing" — obtaining personal information such as home addresses and posting it online — has raised privacy and safety concerns. Under current law, doxing is legal in most cases, so long as the information gathered and shared is from publicly available sources. But some critics question whether it's ethical to dox people who aren't public figures and aren't breaking any laws simply because they hold a controversial opinion. Others point out that this is simply offering easier access to what is already public information. What do you think? Is doxing ever appropriate?

28 LaFrance, Adrienne, *The Convenience-Surveillance Tradeoff*, The Atlantic, Jan. 14, 2016, https://www.theatlantic.com/technology/archive/2016/01/the-convenience-surveillance-tradeoff/423891/.

Additional Sources

Alasaad v. Neilsen, 419 F.Supp. 3d 142 (D. Mass. 2019), *aff'd in part, vacated in part, rev'd in part sub nom. Alasaad v. Mayorkas*, 988 F.3d 8 (1st Cir. 2021).

Ali, Idrees and Culliford, Elizabeth, *Army Examines TikTok Security Concerns After Schumer's Data Warning*, Reuters, Nov. 21, 2019, https://www.reuters.com/article/us-usa-tiktok-army/army-examines-tiktok-security-concerns-after-schumers-data-warning-idUSKBN1XV2N6.

American Civil Liberties Union, *It's Time for a Privacy Update!*, 2017, https://www.aclu.org/issues/privacy-technology/internet-privacy/its-time-privacy-update.

Beres, Damon and Gilmer, Marcus, *A Guide to 'Deepfakes,' The Internet's Latest Moral Crisis*, Mashable, Feb. 2, 2018, https://mashable.com/2018/02/02/what-are-deepfakes/

Byers, Dylan, *The U.S. Wants Smartphone Location Data to Fight Coronavirus. Privacy Advocates Are Worried*, NBC News, Mar. 18, 2020, https://www.nbcnews.com/tech/tech-news/u-s-wants-smartphone-location-data-fight-coronavirus-privacy-advocates-n1162821.

Carnevale, Dan, *Penn Drops Charges Against Student Who Posted Online Photos of Nude Couple*, Foundation for Individual Rights in Education, Dec. 5, 2005, https://www.thefire.org/penn-drops-charges-against-student-who-posted-online-photos-of-nude-couple/.

Cox, Matthew, *Army Follows Pentagon Guidance, Bans Chinese-Owned TikTok App*, Military.com, Dec. 30, 2019, https://www.military.com/daily-news/2019/12/30/army-follows-pentagon-guidance-bans-chinese-owned-tiktok-app.html.

Dickson, E.J., *Can Alexa and Facebook Predict the End of Your Relationship*?, Vox, Jan. 2, 2019, https://www.vox.com/the-goods/2019/1/2/18159111/amazon-facebook-big-data-breakup-prediction.

Duhigg, Charles, *How Companies Learn Your Secrets*, New York Times Mag., Feb. 16, 2012, https://www.nytimes.com/2012/02/19/magazine/shopping-habits.html.

Ferek, Katy Stech, *Trump Signs Order Setting Deadline for TikTok Sale*, Wall Street Journal, Aug. 14, 2020, https://www.wsj.com/articles/trump-signs-order-setting-deadline-for-tiktok-sale-11597457927.

Fraley, et al. v. Facebook, Inc., et al., Civil No. 11-01726 (N.D. Cal. settled 2012), 966 F. Supp. 2d 939 (N.D. Cal. 2013) (approving settlement), *aff'd sub nom. Fraley v. Batman*, 638 F. App'x 594 (9th Cir. 2016), *cert. denied sub. nom. K.D. v. Facebook, Inc.*, 137 S.Ct. 68, 196 L.Ed.2d 34 (U.S. Oct. 3, 2016).

Grabowski, Mark, *To Post or Not to Post: The Ethics of Mugshot Websites*, 8 Journal of Media Law & Ethics 2 (2020), 21–36.

John Wayne Enterprises v. Lucchese, Inc., No. 2017-00917391 (Cal. Super. settled May 2019).

Kaste, Martin, *Is Your Facebook Profile as Private as You Think*?, NPR, Oct. 27, 2009, https://www.npr.org/templates/story/story.php?storyId=114187478.

Nittle, Nadra, *Spend 'Frivolously' and Be Penalized Under China's New Social Credit*, Vox, Nov. 2, 2018, https://www.vox.com/the-goods/2018/11/2/18057450/china-social-credit-score-spend-frivolously-video-games.

Payne, Marissa, *Jason Pierre-Paul* and ESPN Reach *Settlement in Invasion-of-Privacy Lawsuit*, Washington Post, Feb. 3, 2017, https://www.washingtonpost.com/news/early-lead/wp/2017/02/03/jason-pierre-paul-and-espn-reach-settlement-in-invasion-of-privacy-lawsuit/.

Perez, Chris, *White Nationalists Are Being Outed on Twitter — And One Lost His Job*, New York Post, Aug. 13, 2017, https://nypost.com/2017/08/13/white-nationalists-are-being-ousted-on-twitter-and-one-lost-his-job.

Perez, Juan Carlos, *Judge Dismisses Google Street View Case*, PC World, Feb. 18, 2009, https://www.pcworld.com/article/159740/google_street_view:case_dismissed.html.

Perez, Sarah, *House Shoots Down Legislation That Would Have Stopped Employers from Demanding Your Facebook Password*, TechCrunch, Mar. 28, 2012, https://techcrunch.com/2012/03/28/house-shoots-down-bill-that-would-have-stopped-employers-from-demanding-your-facebook-password/.

Pew Research Center, *Americans and Privacy: Concerned, Confused and Feeling Lack of Control Over Their Personal Information*, Nov. 2019, https://www.pewresearch.org/internet/wp-content/uploads/sites/9/2019/11/Pew-Research-Center_PI_2019.11.15_Privacy_FINAL.pdf.

Rainie, Lee and Duggan, Maeve, *Privacy and Information Sharing*, Pew Research Center, Jan. 14, 2016, http://www.pewinternet.org/2016/01/14/privacy-and-information-sharing/.

Riley v. California, 573 U.S. 373 (2014).

Schwartz, Paul M., *From Victorian Secrets to Cyberspace Shaming*, 76 University of Chicago Law Review (2009), 449–490, https://lawreview.uchicago.edu/publication/victorian-secrets-cyberspace-shaming.

Student Press Law Center, *Media Law Presentation: Invasion of Privacy*, 2014, http://www.splc.org/article/2014/08/media-law-presentation-invasion-of-privacy.

Sullivan, Bob, *Online Tracking Dears Are Real*, NBC News, Dec. 6, 2013, http://www.nbcnews.com/id/3078835/t/online-#.WywYAVVKipc.

Sunn, Jung Wong, *Coronavirus: South Korea's Success in Controlling Disease Is Due to its Acceptance of Surveillance*, The Conversation, Mar. 19, 2020, available at https://theconversation.com/coronavirus-south-koreas-success-in-controlling-disease-is-due-to-its-acceptance-of-surveillance-134068.

Taylor, Adrean S., *Common Invasion of Privacy Claims in Social Media*, Wassom.com, July 2013, http://www.wassom.com/from-the-archives-common-law-invasion-of-privacy-claims-in-social-media.html.

U.S. v. Jones, 565 U.S. 400 (2012).

U.S. v. Vergara, 884 F.3d 1309 (11th Cir. 2018), *cert. denied*, 139 S.Ct. 70, 202 L.Ed.2d 47 (U.S. 2018).

Virgil v. Sports Illustrated, 424 F. Supp. 1286 (S.D. Cal. 1976).

Walsh, Diana et al., *Privacy as a Right or as a Commodity in the Online World: The Limits of Regulatory Reform and Self-Regulation*, Electronic Commerce Research (June 2017), https://link.springer.com/article/10.1007%2Fs10660-015-9187-2.

7 Intellectual Property

> The Congress shall have power … To promote the progress of science and useful arts, by securing for limited times to authors and inventors the exclusive right to their respective writings and discoveries.
>
> — U.S. Constitution

Perhaps the most persistent legal issue online involves posting copyrighted videos, movies, photos and music without permission. Any use of someone else's work without their permission is copyright infringement and can result in hefty fines and even criminal penalties. But copyright law also protects original work that you create, and you wouldn't want others stealing your work without asking or paying. This chapter will provide a primer on copyright, the area of law covering ownership of creative works, and the misuse of such works. We will also touch upon other ways that specific types of creative works receive legal protection: namely patents, trademarks and trade secrets.

Just as individuals and entities (such as corporations) can own physical property — like land, a building, a car or a book — the law also allows for ownership of concepts and ideas. Because these things are intangible, these types of property are known as "intellectual property."

Creating a system of intellectual property (IP) protection was actually deemed so important to the development of a strong, healthy society and economy that it was specifically included in the United States Constitution. In order "to promote the Progress of Science and useful Arts," Article 1, Section 8, Clause 8 of the Constitution provides that the government can enact laws that "secur[e] for limited times to Authors and Inventors the exclusive Right to their respective Writings and Discoveries." Copyright and patent law are federal laws; states do not have their own separate laws. Trademarks are also primarily a matter of federal law, but states also have their own laws that give more limited protections within their borders.

At its core, IP law is about encouraging cultural, technological and economic progress. The framers of the Constitution believed that a society can only flourish where there is a steady advancement in its arts, sciences and literature. To bring about such advancement, IP law — in its most ideal form — tries to balance two sometimes competing interests.

On one hand, IP law recognizes that it is important that artists, authors, filmmakers and other "creators" be recognized and fairly compensated for their work. Most writers would be unwilling — and financially unable — to devote many years working on the next "Great American Novel" or the next Hollywood blockbuster if, once they were done, anyone could download their work, make copies and sell their bootlegged version to others on the Internet. IP law promises authors that their investment of time, energy and resources will be protected and ensures that a robust collection of original works is available for public enjoyment and benefit.

On the other hand, IP law recognizes that encouraging people to create new works will provide little benefit to society as a whole if others are not permitted to discuss and learn from them. For example, a system that requires bloggers or others to compensate or seek permission from a scientist or historian before they can talk about or critique their work would be unduly burdensome and stifle progress. Advancing the arts and sciences requires a system that allows others to share information and to learn from and build on the work of others.

Copyright

Copyright is a set of federal laws that grant creators the exclusive right to benefit from their creations. Copyright law can be both a friend and foe for university students. While the law limits students' ability to reproduce the works of others, it also protects students against the unauthorized use of their own work, such as journalism stories, films, academic papers, music, drawings, photographs, code, programs and inventions.

Especially with the Internet, there has never been a time in human history that we have had so much material — most of it copyrighted material — available literally at our fingertips. Similarly, new technologies have turned more of us into publishers and creators of our own copyrighted material. Despite the new mediums of expression, however, the same old copyright questions remain: What can I use? What can't I use? What can I prevent others from using?

The answer is copyright law, but it can get a bit complicated. Lawmakers and courts have tinkered with — and muddied — the rules a number of times over the years, and many of the rules weren't so clear to begin with. Still, the ideas behind copyright law are pretty easy to understand and can help a great deal in recognizing where today's legal boundaries lie.

The basics of copyright are fairly straightforward. A copyright is a property right. A person owns a copyright in much the same way she owns a car. Just as it is against the law to use someone else's Tesla without the owner's permission, it is generally against the law to use someone's copyrighted work without first obtaining her consent. Additionally, just as no one but the car owner can legally sell, give away, allow someone to borrow or change the appearance of their car, no one but the copyright owner, with a few exceptions, may legally transfer, loan or alter a copyrighted work.

A copyright of a particular work gives its owner five exclusive rights: distribution, reproduction, public performance, public display and adaptation (the latter is also known as the right to create "derivative works" based on the original). This is where copyright begins to get complicated, since each of the rights can be individually sold or licensed. Such distribution of rights to a work, plus the fact that many works are the result of collaborations that may result in various individuals and/or entities having ownership of a copyrighted work and the various rights included in the copyright, can make copyright issues very complex.

The popular song "Happy" by Pharrell Williams can illustrate these rights. Williams wrote and performed the song (and did not sell the rights). As the creator of the song, he owns the copyright in the lyrics and musical arrangement (the musical notes), in the form of sheet music. (Less established artists would likely have to surrender their rights to their record company.) This means that he owns all the rights described above: to reproduce the sheet music and the musical notes and lyrics that it contains, as well as the rights to adapt it, to distribute it, to publicly perform it and to publicly display it.

Williams also performed the song and produced the original recording of his performance. Thus Williams also owns the copyright for the original recording of the song, although he has assigned these rights to his music publishing company, Waters of Nazareth, and licensed them to two other music publishing companies in the U.S., EMI Blackwood Music and Warner Chappell Music, and to other publishing companies outside the U.S.

The song was released on November 21, 2013 in a video posted online, as well as in the soundtrack of the film *Despicable Me 2*, and was subsequently included in Williams' 2014 album *Girl*. As copyright owner of his performance(s) of the song, Pharrell licensed all of these distributions and public performances of the song.

Like most owners of musical performance copyrights, Williams allows "performing rights organizations" (known in the industry as "PROs") to license his rights in "Happy" to others who want to either use one of his performances of the song or to perform it themselves. Depending on which version of the song is used, the PROs for "Happy" are ASCAP and/or Global Music Rights. Most users of the song must acquire such a license, and most uses or performances of the song in any public place without such a license is copyright infringement. Note, though, a provision of copyright law unique to sound recordings does allow someone to make and distribute their own performance of an original song, known as a "cover," without the copyright owner's permission as long as they pay the owner a fee. Also, broadcast radio and TV stations need not pay fees, although satellite and online music services have to. The fees for all these uses are collected and distributed by organizations set up for this purpose by the copyright statutes, with the fees based on overall usage, rather than on a song-by-song basis.

In 2018, Williams objected to the use of "Happy" at an Indiana event featuring President Donald Trump. But because the sponsor of the event had obtained a license that included the right to play ("perform") the song, as part of a blanket license to use songs at the event, there was little legal ground for Williams to follow through on his objection. Recently, the licenses that PROs in the U.S. have granted to political campaigns have specifically excluded songs whose artists do not want their work used in such a way.

Williams also licenses companies to sell recordings of his performances: on physical vinyl records, CDs and as electronic downloads from sites such as Apple Music. But the rights you have when you buy "Happy" depend on what form you buy it in. If you bought a physical copy such as a CD, you are allowed to sell that particular copy or make fair uses of it, but you don't own a copyright in the music itself. This means that you cannot make unauthorized copies of the music or post the song online (even as background music to your own video). If you bought a song on Apple Music or another app or service, you have a license to listen to the recording, but not ownership of it: you cannot sell or loan the recording to someone else. Usually these restrictions are enforced by technology built into the music files and platforms themselves.

Music copyrights are particularly complex, but the same copyright principles apply to all copyrighted works.

What Can Be Copyrighted?

So, you now have a general idea of what copyright is (and is not), what it does and why it's important. But what types of work can be copyrighted? There are three main requirements. First, the work must be original. You cannot copyright a work that already exists or that was created by someone else, unless they give their permission. Second, the creator must have shown at least a small spark of creativity when he made the work. The result does not have to be good and the standard is not an especially high one, but some creative effort must be shown. For example, courts have said that simply alphabetizing a list of names, addresses and phone numbers lacks the creativity necessary to qualify for a copyright, but if they are displayed in a unique layout, that layout — but not the data — can be copyrighted. Finally, the work must be "fixed in any tangible medium of expression." This "fixation" requirement means that only works preserved in a tangible form (a book, a newspaper, a photo, a video, a CD-ROM disk, a website, a blog, a computer file, etc.) — as opposed to those existing entirely in an artist's mind — will receive copyright protection. This is one of the reasons that "live" TV and radio programs are simultaneously recorded by the stations or networks that air them: the recording is a "fixation" that allows the programs to be copyrighted.

The "fixation" requirement can be met in a wide variety of formats. Thus, copyright law protects both printed materials (such as books, encyclopedias and photographs) and those stored electronically (such as e-books, Wikipedia entries and digital photos). This includes material on the Internet: just because it is now possible to find and download almost any image, text passage or song that exists with one click of a mouse does not mean it's legal to do so. You should presume that the same copyright rules and restrictions apply to the use of online material as govern your use of print-based works. Using either online or offline works without regard to copyright can result in civil and criminal penalties, as detailed below.

As long as a work satisfies the three requirements, the list of material eligible for copyright protection is a long one. For example, copyright protects literary works, sound recordings, works of art including paintings and sculptures, musical compositions, choreography, architectural works, newspaper and magazine articles, drawings and cartoons, and some computer programs. Even your kid brother's finger painting can be copyrighted. In fact, the U.S. Copyright Office in Washington, D.C. has shelves and shelves of wallpaper which have designs that are original, creative and fixed — and protected by copyright. The design of your computer's "wallpaper" — the background screen design for your operating system — is also likely copyrighted and is in the tangible form of 1s and 0s in the computer's memory. Still, while the copyright eligibility list is extensive, it is not unlimited. There are certain things that copyright does not protect.

What is Not Protected?

Copyright protects a particular expression of an idea but does not protect the idea itself. In other words, copyright law recognizes a distinction between "expression" and "ideas." Only creative expression, and not the creative ideas or thoughts that inspire such expression, qualifies for copyright protection. You might have the "Greatest Idea Ever," but until you record that idea in some more permanent, fixed, expressive form, you can't look to copyright law for protection.

Similarly, the expression of facts is subject to copyright protection, but not the facts themselves. For instance, while the website *Huffington Post* will have a copyright on the exact words and arrangement of an article on teen vaping, the facts and statistics included in *HuffPo*'s reporting belong to no one and can therefore be used as a source for other reporters.

Students are also free to look to other sources for paper ideas of their own or for facts to use in creating their own papers. But students are not free to copy the words of the *Huffington Post* article, since that would be a copyright violation. Students also should be concerned about the separate ethical question of plagiarism, which is copying or using someone else's material without attribution. (Plagiarism is discussed in more detail below.) But even with attribution, copying someone else's words is still copyright infringement unless it qualifies as "fair use" (also explained below), which would include most academic papers.

Another type of material not protected by copyright is anything created by U.S. government officials or employees. These materials, including materials as diverse as federal Environmental Protection Agency reports to NASA photos of the stars and planets, can be used without obtaining prior permission. In addition, all "official" pronouncements (court opinions, statutes, public records and similar official documents) of state and local government are in the public domain. But other works created by state or local government employees (such as a state parks website) may be protected by copyright.

There are also some forms of expression that the U.S. Copyright Office has determined are not protected by copyright, even though they are arguably original and fixed. These include common words, names, short phrases, titles, slogans, instructions, lists of ingredients and familiar symbols or designs. These are generally ineligible for copyright because they lack the necessary originality and creativity necessary to distinguish them from the ideas they represent.

But use of a phrase in a distinctive design may be protectable by copyright, and also as a trademark. For example, the phrase "Oh no they didn't!" cannot be copyrighted and therefore can be used by anyone as a heading for a blog post or as a tweet. However, the actual logo from the popular celebrity gossip blog by the same name cannot be used — barring permission or a "fair use" argument — because unlike the four "bare" words, the design of the logo (with artwork depicting an exclamation point inside a speech bubble to designate the letter "O") is sufficiently creative and can be copyrighted and trademarked as a logo. Similarly, the "bare words" of titles of movies or songs, ingredient lists, short phrases and even advertising slogans are not protectable by copyright.

Statistics are also not copyrightable. In the 2000s, Major League Baseball (MLB) created a lucrative side business licensing out player names and stats to fantasy baseball providers. When one company that provided a fantasy baseball league refused to pay for the information, MLB claimed it owned all game data. But the U.S. Court of Appeals for the Eighth Circuit ruled that, while TV broadcasts of the baseball games themselves were protected under copyright law, facts about the games such as individual players' performances were not copyrightable.[1] An earlier case involving scores of NBA games reached the same conclusion.[2]

Copyright can protect:

- Instagram photos
- Website logos
- Blog posts
- Podcasts
- Videos
- MP3s

Copyright does <u>not</u> generally protect:

- Facts, such as sports statistics
- Federal government content, such as NASA's photos
- Works whose copyright term has expired
- Titles and short phrases

1 *C.B.C. Distribution and Marketing, Inc. v. Major League Baseball Advanced Media, L.P.*, 505 F.3d 818, 823 (8th Cir. 2007), *cert. denied*, 553 U.S. 1090 (2008).

2 *NBA v. Motorola, Inc.*, 105 F.3d 841 (2nd Cir. 1997).

How Long Does Copyright Last?

Unfortunately calculating the duration of copyright protection can be a complicated task. Over the years, Congress has changed the law and time periods of copyright protection several times and there is no single rule that applies to all copyright-eligible works. In order to determine whether a valid copyright exists, you will often need to know when the work was created and when the work was first published (if those dates are not the same). Additionally, if the work is created by one or more individual people — rather than by or for a company — you will often need to know the date of death of the last surviving author.

For copyrighted works created now, current law provides for copyright protection as follows:

- Work by an individual author: Author's lifetime plus 70 years.
- Work by multiple authors: Lifetime of the last surviving author plus 70 years.
- Work by a corporation or organization (including creative work that a company paid someone, either an employee or a contractor, to complete; such a work is known as a "work for hire"): 95 years from first publication or 120 years from creation, whichever expires first.
- Anonymous/pseudonymous works: Same as corporate works.

The medium that a copyrighted work is made in does not matter. The copyright duration for a particular work is the same whether it was published in print or posted on the Internet.

Copyright protection does not last forever. Once a work's copyright expires, it becomes part of the public domain and can be used without permission from the former copyright owner. And while determining the length of copyright is complicated, any work that was published in the U.S. more than 95 years ago is fair game, which does allow for the extensive use of older literature and historical documents or photos without having to worry about first obtaining permission. Of course, good ethics suggest that even works whose copyrights have expired need to be properly attributed to the author in order to avoid plagiarism.

For example, a blogger who wanted to republish the complete works of William Shakespeare can do so without a problem. Shakespeare's works — all of which are now about four centuries old — are not copyright protected and can be freely used. But a specific publication or performance of a Shakespeare play can be copyrighted by the creator of that particular version and has a copyright separate from the public domain work itself.

The title page of the first edition of *The Wonderful Wizard of Oz*, published in 1900. Credit: Library of Congress.

As another example of this, consider *The Wonderful Wizard of Oz*. The original book, by author L. Frank Baum, was published in 1900, with a copyright that under the law in effect at the time lasted until 1956. This copyright protected the story of the book, including its characters (Dorothy, the Wizard, the Cowardly Lion and the rest) and its major plot elements (the Yellow Brick Road, the flying monkeys and Dorothy's silver slippers). Since the book was still protected by copyright, MGM licensed the story to create the 1939 movie *The Wizard of Oz* starring Judy Garland. The license allowed the moviemakers to use characters and plot elements from the book. The movie also added additional elements — such as replacing the silver slippers with ruby slippers, which appeared more vibrant on the screen — that are protected by the copyright on the movie, which under current law lasts until 2034. When the Broadway show *Wicked* debuted in 2003, the creators were free to use the characters and elements of the original book, since the copyright on the original book had expired. But they could not use elements of the MGM film without a license, since it was still protected by copyright. Another film based on the original book, *Oz the Great and Powerful*, released by Disney in 2013, used the book's characters but was careful not to use any elements from the 1939 movie, even going as far as making the Wicked Witch's skin a different shade of green to avoid legal issues.

How to Copyright Your Work

Nowadays, you don't need to do anything special to secure copyright protection for your work. Original works are protected by copyright the moment they are completed and "fixed" in a tangible medium of expression. For example, anytime you take a photo with your phone or write a paper for class, you can probably claim a copyright in your work. You don't need to do anything else. From this moment forward, no one else can use, alter or sell your copyrighted work in any way without your express permission (although if you do it for a class you probably grant implicit permission for your professor to use it for educational purposes).

To reiterate: under current law, all you have to do to have a copyright is to create an original work. There are no other requirements.

By the way, there is no set standard for determining whether a work is "original." Instead, courts will decide this on a case-by-case basis. Of course, this creates some difficulties for creators. They may use some elements of existing copyrighted works, but not too much that the new work essentially is a substitute for the original or lowers the original's economic value.

You do not have to put any sort of copyright notice on the work in order to have a copyright. Such a notice was mandatory, with some exceptions, for works published before March 1, 1989. For works published after that date, however, a copyright notice is optional and does not determine the validity of a copyright. Regardless, it remains a good idea to include a copyright notice on all published works, to remind others of their obligations and as a courtesy to users who may wish to contact the copyright owner. Such a notice can be used in court if there ever is a copyright dispute to show that an alleged infringer had notice that the original work was protected by copyright. The use of a copyright notice is the responsibility of the copyright owner and does not require advance permission from or registration with the Copyright Office.

Similarly, the registration of a new copyrighted work with the U.S. Copyright Office in Washington, D.C. is also voluntary. As mentioned before, a copyright now exists automatically from the moment a work is created.

Registration — or lack of registration — does not alter the validity of that copyright. Nonetheless, registering a copyrighted work and obtaining a certificate of registration can be advantageous to the copyright owner. First, only a copyright owner who has registered her work with the Copyright Office may sue someone who infringes her copyright. Additionally, while you have the right to register your work at any time while your copyright is in effect, certain damages and reimbursement for your attorney fees in any lawsuit are only available to those who formally register their work within three months of publication.

Registration is easy and does not require the help of an attorney. It entails completing a fairly straightforward form (either online or on paper), paying a small fee and submitting some copies of your work. Special registration requirements are available for serial publications (newspapers, weekly magazines, blogs, etc.) that make registration cheaper and easier to accomplish. Because of the "hassle" and expense, student media — which are often of limited value soon after they are published — often forego the benefits of registration. Still, if you anticipate that your published work may have value over time (and this probably includes some student films and software programs), you may want to consider registration.

Who Owns a Copyright?

Generally, the creator or creators of a work own the copyright. However, under the "work for hire" doctrine, an employer owns the copyright of works created by her employees while working in the scope of their employment. For example, copyright for a journalist's stories would belong to the news site that employs her.

Here is the most important rule to remember: if you didn't create the material that you want to use or you don't own the copyright to it yourself, you must obtain permission from the copyright owner before you do.

Contrary to what many people apparently think, the law requires actual permission from the copyright owner, not just attribution. Simply including a credit line along with a copyrighted work (e.g. "Image courtesy of *The New York Times*") — without actually contacting the copyright owner and obtaining explicit permission — is not enough to legally use the material.

Obtaining copyright permission isn't especially complicated — at least not for the uses most university students require — but it does require some legwork, plenty of time, and even some luck. The hardest part of obtaining copyright permission is often determining — and finding — who you need to ask, particularly since registration is not required. In many cases, the creator of the work is also the copyright owner, so contacting the creator is usually a good first step. At other times, however, the original author has sold or transferred ownership of the copyright to a third party. So, you should look for a copyright notice, which identifies the owner of the work at the time of publication. (Again, there may not be such a notice, since it is no longer required.)

If there is such a notice, you should contact that person or company. (Most companies have a "Copyright Permissions Department.") For works registered or renewed after 1978, you can also search the copyright registration records online at the Copyright Office's website to find the original copyright owner. But the Copyright Office records do not reflect subsequent transfers or licenses, and there won't be a record at the Copyright Office if the work was never registered.

While it is probably worth an initial telephone call, particularly at a smaller or less formal organization, most copyright owners require a written or e-mailed request. Your request should include your contact information, the expected date of publication, the number of copies you intend to produce and the price, if any, you will charge. If you are an editor for a non-profit student publication like your school's student newspaper, or making a film just to show at non-commercial events like a student film festival, be sure to make that absolutely clear. It is also important that you include a precise description of what you want to use and, if possible, a copy of your layout or sketch of your plans. Finally, include a (polite) statement regarding your deadline for a response. It is always a good idea to obtain copyright permission in writing. While verbal permission is valid, it can be more difficult to prove, especially following the passage of time. While copyright permission agreements or licenses for commercial uses can get pretty complicated, running several pages and full of "legalese," most student media uses of copyrighted works require much less paperwork. A simple statement giving permission, describing the work and its intended use, signed and dated by the copyright owner or his lawful agent, will generally suffice.

While it is sometimes tough to obtain permission to use a copyrighted work for free, there are a number of companies that are more than happy to give you permission to use copyrighted material, usually for a price. Photo services, news agencies and wire services (such as the Associated Press) make their money by collecting copyright-protected news stories and images and selling them to blogs and news sites. Similar licensing agencies exist that sell the rights to songs and lyrics. While the high cost of some of these services puts them out of reach of most students and student organizations, some are fairly inexpensive, at least for occasional use.

In addition, there are many photos, videos and documents online that are free to be used without permission. Content created by federal employees in the course of their work is unprotected by copyright and can be freely reused. To find such materials, start with federal government (.gov) sites like the White House, the Centers for Disease Control, NASA and others. Also look for materials carrying the Creative Commons (CC) license, a voluntary alternative to copyright that often allows particular uses of a work, with the permitted uses determined by the copyright owner. For example, many CC materials can be used to create new works, as long as it is not-for-profit and proper attribution is given.

SOURCES OF FREE REPRODUCIBLE CONTENT

- Federal government materials created by federal government employees are generally not protected by copyright, so websites of federal agencies and organizations are a good source of materials that can be reused.
- Google image search contains a filter for CC licensed materials (under Tools > Usage Rights).
- Mashable has compiled a list of 25 websites that provide CC content for audio, video, images and other types of content at https://mashable.com/2007/10/27/creative-commons/.
- Wikipedia has a policy of using mainly public domain or CC pictures and illustrations, so it is a good source of such images.

Contributory Infringement

When it comes to respecting copyright, you may be held accountable for more than your own violations. If you create a technology, such as a file-sharing website, that encourages users to duplicate and share copyrighted materials such as music or movies, you could get in trouble with the law for something known as contributory infringement. If a person or business enables copyright infringement by another person, they may be held liable as a contributory infringer if they had knowledge, or reason to know, of the infringement. For example, in 2001 music-sharing site Napster was successfully sued by music studios for allowing users on its site to freely share copyrighted material without getting permission from or paying the copyright owners, and eventually shut down.[3] The music companies also sued individual users for infringing copyright by downloading songs from the site. Subsequent copycat platforms, such as LimeWire[4] and Megaupload,[5] suffered the same fate.

However, duplication technology isn't necessarily illegal. In 1984, for example, the U.S. Supreme Court held that the sale of video tape recorders was not contributory infringement since the device was capable of "substantial non-infringing uses."[6] Although VCRs could be abused to duplicate

3 *A&M Records, Inc. v. Napster, Inc.*, 239 F.3d 1004 (9th Cir. 2001).

4 *Arista Records LLC v. Lime Group LLC*, 784 F.Supp.2d 398 (S.D.N.Y. 2011).

5 *U.S. v. Kim Dotcom*, Crim. No. 12-3, 2012 WL 4788433 (E.D.Va. Oct. 5, 2012) (denying motion to dismiss).

6 *Sony Corp. of America v. Universal City Studios, Inc.*, 464 U.S. 417, 418 (1984).

copyrighted movies, they were also commonly used to play and duplicate personally made videos.

Based on that precedent, manufacturers of 3D printers are arguably free of liability, even though customers may utilize them to duplicate copyrighted items. "Manufacturers of 3D printers have a good defense that, because their printers have substantial non-infringing uses, that they cannot be liable for contributory copyright infringement without engaging in additional conduct," argues the International Trademark Association, which also works on copyright issues. However, it adds that individuals who create or distribute copies or digital files of copyrighted, 3D objects "may be liable for contributory copyright infringement."[7] Besides copyright issues, 3D printers may also raise safety concerns. Several states are currently involved in litigation to prevent computer files for 3D-printed guns from being posted online. Proponents argue that there is a constitutional right to publish the material, but critics counter that it could lead to an increase in untraceable guns and more gun violence.

Streaming

Contributory infringement claims can also be applied to platforms that allow users to stream unauthorized movies, TV shows and broadcasts on their sites, even if users can't download them. Such a transmission is an infringement because the Copyright Act gives a copyright holder the exclusive right "to perform the copyrighted work publicly,"[8] and defines a public performance to include a transmission to the public "by means of any device or process" so long as "the members of the public capable of receiving the performance or display receive it in the same place or in separate places and at the same time or at different times."[9] So, streaming somebody else's work without their consent is infringement. Streaming platforms such as Netflix and Hulu pay millions of dollars annually for the right to legally stream content, leading the U.S. Court of Appeals for the Second Circuit to rule that streaming without permission would "substantially diminish the value of the programming."[10]

Fair Use: An Important Exception

So, the general rule of copyright is that you need permission to use other people's work. But there is an important exception that students, journalists,

7 3D Printing Task Force, International Trade Assn, 3D Printing: Key Legal Issues and Options for Change 6–7 (2017), https://www.cantorcolburn.com/media/news/428_3D%20Printing%20Report%2027.09.2017.pdf.

8 17 U.S.C. § 106(4).

9 17 U.S.C. § 101.

10 *WPIX, INC. v. ivi, Inc.*, 691 F.3d 275, 285 (2d Cir. 2012).

graphic artists, social media influencers and computer programmers in particular need to know about: fair use.

Remember the balance we talked about earlier between protecting copyright owners' rights and recognizing society's need for readily accessible information? "Fair use" is an exception to the general copyright rule where that balancing act really comes into play. The Fair Use Doctrine is, in effect, a compromise and allows for the use of limited amounts of copyrighted works for important purposes like news reporting, commentary, critiques, teaching, research, education, library archiving and Internet search engine results, as long as the use does not cause the copyright owner to lose potential revenue from the original copyrighted work. No permission is needed if fair use applies.

For example, short quotations will usually be fair use, not copyright infringement. So, students can cite portions of an academic journal article in a term paper (with proper attribution to avoid plagiarism), a blogger can generally reprint a short passage from a new book to accompany a book review, and a podcast is usually safe to include a short clip from a movie to illustrate its discussion or review of the motion picture. Other fair uses probably include the use of a single frame from a comic strip to illustrate a news article reporting the retirement or death of the strip's creator, republishing an e-cigarette advertisement taken from a website to illustrate a blog post on the effect of vaping advertising on minors, reprinting two lines from a song in a news article about a controversy involving the song, or copying a small portion of information from a website and distributing it to students in a class.

But "fair use" is not a universal "get out of jail" card. Keep in mind that students, journalists, programmers and others cannot always claim a fair use whenever they use someone else's work. But unless their use meets the fair use criteria, they must first obtain permission. For example, in 2013, a federal court ruled that two news outlets should have asked for permission before using images a photographer took and posted on his Twitter account of a devastating earthquake in Haiti. A jury found that Agence France-Presse and Getty Images willfully violated the Copyright Act by simply downloading the photos and then distributing the photos to their subscribers, and awarded the photographer a $1.2 million payout.[11]

Unfortunately, determining whether a use would qualify as a fair use can often be a tough call. Despite what you may have heard, there is no simple formula or clear-cut threshold. Still, it is essential to understand the basics of fair use and keep this important exception in mind. In trying to determine whether or not a particular use is a fair use, courts have looked at four different factors.

The first question a court will ask is: what is the purpose and character of the use? Non-commercial uses for purposes like news reporting, teaching, academic research, criticism or commentary are more likely to be fair. Such uses tend to "add something new" and are not merely a substitute for the original.

11 *Agence France-Presse v. Morel*, 934 F.Supp.2d 584 (S.D.N.Y. 2013).

For example, including a few lines from *SpongeBob SquarePants* to illustrate your critique of the popular TV cartoon show would more likely be considered a fair use than publishing those same quotes — by themselves — to "decorate" a website. Uses that are not directly or indirectly motivated by profit are more likely to be held to be "fair use," while uses that are primarily intended for commercial gain are less likely to be considered "fair use." But, since there's no exact equation for determining this, different courts may reach different conclusions over whether a line was crossed. For example, a tattoo artist who created a tattoo for boxer Mike Tyson sued when the film *The Hangover Part II* replicated the tattoo on a character in the movie.[12] The film company settled after the court indicated that the company's fair use argument was likely to fail. But another court dismissed a lawsuit by a tattoo artist whose tattoos for LeBron James were reproduced in a basketball video game, with the court finding that the use of the tattoo designs was minimal and was thus fair use.[13]

Second, a court will ask, what is the nature of the copyright-protected work? Uses of works containing mostly factual material like maps or biographies are more likely to be fair than uses of highly creative and original works like illustrations and novels.

Third, how much of the original work is used? In order for a use of a copyrighted work to be a "fair use," the use should be no more of the work than what is necessary. The test is both quantitative (for example, how many words of a 250,000-word book are reproduced?) and qualitative. Using the "core" or "heart" of a work — no matter how small — is less likely to be a "fair use."

While it would certainly make life easier, there is no established word limit for determining whether a particular use would qualify as a fair use. Neither is there a set amount of time of a song or a movie that you can safely use as a clip. A news magazine was once successfully sued for copyright infringement for using a mere 300 words from a 500-page book because it didn't get the book publisher's permission. The court determined that the 300 words were the "core" or most important information of the book and, by publishing a news story about it, the book publisher lost out on potential book sales and on an exclusive preview that it had sold to another magazine.[14]

Finally, in determining whether fair use applies, courts examine, what is the effect of the use on the potential market value of the original work? This may be the most important factor, since the major point of copyright is to protect the economic interests of creators. If consumers are likely to buy something that uses a copyrighted work as a substitute for the original, it probably will not qualify as a fair use. The fact that the copyright owner lost the ability to

12 *Whitmill v. Warner Bros. Entertainment, Inc.*, Civil No. 11-752 (E.D. Mo. dismissed pursuant to settlement 2012).

13 *Solid Oak Sketches, LLC v. 2K Games, Inc.*, 2020 WL 1467394, 449 F.Supp.3d 333 (S.D.N.Y. 2020).

14 *Harper & Row Publishers, Inc. v. Nation Enterprises*, 471 U.S. 539 (1985).

sell the rights to use their work to you (especially if that is their business) could diminish the likelihood of a fair use determination as well.

There are some things you can do to minimize the effect of a use on the market value of the original. For example, a blogger using an image at a significantly smaller size and a lower resolution or reproducing it in black and white instead of full color are a few things that would make it less likely a consumer or a court would look upon such a use as a substitute for the original.

Now that you have a general understanding of the purpose behind fair use, here are some common examples generally regarded as fair use:

- Small excerpts in a review or criticism for purposes of illustration or comment.
- Quotations from a speech, address or position paper in a news report.
- Limited copying made by a student for academic work.
- A professor copying a small part of a book and posting it on the university's online class system or handing it out to students for class discussion.

A seminal case involved Google, which launched Google Books in the early 2000s by digitizing library books so that users could search the full text of all the books in its database. Although users could only view snippets of copyrighted books and only download and view full copies of books whose copyrights had expired, the Authors Guild and Association of American Publishers filed a class action lawsuit. After a long court battle, the Second Circuit Court of Appeals handed Google a clear victory, soundly rejecting claims that Google Books constituted copyright infringement.[15]

Other Copyright Exceptions

Besides fair use, there are some other noteworthy exceptions to copyright claims.

Digital Millennium Copyright Act

If you manage a blog that allows users to submit comments or run a website that allows users to post content, you can avoid being held responsible for copyright infringement by users. The federal Digital Millennium Copyright Act (DMCA) allows website operators to escape liability for copyright infringement in materials posted by users, but only as long as the site promptly pulls down infringing material posted by outside parties (not staffers) after getting notice of the infringement. To qualify for protection the website operator must also register with the Copyright Office, designate whom to contact regarding alleged infringement on the site and pay a fee.

15 *Authors Guild v. Google, Inc.*, 804 F.3d 202 (2d Cir. 2015) (affirming dismissal), *cert. denied*, 136 S.Ct. 1658, 194 L.Ed.2d 800 (U.S. 2016).

Links, Embedded Videos and Thumbnails

While copying and posting material from another site without permission is infringement, linking to copyrighted material, embedding copyrighted videos from another site (such as YouTube) and using thumbnails of copyrighted images on your site are generally OK. So far, U.S. courts have not found these practices to be a copyright violation, even though websites complain that it steals traffic away from their sites. Australia and the European Union have taken a different approach, moving towards requiring sites that aggregate news from other sites to compensate those sites.

Parody and Spoofs

Copyright law also gives parodies and spoofs a fair amount of breathing room. The courts recognize that a parody must to some extent mimic the original to make its point. For example, the U.S. Supreme Court held that 2 Live Crew's parody of Roy Orbison's song "Pretty Woman," which used the same basic tune and much of the same lyrics, was a parody — and not copyright infringement — because it made a comment about the original work and was dissimilar enough and appealed to a different audience so as not to cause consumer confusion.[16]

But this does not mean that simply changing the lyrics to a popular song is fair use. It is probably not fair use to change some words of a Britney Spears song so that it comments on the members of your sorority and to then make a YouTube video of the altered lyrics — no matter how funny the end result — because you could have paid Spears (or her record company) to use the tune. On the other hand, it probably would be considered a fair use to change a small portion of the song's lyrics to make fun of Britney Spears herself.

In short, it is much more difficult to prove fair use if you just borrow from a popular song or cartoon character as a gimmick rather than using the borrowed material to satirically attack something other than the original work or its creator. In order to safely parody a copyrighted work without permission from the copyright owner, the parody must be obvious. The audience must reasonably perceive that the use is a criticism or commentary of the original. (Hence why shows like *Saturday Night Live* are able to avoid infringement claims for their skits.)

Second, an artist who wants to parody an original must not use any more of the original work than is necessary to "conjure-up" or evoke thoughts of the original in the minds of the audience. If only a mannerism, a classic line of dialog or a physical attribute of a character is necessary to make the parody succeed — for example, blue overalls and red hat with the letter "M" to depict the video game character Super Mario — then only those elements should be used and not more. Creativity also counts. Anything you can do to distinguish your

16 *Campbell v. Acuff-Rose Music*, 510 U.S. 569 (1994).

parody from the original and add something new helps. Finally, the parody must not directly threaten the market value of the original work. If a court is presented with evidence that the public will buy the parody instead of buying the original, it is more likely to rule that the use is probably not fair use.

Internet memes occupy a grey area of copyright law. On one hand, a meme is usually a derivative work, as meme creators will simply add text to a copyrighted image. On the other hand, memes often involve parody and may require some creativity, so a fair use argument could be made. While many copyright owners may not press the issue because they don't care or may even appreciate the publicity, it's safest to only use images for which you either have a license or own the copyright. For example, the photo licensing agency Getty Images demanded payment from several individuals who posted memes based on the "Awkward Penguin" photograph by George Moberly of *National Geographic* magazine, for which Getty owns the licensing rights.

Even the president isn't above the law. In 2019, the musical group Nickelback got Twitter to remove a parody of its "Photograph" music video that President Trump posted in response to his impeachment. The use of memes based on copyrighted material can be especially legally risky in advertising, since the advertiser would normally have to pay for such a use.

This "distracted boyfriend" image was originally snapped by photographer Antonio Guillem who uploaded it online in 2015 to sell on stock photo websites. It wasn't until two years later that the image became a popular meme with simple captions added to the image to represent real-life things people are distracted by. Although copyright infringement of his photo is rampant, Guillem told *The Guardian* he won't be taking legal action except in cases of "bad faith": "What really worries us — and we are not going to allow it, taking the appropriate legal measures — is the use of the images in a pejorative, offensive or any way that can harm the models or me." Credit: Antonio Guillem.

Reverse Engineering

Another tricky area of determining fair use is "reverse engineering" or "back engineering," which is examining already published software, devices and other products to figure out how they work and then duplicate the process. Under both the DMCA and fair use doctrine, this practice is legal under certain conditions.

For example, reverse engineering is often performed on computer programs to make them compatible with other programs or allow add-on features. In order to legally reverse engineer the software, it must be legitimately acquired and used in good faith for the sole purpose of identifying and analyzing the parts of the program needed for interoperability. Reverse engineering is also often used in "white hat hacking," in which ethical hackers identify security vulnerabilities and exploits and then responsibly disclose them to a manufacturer or client organization. In addition, some software authors explicitly encourage others to copy their code, learn from it, modify it or share it by using "open source" licenses. The cryptocurrency Bitcoin is an example of open-source code. Nobody owns or controls Bitcoin's software and anyone can take part in its network. Many other cryptocurrencies have been created by copying Bitcoin's underlying code and adding new features to it.

However, most tech companies limit other's rights to reverse engineer their products through Terms of Use or End User License Agreements. Such policies give the creator exclusive control over the product and preclude anyone who attempts to modify it from using the fair use defense. In a 2005 case involving *World of Warcraft*, a few fans of the game successfully reverse engineered the software and created a network which allowed far-flung players to compete against each other online instead of using the video game company's network. When the company sued, the fans argued that the Copyright Act expressly permits reverse engineering in order to achieve "interoperability," the ability of parts made by different companies to work together, but a federal appellate court concluded that they had waived that right by agreeing to the game maker's Terms of Service.[17]

Some tech companies — and even non-tech companies, such as makers of farm tractors — also include provisions in the Terms of Use and/or End User License Agreements of the electronic components of their products that ban service and repairs from anyone other than authorized persons, on the grounds that repairs by others violate their copyrights and patents. Bills introduced in Congress and several state legislatures would ban such practices.

When the goal of reverse engineering is to duplicate a copyrighted item, with only minor changes, it may or may not be copyright infringement. In 2021, the Supreme Court held that using copyrighted computer code from Oracle's Java platform in Google's Android platform was fair use.[18]

17 *Davidson & Associates DBA Blizzard Entertainment, Inc. v. Jung et al.*, 422 F. 3d 630 (8th Cir. 2005).

18 *Google LLC v. Oracle America, Inc.*, No. 18-956 (U.S. Apr. 5, 2021).

Animals and Artificial Intelligence

It may be "speciesist," but copyright applies only to humans. In 2011, People for the Ethical Treatment of Animals (PETA) filed a federal lawsuit against a photographer who profited off of "selfies" that were taken by a Celebes crested macaque named Naruto, using the photographer's camera. The court faced a novel issue: who owned the copyright to photos taken by a monkey? The federal Court of Appeals for the Ninth Circuit ruled U.S. copyright law does not give animals the rights to photographs or other original work, and that copyright infringement can only be claimed by humans.[19] That left the photo ostensibly author-less, and in the public domain. This precedent seems to suggest that artificial intelligence (AI) will not be entitled to copyright protection if it creates content. However, it could be that copyright will belong to the programmer who created the AI. Undoubtedly, this issue will arise in the future and a court will have to decide whether AI can own copyright. For now, all we can do is speculate as to the result.

This infamous "selfie" photo, captured when the monkey pressed the shutter, became the subject of a years-long copyright dispute that left the human photographer who claimed ownership financially broke. Credit: Naruto.

Penalties for Copyright Infringement

Keep in mind that merely claiming your infringement qualifies for fair use is not sufficient to make it so. Whether the doctrine applies is ultimately for a court to determine. Usually it's best to get the copyright owner's permission or pay their licensing fee, even if you're pretty sure you don't need it.

19 *Naruto v. Slater*, 888 F.3d 418 (9th Cir. 2018), *reh'g en banc denied*, 916 F.3d 1148 (9th Cir. 2018).

Legal threats and lawsuits can be a big headache — and are likely to be costly. Copyright owners can sue for copyright infringement if they believe someone has used their work without permission or in a way that would not be considered a fair use. If the copyright owner wins, the court may award either actual damages, based on the copyright owner's lost revenue plus any profits made by the infringer, and/or statutory damages, which range from $200 to $150,000 per infringement depending, in part, on whether the infringement was "innocent" or "willful." In addition, the judge can order injunctive relief to stop sale of the infringing material and confiscation of that material. Even poor college students who claim ignorance aren't immune. In 2005, the Recording Industry Association of America (RIAA), the trade organization which represents the music industry, won a $222,000 judgment against a single mother of four who shared 22 copyrighted songs on a file-sharing website, making them available for others to download.[20] Following bad publicity for the lawsuit, which led to the mother declaring bankruptcy and was criticized as heavy-handed, the RIAA now typically works with Internet service providers — including universities — to identify and initially warn violators before pursuing litigation against repeat offenders.

Adelphi University, where one of the textbook authors teaches, receives about 600 notices of copyright infringements per year, mostly related to students illegally downloading movies, TV shows and music. Because of the DMCA, Adelphi is shielded from liability. However, students may be hit with fines. At a minimum, a student who commits copyright infringement will probably be summoned to the Student Affairs Office for a stern talk. Remember, if you illegally download a song, TV show or game using your college's network, the IT department can likely figure out your identity.

Copyright v. Plagiarism

Another area of concern for college students — and one that is often confused with copyright — is plagiarism. Plagiarism is not really an IP infringement, but an ethical violation that can occur when one fails to give an author of a work proper credit.

Simply stated, a plagiarist is a person who poses as the creator of words, ideas or methods that are not his own. By contrast, a person infringes another's copyright when he makes unauthorized use of material that is protected by copyright, even if the user gives credit to the creator. Often plagiarism and copyright overlap. But not always.

For example, a person could plagiarize information from a U.S. government website by not giving the government proper credit. He would not, however, be guilty of copyright infringement because federal government works

20 *Capitol Records, Inc. v. Thomas-Rasset*, 692 F.3d 899 (8th Cir. 2012), *cert. denied*, 568 U.S. 1229 (2013).

cannot be protected by copyright and are in the public domain. You will not be punished by a court of law if you are found guilty of plagiarizing someone else's work, but you might be subject to punishment by your professor and your university's Academic Honesty Committee. And you should certainly be embarrassed.

On the other hand, if you were to copy and paste an article from *The New York Times* on your blog, noting that the article was published by the newspaper and not you, this would not be considered plagiarism because you are properly citing the source. However, if you did not get *The Times*' permission to repost the article on your site, it might constitute copyright infringement.

Other IP Laws

Copyright is just one means of providing legal protection for creative works. Patent law protects inventions, such as computers, smartphones and photo filtering software. Trademark law protects the symbols and slogans that identify businesses to their consumers. Trade secret laws help keep a company's valuable information confidential through legal agreements. Together with copyright, these legal issues comprise the area of the law known as IP. Let's take a closer look at each.

Patent Law

Patent law protects inventors' IP rights. To receive a patent, the inventor must invent an item or process that is novel, useful and not obvious from preexisting patented items. Patents generally last 20 years and can be obtained by filing an application with the U.S. Patent and Trademark Office (USPTO). Like infringement of copyrights, patent holders may sue for infringement of their IP.

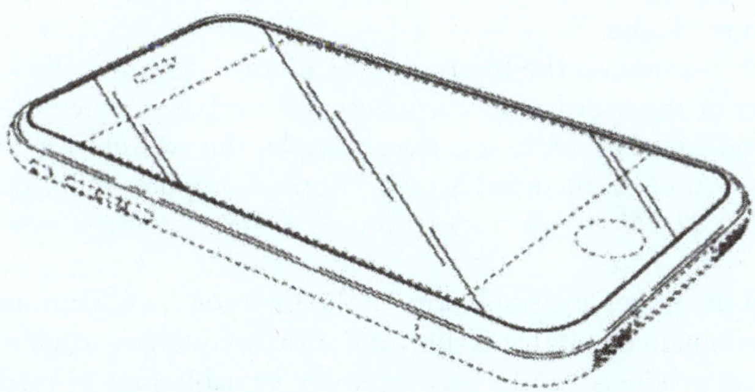

An illustration from the design patent (Number US D672769 S) for the original iPhone, granted in 2007. Credit: U.S. Patent and Trademark Office.

Tech-related patents are available for utilities, designs and business methods. For example, Apple owns both utility and design patents for the iPhone. The utility patent covers the machinery of the device while the design patent protects the iPhone's aesthetics: what it looks like. Whenever Apple invents a new product, or even makes an upgrade for an existing product, such as a seal to waterproof iPhones, it can apply for a patent on that innovation.

In 2010, the U.S. Supreme Court expanded patent protection to include business methods.[21] Such patents are commonly sought for e-commerce purposes. For example, Amazon held a patent on a "1-Click shopping" system that simplifies online shopping by allowing consumers to purchase items by clicking an order button on a website. This patent expired in 2017, so other sites may now use the technology freely.

Trademark Law

While copyright and patent protect a creator's rights, trademark law should be viewed more as a protection for consumers. Trademarks that identify products — for example, the Apple Computer symbol or the brand name "Google" — and service marks, which identify services — for example, the blue bird synonymous with Twitter — are unique symbols, names or other "marks" that companies use and consumers rely upon to distinguish one product or service from another. Trademark law is generally only a problem when a trademark or service mark is used in a way that would confuse a potential consumer.

If there is no likelihood that a consumer would be confused by the use of a trademark, there is generally no violation. That's why, for example, there would be no problem in a blog publishing a photograph of the new iPhone (complete with the well-known Apple trademark) to review the product. There is, obviously, no likelihood that a blog visitor would read the blog post thinking it was an actual iPhone. On the other hand, many years ago Coca-Cola successfully sued to stop a competitor from selling a different beverage under the name "Koke."[22]

Trademark disputes on the Internet often involve domain names. A domain name consists of the words and characters that website owners designate for their registered Internet addresses. For example, the website for McDonald's restaurants is found at mcdonalds.com, Apple computer's domain name is apple.com, and *The New York Times*' domain name is nytimes.com — you get the idea.

Because of the increasing popularity of the Internet, merchants have realized that having a domain name that is the same as their company name or the name of one of their products can be an extremely valuable part of establishing an

21 *Bilski v. Kappos*, 561 U.S. 593 (2010).

22 *Coca-Cola Co. v. Koke Co.*, 254 U.S. 143 (1920).

Internet presence. However, sometimes opportunistic individuals will reserve a domain name on the Internet that uses a company's trademark and then seek to profit by selling or licensing the domain name to the company that has an interest in being identified with it. This practice is known as "cybersquatting." When a company finds that the domain name corresponding to their corporate name or product trademark is owned by someone else, the company can (1) choose a different name, (2) attempt to negotiate to purchase the name from the current owner, or (3) fight to get the domain name back from its current owners by filing a trademark infringement lawsuit. Brand owners can rely on ICANN's Uniform Domain-Name Dispute Resolution Proceedings or the U.S. Anti-Cybersquatting Consumer Protection Act, which allows a trademark owner to bring a lawsuit against an individual or entity that registers a domain name that is similar enough to a trademark that it confuses customers and web users.

Some well-publicized examples of these types of domain names disputes are:

- zippo.com: Zippo News, a news site, was ordered by a federal court to relinquish its domain name after being sued by the manufacturer of well-known Zippo tobacco lighters, which owned the Zippo trademark. The case also established a precedent for determining jurisdiction for Internet disputes involving parties from different states, which is discussed in Chapter 2.[23]
- candyland.com: A pornography business beat toy company Hasbro in registering the domain name candyland.com. Hasbro was able to obtain the name after suing.[24]
- mcdonalds.com: A writer for *Wired* magazine registered this domain while writing a story on the value of domain names. The writer eventually gave the domain name to McDonald's after the burger chain donated $3,500 to a New York grade school for new computers.
- micros0ft.com: The maker of Windows obtained this URL (with the number zero in place of the second "o" letter) after it filed a protest against Zero Micro Software, which had initially obtained a registration for it.
- peta.org: People for the Ethical Treatment of Animals (more commonly known by its acronym PETA) was able to obtain the domain name peta .org after the registration of the domain by an organization known as "People Eating Tasty Animals" was suspended.
- .amazon: In 2019, after a seven-year dispute, online shopping giant Amazon — which already owned the domain amazon.com — was also allowed to register the ".amazon" domain name extension over the strong objections of a coalition of South American governments that had

23 *Zippo Manufacturing Co. v. Zippo Dot Com, Inc.*, 952 F. Supp. 1119 (W.D. Pa. 1997).

24 *Hasbro, Inc. v. Internet Entertainment Group, Ltd.*, 1996 WL 84853 (W.D.Wash., Feb. 9, 1996), *modification denied*, 1996 WL 84858 (W.D.Wash. Feb. 22, 1996).

argued the name referred to their geographic region and should belong to them.

Trade Secrets

In contrast to patents, which are filed with the government and eventually become publicly accessible, a trade secret is by definition not publicly known. Rather, it is information such as a practice, formula or technique that is kept confidential within a company because it gives the company an economic advantage over its competitors — such as a way to make a superior product — and is often a product of internal research and development. For example, the algorithms used for Google's search engine and the algorithms used to create *The New York Times*' bestseller list are both trade secrets. So is the "secret" formula for Coca-Cola. Because protection of trade secrets can, in principle, last indefinitely, it may provide an advantage over registered IP rights, which last only for a specific duration.

The formula for Coca-Cola, which is legally protected as a trade secret, is held in this vault at the company's museum in Atlanta. Credit: Coca-Cola Company.

Trade secrets are protected by the federal Economic Espionage Act of 1996. In addition, most states have also enacted laws to help companies protect their trade secrets. To ensure secrecy, a worker may be required to sign agreements to not reveal their prospective employer's proprietary information, to surrender or assign ownership rights to any intellectual work produced during employment to their employer, and to not work for a competitor for a given period of time. Violation of the agreement generally carries the possibility of heavy financial penalties.

Companies that benefit from such theft may also take a hit. For example, in 2017, a federal jury ordered Facebook to pay $304 million after a jury found that it had hired another company's employee in order to steal its trade secrets needed to create its Oculus Rift virtual reality headset. The parties subsequently settled rather than prolong the litigation with appeals.[25]

Governments often engage in industrial espionage. In the late 1980s, for example, French intelligence officials targeted U.S. electronics companies including IBM and Texas Instruments in an attempt to bolster a failing state-owned French computer firm. The efforts mixed electronic surveillance with attempted recruitment of disgruntled personnel, according to the FBI. Huawei, a technology firm with close ties to China's government, has been accused of stealing trade secrets from several other North American tech firms, and in 2019 was criminally indicted for allegedly stealing secret robotic technology from American telecom giant T-Mobile.[26] In 2019, U.S. government officials indefinitely banned Huawei from selling its products to Americans.

International Intellectual Rights

Protection against unauthorized use of a copyrighted work, patent or trademark in a particular country depends the national laws of that country. As a result, there is no such thing as an international IP right that will automatically protect a work throughout the world. However, as discussed in Chapter 2, the U.S. and many other countries have signed bi-lateral and multilateral treaties in which they agree to offer protection to IP from other countries under certain conditions. Major international treaties include the World Intellectual Property Organization Copyright Treaty and the Berne Convention for the Protection of Literary and Artistic Works. Under the Patent Cooperation Treaty, inventors who apply for patents with the USPTO can simultaneously seek protection in more than 100 other countries.

25 *ZeniMax Media Inc. et al. v. Oculus VR, Inc.*, Civil No. 4-01849 (N.D. Tex. Mar. 14, 2019) (approving settlement).

26 *U.S. v. Huawei Device Co., Ltd.*, Crim. No. 19-10 (W.D. Wash. filed Jan. 16, 2019).

CLOSING ARGUMENTS

By protecting the economic incentives to create content, copyright law is a fundamental basis of the vast industry of information produced for offline and online venues. But there are many who feel that the absolute protection that American copyright law provides to works for lengthy periods of time actually constrains innovation by severely limiting reuse of existing materials in new ways. The principle of "fair use," they argue, does not go far enough to allow such reuse, particularly because of its vague nature. Does copyright law give too much protection? Or is such protection necessary to the creation of new content?

Additional Sources

Balsamo, Michael and Grygiel, Chris, *Coalition of States Sue over Rules Governing 3D-Printed Guns*, Associated Press, Jan. 23, 2020, https://apnews.com/0a34a17d6ee5f9f77af6b51a3280f310.

Barnes, Brooks, *We Aren't in the Old Kansas, Toto*, New York Times, Feb. 28, 2013, https://www.nytimes.com/2013/03/03/movies/oz-the-great-and-powerful-disneys-wizard-of-oz-prequel.htm.

Bloomberg News, *Why Australia Forcing Facebook, Google to Pay Publishers for News Isn't a Good Idea*, The Print, Aug. 15, 2020, https://theprint.in/world/why-australia-forcing-facebook-google-to-pay-publishers-for-news-isnt-a-good-idea/482336/.

Boboltz, Sara, *Getty Is Quietly Charging Bloggers for "Socially Awkward Penguin" Meme*, Huffington Post, Sept. 5, 2015, https://www.huffpost.com/entry/getty-socially-awkward-penguin_n_55e9dbece4b03784e275c935.

Business Insider Intelligence, *Amazon's Patent on One-Click Payments to Expire*, Business Insider, Jan. 5, 2017, https://www.businessinsider.com/amazons-patent-on-one-click-payments-to-expire-2017-1.

Drozdiak, Natalia, *Google Considering Pulling News Service from Europe*, Bloomberg, Jan. 21, 2019, https://www.bloomberg.com/news/articles/2019-01-22/google-says-it-s-considering-pulling-news-service-from-europe.

Feist Publications, Inc. v. Rural Telephone Service Co., 499 U.S. 340 (1991).

Flava Works, Inc v. Gunter, 689 F.3d 754 (7th Cir. 2012).

Hvistendahl, Mara, *The Oldest Game: The Very Long History of Industrial Espionage*, Foreign Policy, Apr. 27, 2019, https://foreignpolicy.com/2019/04/27/the-oldest-game-industrial-espionage-timeline/.

Keane, Sean, *Huawei Ban Timeline: Trump Administration Says Company Is Backed by Chinese Military*, CNET, June 25, 2020, https://www.cnet.com/news/huawei-ban-full-timeline-us-government-china-trump-security-threat-p40/.

Lindquist, David, FFA: *President Trump Didn't Call the Tune for Pharrell Williams' 'Happy' in Indianapolis*, Indianapolis Star, Oct. 30. 2018, https://www.indystar.com/story/entertainment/music/2018/10/30/ffa-president-trump-didnt-call-tune-pharrell-williams-happy-indianapolis/1821448002/.

Lloyd, Craig, *What Are "Right to Repair" Laws, and What Do They Mean for You?*, How to Geek, Jan. 20, 2019, https://www.howtogeek.com/339925/what-are-%E2%80%9Cright-to-repair%E2%80%9D-laws-and-what-do-they-mean-for-you/.

Perfect 10, Inc. v. Amazon.com, Inc., 508 F.3d 1146 (9th Cir. 2007).

Quittner, Josh, *Billions Registered*, Wired, Oct. 1, 1994, https://www.wired.com/1994/10/mcdonalds/.

Religious Technology Center v. Netcom On-Line Communication Services, Inc., 907 F.Supp. 1361 (N.D. Cal. 1995).

Roberts, Jeff John, *Twitter Took a Trump Tweet Down, But Should It Have? And Is Nickelback to Blame?*, Fortune, Oct. 3, 2019, https://fortune.com/2019/10/03/donald-trump-twitter-nickelback-photograph-tweet/.

Student Press Law Center, *SPLC Guide to Fair Use*, Apr. 26, 2011, https://splc.org/2011/04/splc-guide-to-fair-use/.

Student Press Law Center, *Student Media Guide to Copyright Law*, Aug. 5, 2015, https://splc.org/2015/08/the-student-media-guide-to-copyright-law/.

8 Online Business and the Law

> Today's big tech companies have too much power — too much power over our economy, our society, and our democracy. They've bulldozed competition, used our private information for profit, and tilted the playing field against everyone else.
>
> — Senator Elizabeth Warren

The growth of e-commerce was already skyrocketing before the coronavirus pandemic sent it out of this world. In 2019, e-commerce was responsible for around $602 billion in sales in the United States,[1] and the pandemic spiked sales to $792 billion nationwide in 2020.[2] In short, nowadays we're all doing business online. Whether you're selling or buying items online or even just surfing the web and using social media, there are some important laws regarding e-commerce that you should know.

In addition, just like offline businesses, online businesses and tech companies in the U.S. must comply with various regulations imposed by the federal, state and local governments that apply to all businesses. This typically means things like paying taxes, not engaging in discriminatory hiring practices, following environmental standards and other requirements. But certain business regulations that apply to all businesses are of particular concern for businesses that offer products or services online, especially when the regulations are completely different depending on location. Meanwhile, consumers should be aware of what protections they have — and don't have — when using the Internet. This chapter summarizes some of the key regulations applicable to businesses and consumers online.

Anti-Trust Laws

In free market economies such as the U.S., consumers and businesses shape commerce through supply and demand. There is little interference from the

1 Young, Jessica, *Global Ecommerce Sales to Reach Nearly $3.46 Trillion in 2019*, Digital 360 Commerce, Nov. 13, 2019, https://www.digitalcommerce360.com/article/global-ecommerce-sales/.

2 U.S. Department of Commerce, *Quarterly Retail E-Commerce Sales*, U.S. Census Bureau News, Feb. 19, 2021, https://www.census.gov/retail/mrts/www/data/pdf/ec_current.pdf.

government. But in the late 19th and early 20th centuries, large corporations came to be so dominant in certain types of businesses that the federal and state governments passed laws barring individual companies from becoming so powerful that they effectively control their entire market. For example, oil tycoon John D. Rockefeller's Standard Oil Company gained control of nearly 90% of its market, allowing it to prevent competition, abuse labor and engage in price-fixing. After the passage of anti-trust laws, Rockefeller was eventually forced to sell off parts of his company to new owners.

A company in such a position is known as a "monopoly," and a combination of companies that coordinate their activities in this way is known as a "trust." Monopolies aren't always bad or prohibited — water and electric companies, for example, often have monopolies in a local area — but they can become problematic when there's not enough competition to ensure economic efficiency and consumer choice. Trusts are problematic for the same reasons.

In the Internet Age, competition issues have arisen with a handful of tech companies. Google, Apple, Facebook, Amazon and Microsoft — or "The Frightful Five" as they're sometimes collectively called — have accrued a tremendous amount of power and influence over their industries that make serious competition from startups nearly impossible. In the U.S., Google is used for more than 90% of Internet searches,[3] 95% of young adults on the Internet use a Facebook product (such as Facebook, Instagram or WhatsApp),[4] and 75% of sales of e-books occur on Amazon.[5] In other markets, these firms may not have a monopoly, but instead be part of a duopoly: Google and Facebook share 60% of online ad spending,[6] Google and Apple provide 99% of mobile phone operating systems,[7] and Apple and Microsoft supply 95% of desktop operating systems.[8] As a result, these tech giants and their owners have become obscenely rich. Apple and Google are wealthier than many large nations and Amazon's Jeff Bezos, Microsoft founder Bill Gates and Facebook's Mark Zuckerberg are

3 Clement, J., *Distribution of Total and Mobile Organic Search Visits In the United States As of 1st Quarter 2020, By Engine*, Statista, Aug. 19, 2020, https://www.statista.com/statistics/625554/mobile-share-of-us-organic-search-engine-visits/; Clement, J., *Worldwide Desktop Market Share of Leading Search Engines from January 2010 to April 2020*, Statista, Sept. 2, 2020, https://www.statista.com/statistics/216573/worldwide-market-share-of-search-engines/.

4 Ip, Greg, *The Antitrust Case against Facebook, Google and Amazon*, Wall Street Journal, Jan. 16, 2018, https://www.wsj.com/articles/the-antitrust-case-against-facebook-google-amazon-and-apple-1516121561.

5 *Id.*

6 Perrin, Nicole, *Facebook-Google Duopoly Won't Crack This Year*, eMarketer, Nov. 4, 2019, https://www.emarketer.com/content/facebook-google-duopoly-won-t-crack-this-year.

7 O'Dea, Simon, *Mobile Operating Systems Market Share Worldwide From January 2012 to July 2020*, Statista, Aug. 17, 2020, https://www.statista.com/statistics/272698/global-market-share-held-by-mobile-operating-systems-since-2009/.

8 Liu, Shanhong *Global Market Share Held by Operating Systems for Desktop Pcs, from January 2013 to July 2020*, Statista, Aug. 17, 2020, https://www.statista.com/statistics/218089/global-market-share-of-windows-7/.

the richest people in the world, with an estimated net worth of more than $100 billion each.

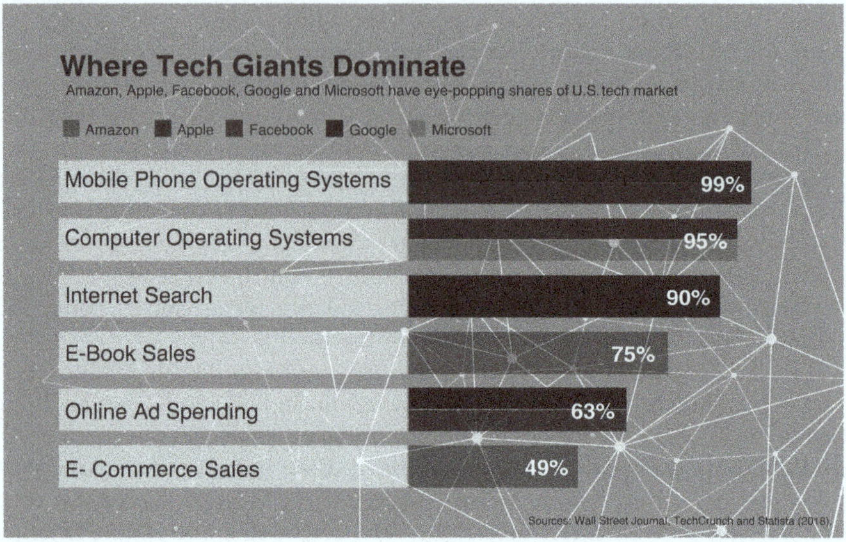

Consequently, a growing number of critics think these tech giants need to be broken up or regulated as Standard Oil was. Their alleged sins run the gamut from disseminating fake news and fostering addiction to laying waste to small towns' shopping districts. But in recent years antitrust regulators have used a narrow test for antitrust: does a company's size leave consumers worse off? Most of these companies' services are free to users, making it hard to show harm under this standard. But some consumer advocates argue this antitrust standard is out of date.

In 2020, the Federal Trade Commission, the Justice Department and Congress all began investigating the conduct of these big tech companies and whether they are engaging in anti-competitive practices such as using their market power to undermine potential competitors. A reckoning appears to loom. In October 2020, the U.S. House of Representatives Judiciary Subcommittee on Antitrust, Commercial and Administrative Law issued a sweeping report which found Facebook, for example, "has monopoly power in the market for social networking," and that power is "firmly entrenched and unlikely to be eroded by competitive pressure" from anyone at all due to "high entry barriers — including strong network effects, high switching costs, and Facebook's significant data advantage — that discourage direct competition by other firms to offer new products and services."[9] A week later, the Justice Department

9 U.S. House of Representatives Judiciary Subcommittee on Antitrust, Commercial, and Administrative Law, Investigation of Competition in Digital Markets (2020), https://judiciary.house.gov/uploaded-files/competition_in_digital_markets.pdf.

sued Google for abusing its dominance in online search and advertising. And in December 2020 the federal government and attorneys general from 46 states filed an antitrust lawsuit against Facebook, accusing it of using its power to buy out competitors such as Instagram and WhatsApp. The two cases are arguably the U.S. government's most significant attempts to protect competition in the 21st century. Depending on how federal courts rule, Facebook and Google could be forced to limit their growth or divest earlier acquisitions and divisions.

There are arguments both for and against reining in Silicon Valley's tech titans. On one hand, tech giants' market dominance hasn't harmed consumers' pocketbooks. Twitter, for instance, is free to use and, until 2019, it didn't make a profit. And while Google and Facebook are extremely profitable companies, they are hardly price gougers. Most of their products are free to consumers and the price that advertisers pay per click has dropped significantly in recent years. Both companies remain innovation powerhouses, creating and investing in new products and services.

"It used to be that you should not let a firm get too big … if it gets too big, break it up, [like what happened with] AT&T [the U.S. telecommunications firm]," said Arun Sundararajan, a business technology professor at New York University. "With these tech platforms, 'breaking it up' is hard to define and not in the interest of consumers. You'll weaken the network effects without sorting the problems. If you broke up Facebook and Instagram, it would not stop Facebook copying Instagram's features."[10]

Yet tech giants' monopoly status means that some features and prices that were offered by competitors never made it to customers. For example, in 2004 Yelp began aggregating detailed information and user reviews of local services, such as restaurants and stores. Yelp claims that Google altered its search results to hurt Yelp and promote its own competing service. While Yelp survived, it has retreated from Europe, and several other, similar local search services have faded. Google has also acquired several upstarts and incorporated their innovations into its dominant platform, making it even more useful to consumers and also more economically powerful.

So, there has perhaps been a hidden cost to consumers. By allegedly directing web traffic to its own business listings and reviews through its search results, Google may be depriving Yelp of visitors and the valuable data-mining and advertising revenues that come with them.

"Today's big tech companies have too much power — too much power over our economy, our society, and our democracy," argues U.S. Senator Elizabeth Warren. "They've bulldozed competition, used our private information for

10 Fullerton, Jamie, *Top Quotes on Tech Monopolies*, World Economic Forum, July 1, 2019, https://www.weforum.org/agenda/2019/07/these-are-some-of-the-best-quotes-about-technology-monopolies-in-2019/.

profit, and tilted the playing field against everyone else. And in the process, they have hurt small businesses and stifled innovation."[11]

The U.S. government has cracked down on some of these controversial practices in the past. For example, Microsoft barely escaped being split up in the early 2000s after a court ruled that it had an unlawful monopoly over web browsing software.[12] The court found that Microsoft used its stranglehold on the PC operating system market to integrate its Internet Explorer browser into its Windows operating system and thus cripple competitors such as Netscape's Navigator browser. A court settlement between Microsoft and the U.S. government in 2002, in which Microsoft agreed to pay $750 million to Netscape's parent company and curb its anti-competitive practices, saved the company from being split up.

Anti-competitive practices by tech giants could worsen without net neutrality rules in place. For example, the Frightful Five could work with the most powerful mobile carriers and Internet providers for the sake of their own financial benefit — and at the expense of their customers. In 2009, for example — before the adoption of any net neutrality regulations — Apple was found to be blocking Skype calls at the request of AT&T because the wireless provider wanted consumers to pay for more expensive plans instead of accessing the cheaper alternative to placing calls overseas.

The regulation debate on Capitol Hill will continue as consumers become more and more reliant on the Internet and tech giants become even more powerful. But unless a significant amount of voters care as much about tech policy as the economy, abortion, immigration and other major campaign issues, it may be a difficult battle. Google, Facebook and Amazon are among the highest spenders on lobbying in Washington, D.C.[13]

But consumers can fight back in other ways. The Internet is still in its infancy and popular websites and apps come and go based on consumer demand. Consider: back in 2007, MySpace was the most popular social media website. Of course, that site was eventually surpassed by Facebook as the dominant social media platform. Now Facebook, reeling from data-sharing and fake news scandals related to the 2016 presidential election, finds itself suddenly facing a steep and sudden decline in popularity. Soon, a whole new set of companies could be dominating the tech scene. Market forces could — and perhaps should — ultimately fix the situation.

11 Warren, Elizabeth, *Here's How We Can Break up Big Tech*, Medium, Mar. 8, 2019, https://medium.com/@teamwarren/heres-how-we-can-break-up-big-tech-9ad9e0da324c.

12 *U.S. v. Microsoft Corporation*, 253 F.3d 34 (D.C. Cir. 2001) (affirming some findings of antitrust violation, while reversing others), *reh'g denied* (D.C. Cir. Aug. 2, 2001), *cert. denied*, 534 U.S. 952 (2001).

13 Romm, Tony, *Tech Giants Led by Amazon, Facebook and Google Spent Nearly Half a Billion on Lobbying over the Past Decade, New Data Shows*, Washington Post, Jan. 22, 2020, https://www.washingtonpost.com/technology/2020/01/22/amazon-facebook-google-lobbying-2019/.

E-Contracts

If you use the Internet regularly, even if it's just to check Gmail or peruse photos on Instagram, you've almost certainly entered into contractual agreements, whether you realize it or not.

An electronic contract, or e-contract, is a binding agreement made by means of a computer or other electronic or automated technology. In today's online-centered world, the use of e-contracts has become prevalent. Website owners and website users are necessarily reaching such agreements all the time.

For example, many online merchants enter into contracts with customers in which the merchant agrees to provide a product in exchange for the customer's payment. Parties can even agree to the transaction using an electronic signature service such as DocuSign. But many e-contracts don't involve the exchange of money. Social media platforms and apps (such as Facebook, Snapchat and Instagram) that don't charge a fee often require users to consent to Terms of Service or Terms of Use agreements which include a variety of provisions, ranging from copyright license agreements (allowing the sites to display material that users upload) to privacy policies (covering what the website will do with the information it has about its users) to choice of law (stipulating which state's — or even nation's — law applies, and in which court disputes can be heard). In exchange for using a social media app or site, you may agree, for example, to allow the company to collect your data and share it with third parties such as advertisers. If you don't follow the app's policies for using the site — for example, Twitter prohibits harassing other users and YouTube prohibits posting copyrighted movies — you may have your account terminated under the Terms of Service.

Courts typically have grouped these contracts into "browsewrap" or "clickwrap" agreements, depending on the manner in which the consumer has notice of or agrees to the terms of the agreement. Browsewrap agreements have hyperlinked Terms of Use that are typically found on a separate webpage, which the user does not have to visit to continue using the website or its services: the Terms of Service provide that merely using the site and its features constitutes agreement to the terms. Clickwrap agreements require a user to affirmatively click a box acknowledging agreement to the Terms of Service, which are often available in a scrolling text box, before the user is allowed to proceed.

	Browsewrap agreements	*Clickwrap agreements*
Notice of Terms of Service	Via hyperlink on page; opening link or reviewing terms not required to use site	Presented to user as text on main page, via link, or in pop-up window
How user agrees to Terms of Service	Use of website/app or services	User must click "I agree" box

Given that the Terms of Service usually involve an exchange of rights and obligations between a website owner and user, disputes often arise over the enforceability of such agreements. Generally, courts have declined to enforce browsewrap agreements because the fundamental elements of notice of the terms and of users' agreement to the terms is lacking. Because no affirmative action is required by the user to agree to the terms other than use of the website, the validity of a browsewrap turns on whether a user is aware of a site's terms. On the other hand, courts have routinely upheld clickwrap agreements. The enforceability of these agreements turns on whether the party had adequate notice of the terms of the agreement and thus agreed to be bound by them.

Popular websites such as Facebook, Google and LinkedIn are frequently criticized for having poorly worded and misleading Terms of Service, with complex legal language that is not user-friendly and allows the companies to collect private user information and provide it to third parties. (This is why the ads you see on Gmail and Facebook often relate to your searches and e-mails.) Unfortunately, most people simply scroll through pages of uninviting text and click "I agree" without understanding what they agreed to. Even those who are aware of controversial Terms of Service provisions often assent anyway for fear of missing out if they don't use a popular app. Also, most Terms of Service provide that they can be changed after the user agrees to them, and that continued use constitutes assent to such changes.

There are limits, however. Terms that are illegal or unconscionable aren't enforceable and may face lawsuits: Facebook, for example, couldn't stipulate that you must donate your kidney to use its network. And controversial terms often face backlash in the court of public opinion. For example, in 2012, Instagram announced a change to its Terms of Use that caused a widespread outcry from its user base. The problematic clause stated: "You agree that a business or other entity may pay us to display your username, likeness, photos (along with any associated metadata), and/or actions you take, in connection with paid or sponsored content or promotions, without any compensation to you." In short, this meant that user content could be used in ads without notice or compensation. There was no apparent option to opt out of the change. While the provision was not illegal, the move garnered severe criticism from privacy advocates concerned about misuse of users' information. After one day, Instagram apologized, saying that it would remove the controversial language from its terms.[14]

Taxes

Over the years, there have been many legislative proposals to impose Internet-only taxes, such as a tax on each e-mail sent. The 1998 Internet Tax Freedom

14 Bromberg, Karen H., *Instagram Retreats on Privacy Policy Change but Gets Sued Anyway*, Cohen & Gresser LLP, Dec. 28, 2012, https://www.cohengresser.com/publication/instagram-retreats-on-privacy-policy-change-but-gets-sued-anyway/.

Act prohibits such taxes in the U.S. However, like traditional brick and mortar businesses, online businesses must pay federal, state and local income and other taxes.

For example, online businesses may have to charge customers sales taxes depending on where the customer is located. This is a recent change to the law. Prior to 2018, if an online merchant didn't have a "physical presence" in a customer's state, it was not required to collect taxes on purchases. Consequently, many online merchants officially registered their business in states without sales taxes, such as Delaware. Officials in the states with sales taxes got upset about all the potential tax revenues they were missing out on by not being able to collect taxes from online purchases. So, they sued and the U.S. Supreme Court held that online merchants must pay sales taxes on all sales, since sending products to recipients in sales-tax states meant that the sellers had a presence in that state.[15] Sellers are responsible for collecting and submitting sales taxes, but after the Supreme Court's decision most states have passed laws requiring marketplace websites such as Etsy and eBay to collect such taxes on behalf of sellers.

Advertising

The government imposes restrictions on advertising, whether online or offline. Ads that promote fake prices or false claims are illegal. So are ads that feature fake test results, or endorsements from people who appear to be experts — such as by wearing a doctor's lab coat — but are not. Misleading ads are also illegal. These are ads that leave out important information or otherwise give customers the wrong impression.

Whether an ad is deemed to be misleading hinges on the "reasonable consumer standard" — i.e. would a reasonable consumer find the ad to be misleading? For example, a lawsuit claiming that ads for Ben & Jerry's ice cream saying that the product came from "happy cows" was dismissed on the grounds that a reasonable customer would not necessarily interpret the phrase to imply particular standards of animal husbandry.[16] On the other hand, another court refused to dismiss a lawsuit claiming that ads saying that "Red Bull gives you wings" falsely implied that the drink increased athletic performance; the company ended up settling the lawsuit.[17] Keep in mind that these regulations only apply to the advertisers (i.e. the people and businesses who create the ads). Websites and apps that host false or misleading ads are shielded from liability by Section 230 of the Communications Decency Act, discussed in Chapter 4. But they may face criticism for hosting such ads. Facebook, for example, came

15 *South Dakota v. Wayfair, Inc.*, 585 U.S. ___, 138 S.Ct. 2080, 201 L.Ed.2d 403 (2018).

16 *Ehlers v. Ben & Jerry's Homemade Inc.*, Civil No. 19-00194, 2020 WL 2218858 (D.Vt. May 7, 2020).

17 Class Action Complaint at 2, *Careathers v. Red Bull North America Inc.*, No. 1:13-cv-00369 (S.D.N.Y. Jan. 16, 2013).

under fire in 2020 for refusing to ban political ads that make false claims. Twitter, meanwhile, decided to ban political ads altogether.

In addition to false and misleading ads, advertisements that promote unlawful activities such as prostitution (except in parts of Nevada, where it's legal) and discrimination in housing or employment are also illegal. Both advertisers and websites hosting the ads can be punished for running online ads associated with illegal products, services or activities. For example, Craigslist in 2010 shut down its "Adult Services" listings after receiving pressure from several states' attorney generals who alleged that "ads for prostitution — including ads trafficking children — are rampant" on the site.[18] In recent years, so-called "sugar baby" sites have come under scrutiny. Sites such as SeekingArrangement.com promise to hook-up wealthy men — or "sugar daddies" — with younger women known as "sugar babies." Some critics say these sites facilitate thinly veiled prostitution and should be banned. But listing a profile on such sites is currently legal in the U.S.

The Federal Trade Commission released its "Disclosures 101 for Social Media Influencers" brochure in 2019. It is available at www.ftc.gov. Credit: Federal Trade Commission.

18 Bluemental, Richard, et al., Re: Adult Services Section on Craigslist (letter), State Attorneys General, Apr. 24, 2010, https://themarginalized.files.wordpress.com/2010/08/craigslist-joint-letter-from-attorneys-general.pdf.

Social media influencers — celebrities, athletes, bloggers and others with large social media followings who make endorsements on their Instagram, Twitter and other social media accounts — are required by Federal Trade Commission (FTC) regulations to publicly disclose if they are being paid (in either cash or reduced-price or free products or services) to endorse products or services. Such disclosures must be clear and conspicuous.

The FTC explains that "The reason is obvious: Knowing about the connection is important information for anyone evaluating the endorsement. Say you're planning a vacation. You do some research and find a glowing review on someone's blog that a particular resort is the most luxurious place he has ever stayed. If you knew the hotel had paid the blogger hundreds of dollars to say great things about it or that the blogger had stayed there for several days for free, it could affect how much weight you'd give the blogger's endorsement. The blogger should, therefore, let his readers know about that relationship."[19] Those who violate the disclosure policy face stiff fines.

Finally, federal law places some limits on marketing via electronic communications, such as e-mail, texts and phone calls. Under the 2003 CAN-SPAM Act, businesses sending advertising e-mails must (1) use their actual e-mail address in the "from" field; (2) use a subject line that reflects what's actually in the e-mail; and (3) give e-mail recipients a way to unsubscribe. Violations can result in a $40,000 fine. But solicitations via phone, which are covered by a different law, are OK with some limitations. The Telephone Consumer Protection Act of 1991 prohibits telemarketing calls before 8 a.m. or after 9 p.m., local time. It also requires businesses to honor the National Do Not Call Registry and to maintain their own "do-not-call" lists of consumers who asked not to be called. And in order to send text messages, a business must have recipients' consent and allow them to opt out. Note that if a company already has a relationship with you, it can send you electronic or telephone communications. In addition, these restrictions do not apply to non-commercial messages, such as political surveys or fundraising messages.

Data Protection

Online businesses and wired devices frequently collect and store all kinds of personal information about their customers and website visitors, such as name, address and billing information. While certain industries, such as healthcare and banking, have laws regulating what info can be collected and how it can be shared, there are no nationwide laws in the U.S. pertaining to data collection. As discussed in more detail in Chapter 6, this largely allows online businesses

19 Federal Trade Commission, *The FTC's Endorsement Guides: What People Are Asking*, Sept. 2017, https://www.ftc.gov/tips-advice/business-center/guidance/ftcs-endorsement-guides-what-people-are-asking.

and social media sites to collect all kinds of information about you and share it with third parties such as advertisers.

One exception where federal law gives some privacy protection involves children. Under the federal Children's Online Privacy Protection Act (COPPA), websites are forbidden from collecting any personal information from anyone that the website operator knows or should know is under the age of 13 without first obtaining parents' permission.

In the absence of a federal law, a few states — notably California — have passed their own online privacy laws. California's Consumer Privacy Act, which went into effect in 2020, gives consumers the right to opt out of the selling of their personal information, and requires companies that collect such data to make individual users' information available to those users. Because of the size of its market, California's law may become a *de facto* national standard in the U.S.

Additionally, online businesses and websites typically must notify consumers when their personal info is stolen. Nearly all states now have laws requiring businesses to notify consumers when hackers steal customers' personal information that's stored electronically. In recent years, several major American companies, including Target, Yahoo and Equifax, have reported extensive data breaches.

ADA Compliance

Courts differ on whether companies that provide their services exclusively online through a website or mobile app are required by the federal Americans with Disabilities Act (ADA) to make sure their website can be utilized by people with disabilities, including the blind and deaf.[20] The underlying purpose of the ADA is to ensure disabled individuals are not subject to discrimination and have as full and equal access to spaces open to the public as non-disabled individuals. In the physical world, the ADA is the reason we have things like disabled parking requirements, service counter height requirements and wheelchair ramp mandates in building codes.

If it applies online, the ADA requires that websites and apps facilitate use of compatible software (such as screen readers) and hardware (such as braille

20 Compare *Magee v. Coca-Cola Refreshments USA, Inc.*, 833 F.3d 530, 534 (5th Cir. 2016), *cert. denied*, 138 S.Ct. 55, 199 L.Ed.2d 18 (2017); *Weyer v. Twentieth Century Fox Film Corp.*, 198 F.3d 1104, 1114 -15 (9th Cir. 2000); *Ford v. Schering-Plough Corp.*, 145 F.3d 601, 613 -14 (3d Cir. 1998); *Parker v. Metro. Life Ins. Co.*, 121 F.3d 1006, 1014 (6th Cir. 1997) (*en banc*); and *Gil v. Winn-Dixie Stores, Inc.*, No. 17-13467, 2021 WL 1289906, 2021 U.S.App. LEXIS 10024 (11th Cir. Apr. 7, 2021) (all holding that ADA requirements apply only to physical facilities), with *Carparts Distribution Ctr., Inc. v. Auto. Wholesaler's Ass'n of New England, Inc.*, 37 F.3d 12, 19 (1st Cir. 1994) (holding the ADA requirements apply to web-only services), *Pallozzi v. Allstate Life Ins. Co.*, 198 F.3d 28, 32 (2d Cir. 1999) (citing Carparts with approval), *Doe v. Mutual of Omaha Insurance Co.*, 179 F.3d 557, 559 (7th Cir. 1999) (approving the *Carparts* application of the ADA to websites), and *Morgan v. Joint Administration Board*, 268 F.3d 456, 459 (7th Cir. 2001) (same).

displays) that allow differently abled individuals to access and use them. In addition, web developers must ensure that images are properly labeled and have alternate text embedded in them and that videos have captions, among other things.

Websites often do not meet these standards because these issues were not considered in creating the sites. But this is risky, since companies that operate websites that are not programmed in these ways can face lawsuits and have to pay out huge sums in damages. In 2019, there were more than 2,500 ADA website lawsuits filed in federal courts across the nation. One such lawsuit was filed against Beyoncé, who was sued by a blind woman claiming the singer's website was inaccessible because it was presented as a "purely visual interface" that made it impossible for blind and low-vision people to use.[21] (The lawsuit was eventually withdrawn by the plaintiff.) According to the ADA, these kinds of barriers to access are a violation of civil rights, limiting communication and participation in society.

Online Reviews

Before the widespread use of the Internet, if you had a bad experience with a business, at most you could tell your friends and acquaintances, and perhaps complain to the local Better Business Bureau, which collects and seeks to resolve consumer complaints. Now you can let the whole country or even the entire world know.

In the U.S., consumers are generally free to give businesses negative reviews online. Most reviews are protected under the First Amendment's right to free speech. In recent years, some businesses had inserted anti-disparagement clauses into their forms and attempted to sue customers who didn't bother reading the fine print and wrote a bad review. But a 2016 federal law, known as the Consumer Review Fairness Act, prohibits companies from adding so-called "gag clauses" to certain contracts that would restrict a consumer's ability to criticize the business or penalize them for doing so.

However, the new law isn't a license for consumers to post whatever they want. A court can still find a reviewer guilty of defaming a business if she posts factually incorrect accusations that seriously damage the business's reputation. Freedom of speech typically boils down to whether someone is expressing their opinion or asserting a fact. So, if you post on Yelp that a restaurant has awful service and bad food, that's perfectly legal. But if you hurt a restaurant's reputation by claiming that it sells dog meat in its burgers — and it doesn't — you could be liable for defamation. Note that adding opinion-like language (e.g., "*I think* that restaurant sells dog meat") does not magically convert a factual statement into an opinion. This is explained in more detail in Chapter 5.

21 *Conner v. Parkwood Entertainment LLC*, No 1:19-cv-00053 (S.D.N.Y. 2019).

To counter negative reviews and other bad online content, some businesses hire people to write positive reviews for them. This practice, known as "astroturfing," raises both ethical and legal issues. The reviews are essentially fake; the reviewers have likely never interacted with the product or business and are only providing a positive review because they're being paid to. If the business does not disclose that it paid for these reviews, it is arguably a form of deceptive advertising. This could lead to enforcement actions by the FTC, as well as private lawsuits. In 2015, online retailer Amazon.com sued 1,114 people who were paid to publish fake five-star reviews for products on its site.[22] These reviews were created using a website for microtasks, fiverr.com. Several other companies offer to post fake Yelp and Facebook reviews for a price.

International E-Commerce Laws

As discussed in Chapter 2, each nation has its own set of expectations and standards when it comes to the Internet. This can cause headaches for online businesses that sell products or services internationally, like Amazon, or locate offices or servers in countries around the world, as Facebook does. In these cases, these companies likely must comply with laws that differ significantly from laws in the U.S.

For example, the European Union is arguably even less tolerant of monopolies than the U.S. Google learned this the hard way in 2017 when European antitrust officials fined it nearly $3 billion for unfairly favoring some of its own services, such as Google Reviews, in its search results over those of rivals such as Yelp.[23] In 2018, the E.U.'s General Data Protection Regulations went into effect, imposing much stricter data security regulations on business than in place in the U.S.

In other situations, businesses may have to comply with regulations that would be unfathomable in the U.S. In some countries, meeting these legal demands may force businesses to choose between following their values and ethics or making a profit. Facebook, for example, has received much criticism from free speech and human rights activists for acquiescing to the censorship demands of authoritarian governments such as Vietnam. At worst, online businesses may be completely banned from offering their products and services. For example, Singapore and South Korea both banned AshleyMadison.com, a website that helps arrange extramarital affairs, on the grounds that it's morally offensive. The Chinese government has banned several large U.S. tech companies, including Facebook and Google, in part to help ensure China's homegrown tech companies succeed by not facing foreign competition. The

22 *Amazon v. John Does 1-1114*, Case No. 15-2-25395 (Wash. Sup. Ct. Oct. 16, 2015).

23 Scott, Mark, *Google Fined Record $2.7 Billion in E.U. Antitrust Ruling*, New York Times, June 27, 2017, https://www.nytimes.com/2017/06/27/technology/eu-google-fine.html.

so-called "Great Firewall of China" isn't just used to censor Western content; it also serves as an economic embargo.

Meanwhile, the U.S. has asserted it has jurisdiction over foreign tech companies and online businesses if they do business with Americans, accept U.S. dollars, use U.S. subcontractors or host their website on a .com or .net domain.

Intellectual Property

Finally, e-commerce raises many intellectual property issues, such as trademarks, patents and copyright, which are covered in depth in Chapter 7.

> **CLOSING ARGUMENTS**
>
> Google, Facebook, Amazon, Apple and Microsoft dominate tech — and the U.S. economy, for that matter. This worries many people, who say they've become too powerful and nicknamed them the "Frightful Five." Some lawmakers say these tech giants have become evil monopolies and it's time to break them up. But others, including Apple's Tim Cook and Microsoft's Bill Gates, disagree and worry doing so could hurt innovation. What do you think? Are big tech companies too powerful? Or has recent experience online — for example, the one-time dominance of MySpace giving way to Facebook — shown that, despite their current power, these major Internet companies are always vulnerable to newer, sprier competitors?

Additional Sources

Associated Press, *U.S. Regulators Expand Antitrust Probe into 5 Giant Tech Companies,* PBS NewsHour, Feb. 11, 2020, https://www.pbs.org/newshour/economy/u-s-regulators-expand-antitrust-probe-into-5-giant-tech-companies.

Balmsamo, Michael and Gordon, Marcy, *Justice Dept. Files Landmark Antitrust Case Against Google,* Associated Press, Oct. 20, 2020, https://apnews.com/article/google-justice-department-antitrust-0510e8f9047956254455ec5d4db06044.

Conner v. Parkwood Entertainment LLC, Civil No. 19–00053 (S.D.N.Y. withdrawn Apr. 9, 2019).

Fiegerman, Seth, *Twitter Records Its First Annual Profit, but it Is Losing Millions of Users,* CNN, Feb. 7, 2019, https://www.cnn.com/2019/02/07/tech/twitter-earnings-q4/index.html.

Ortutay, Barbara and Anderson, Mae, *Facebook Again Refuses to Ban Political Ads, Even False Ones,* Associated Press, Jan. 9, 2020, https://apnews.com/90e5e81f501346f8779cb2f8b8880d9c.

9 Network Neutrality

> High-speed Internet service must be treated as the new electricity.
>
> — Senator Bernie Sanders

You've undoubtedly heard a lot in the news in recent years about network neutrality. Also sometimes referred to as "net neutrality," "Internet neutrality" or "open Internet," network neutrality is the principle that Internet service providers (ISPs) such as AT&T, Verizon, Comcast, Cox and Spectrum should treat all data on the Internet equally, and should not limit access or charge differently by user, content, site, application or device.

For example, under this principle, a company that provides both Internet access and cable TV would not be allowed to charge users of its Internet access services extra for video streaming services such as Netflix that compete with the cable TV services. The ISP/cable company would also be prohibited from inequitably charging services like Netflix for access to its Internet customers. Calls for net neutrality came in response to controversial practices by ISPs, such as charging some websites additional fees to process their web traffic faster and slowing traffic to other websites that competed with ISPs' business interests.

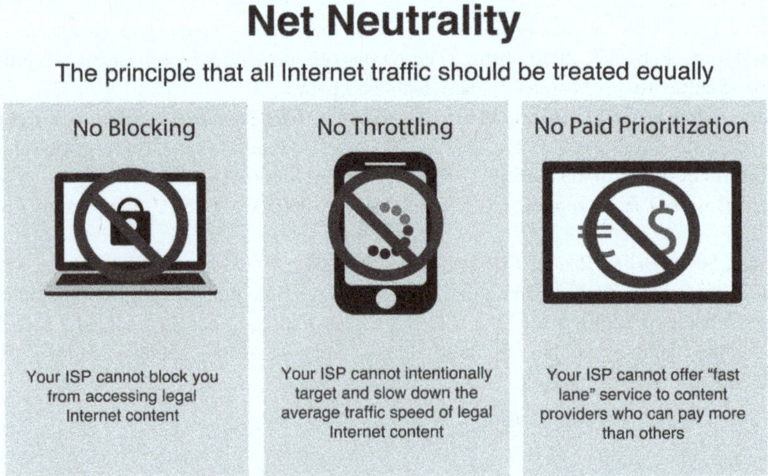

There has been extensive debate worldwide about whether net neutrality should be required by law. Some experts warn that implementing net neutrality could stifle innovation, but examples from other countries suggest that it improves Internet service. In the United States, net neutrality is currently in a state of legal limbo. Polls show that Americans overwhelmingly favor net neutrality. But policymaking has been ensnared by special interests and politics. After federal rules requiring net neutrality were repealed in 2017, several states responded by implementing their own net neutrality regulations. Court and policy battles over the issue seem likely to continue indefinitely.

What Is Network Neutrality?

At its core, the net neutrality movement in the U.S. refers to efforts to keep the Internet open, accessible and "neutral" to all users, application providers and network carriers. Technology law professor Tim Wu of Columbia University explained this principle by comparing it to the electric grid, which is implicitly built on a neutrality theory.[1] The general purpose and neutral nature of the electric grid are some of the things that make it extremely useful. The electric grid does not care if you plug in a lamp, an air conditioner or a computer. Consequently, it has survived and supported giant waves of technological innovation. The same electric grid that worked for the radios of the 1930s now works for the smart TVs of the 2020s. For that reason, the electric grid is a model of a neutral, innovation-driving network. Should the Internet in the U.S. operate the same way?

Some advocates argue that without network neutrality, the Internet will profoundly change and no longer be a platform for free speech and innovation. To draw a simple illustration, take two content providers such as AT&T's WarnerMedia video streaming service and Netflix. Both platforms provide TV shows and films. If net neutrality existed and if all else is equal, any bit of information from AT&T's WarnerMedia service will be sent and received in the same way and at the same price as one from Netflix. There would be no roadblocks or shortcuts that either platform could utilize that would give them an advantage over the other with users.

However, without a neutrality mandate, ISPs can choose to discriminate against particular websites and apps and decide how fast or slow data will be transmitted, the quality of the data and/or whether to impose an additional charge for the transmission of such data. So, in our example, if AT&T (which is also an ISP) chooses to prioritize data from its own WarnerMedia video streaming service over content from Netflix, content from AT&T will then be more accessible to the end user because it will be much faster than content from Netflix, giving AT&T a competitive edge. Imposing such limitations of a particular provider's content is known as "throttling." Alternatively, AT&T

1 Wu, Tim, *Network Neutrality FAQ*, http://www.timwu.org/network_neutrality.html.

could require Netflix to pay a fee to have its data transmitted as fast as AT&T's own data.

Is it fair that AT&T has these advantages over Netflix? What would happen if all ISPs degrade their service for specific content providers? What if ISPs bar content providers they believe threaten their business interests from using their networks at all? These are just some of the many questions that plague the net neutrality debate.

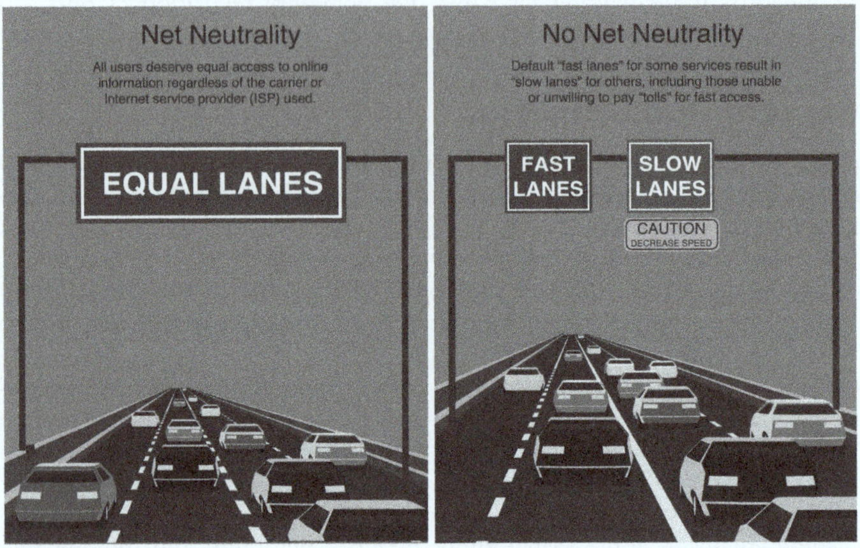

Companies whose primary business is providing content online like Netflix, Google and Facebook are concerned about this and strongly favor net neutrality. Without it, they say, they could be forced to fork over some of their revenues to ISPs like AT&T. In addition, consumer and advocacy groups such as the American Civil Liberties Union favor net neutrality because they say that without it ISPs could censor websites and speech online. For example, AT&T could easily block an anti-AT&T blog from being accessed by those using AT&T's ISP service.

Opponents of net neutrality dismiss such concerns as hysteria. They argue that net neutrality could actually stifle Internet innovation such as technologies to move data more efficiently. Also, it is sometimes desirable and even necessary to prioritize certain data on the Internet, or to block some of it entirely. Traffic management provides a prime example, they say. When web traffic surges beyond the network's ability to handle it, something is going to be delayed. When deciding what gets delayed, it makes sense to allow a network to prioritize traffic from, say, a patient's heart monitor over traffic delivering a movie download. It also makes sense to allow network operators to restrict harmful traffic, such as viruses and spam. Net neutrality opponents also argue that the ISPs should have the freedom to determine which and how services use their privately owned computer systems.

Pricing raises similar issues. To date, Internet pricing has been relatively simple, based on upload and download speeds or data usage. But, based on experience in comparable markets, pricing and service models should arguably be expected to evolve. For example, new services with guaranteed delivery quality might emerge to support applications such as medical monitoring that require higher levels of reliability than typical Internet service can provide. Suppliers would likely charge higher prices for such premium services, net neutrality opponents argue, and imposing net neutrality may deter such premium services. Even the electric grid charges rates based on how much electricity customers use, so why shouldn't ISPs similarly be able to charge higher prices to customers who use more data? "No one would propose that the U.S. Postal Service be prohibited from offering Express Mail because a 'fast lane' mail service is 'undemocratic,'" argued a group of prominent computer science and law professors in a *Washington Post* op-ed. "Yet [net neutrality] could do exactly this for Internet services."[2]

ISPs also argue that it's unfair that they should have to abide by net neutrality, but popular websites and apps don't have to. Google, Facebook and Twitter are free to censor data on their sites, and often do: for example, all three of these sites limit what they deem hate speech. The ISPs argue that they, too, should be able to control the content available through their services.

The History of ISP Regulation in the U.S.

In order to understand how this debate over net neutrality emerged and reached this point of uncertainty, it helps to review the history of regulation of ISPs.

In America, the Internet was initially subjected to very strict regulations that went beyond network neutrality. Before the Internet, telephone companies were considered "common carriers" subject to government regulation. This legal concept dates back to medieval England, where a village's sole dock, inn or surgeon was required to serve all customers at a reasonable price. It was eventually adopted in the U.S. and evolved to include businesses that were considered public services such as railroads, electric utilities and the telephone. Due to a lack of competition, these companies often have great power over their customers, who often have no choice in the providers. In addition, at the time telephones would only work if everyone was connected to the same network. Thus, common carrier regulations were implemented with the intention of protecting consumers by requiring companies to serve all customers in a particular area on a non-discriminatory basis, charging reasonable, often-regulated, rates.

2 Farber, David and Katz, Michael, *Hold Off on Net Neutrality*, Washington Post, Jan. 19, 2007, https://www.washingtonpost.com/archive/opinions/2007/01/19/hold-off-on-net-neutrality/bf43c766-4574-4c65-94d2-03f1951a33c4/.

In its early days, consumers connected to the Internet through a call over a telephone line to an ISP such as America Online (AOL), CompuServe or Prodigy. Because the company providing the local telephone wire was already considered a common carrier, it was open to any ISP to pump its Internet service through. This gave small firms equal footing with dial-up ISP giants at the time. "America's Internet flourished in the dial-up era because federal regulators … forced local phone companies to act as common carriers, allowing competing service providers to use their lines," according to Nobel Prize–winning economist and *New York Times* columnist Paul Krugman.[3]

All that began to change in the late 1990s. Cable TV companies commenced a major upgrade of their infrastructure and began to distribute their service in a new way: through fiber optic and coaxial cable. These "broadband" networks could provide not only cable TV, but also telephone service, high-speed Internet access and other services, all on a single wire into the home. The upgrade to broadband networks enabled cable companies to introduce high-speed Internet access to customers in the mid-1990s, and competitive local telephone, digital cable TV and data services later in the decade.

Also in the late 1990s, deregulation — which had earlier been applied to transportation common carriers such as trucks, railroads and airlines — came into vogue for telecommunications. Cable and telephone companies assured Congress they would enter each other's markets and compete against each other if the government would relax regulations. Lawmakers agreed to deregulation, believing that the resulting competition would remove the need for public oversight.

The Clinton Administration and Congress took the first steps toward deregulation when they overhauled telecommunications law for the first time in more than 60 years via passage of the Telecommunications Act of 1996. After President George W. Bush took office in 2001, his Federal Communications Commission (FCC) continued with deregulation. Eventually, ISPs were no longer subject to common carrier regulation and had very few restrictions on their business.

One of the results of this deregulation was that ISP giants like Verizon and Comcast were not required to open their lines to competing ISPs. This created a roadblock for start-up ISPs that wanted to compete for the growing demand for Internet service while using existing cable and phone wires. These start-ups challenged the FCC's new policy, but the U.S. Supreme Court ruled in favor of the FCC in 2005.[4]

With few restrictions and little competition, ISP giants began engaging in anti-competitive practices. For example, Comcast began limiting the speeds of its customers' access to the web service BitTorrent because it competed

3 Krugman, Paul, *The French Connections*, New York Times, July 23, 2007, https://archive.nytimes.com/www.nytimes.com/ref/college/coll04-french.html.

4 *National Cable & Telecommunications Association v. Brand X Internet Services*, 545 U.S. 967 (2005).

with Comcast's video-on-demand services. Verizon blocked an abortion rights organization from sending text messages over its mobile network because they were "controversial" and "unsavory." AT&T banned its Internet users from making critical remarks about the company online and also got Apple to block downloading of Skype communication software and certain online TV apps onto the iPhone because it said these apps strained its mobile network. All these ISPs later reversed their policies following public backlashes.

Lawmakers eventually came to realize that the grass was not greener in the new cyber landscape. In 2008, with President Bush on his way out, FCC administrators finally conceded deregulation may have gone too far and there was a need for some Internet protections. "The Bush FCC hoped that deregulation would prompt greater competition in Internet access services," explained Harvard Law School professor Susan Crawford, a former special assistant to President Barack Obama for science, technology and innovation policy. "But a wave of mergers of small ISPs into large, national ISP companies instead ended up reducing it. Prices stayed high and speeds slow. And eventually the carriers started saying that they wanted to be gatekeepers — creating fast lanes for some websites and applications and slow lanes for others."[5]

After two prior attempts by the FCC to impose net neutrality regulations were stymied in the courts,[6] in 2015 the FCC officially adopted new regulations banning ISPs from getting paid to offer faster access to certain content providers, such as Netflix and Amazon, and from blocking content from non-paying providers. However, the new regulations were not as strict as the common carriage regulations had been. For example, the FCC said it would not force cable companies to let any would-be Internet service provider use the wires that the cable companies had previously installed. While these new rules were upheld in court,[7] these initiatives were abandoned once President Donald Trump took office, and their repeal was also upheld in court.[8] As a result, after 2018, even these minimal restrictions on ISPs don't exist. But they may reemerge under the Biden Administration.

5 Crawford, Susan, *An Internet for Everybody*, New York Times, Apr. 10, 2010, https://www.nytimes.com/2010/04/11/opinion/11crawford.html.

6 *Comcast Corp. v. FCC*, 600 F.3d 642 (D.C. Cir. 2010) (striking down FCC's 2008 net neutrality regulations); and *Verizon v. FCC*, 740 F.3d 623 (D.C. Cir. 2014) (striking down FCC's 2010 net neutrality regulations).

7 *American Cable Associationn v. F.C.C.*, 139 S. Ct. 454, 202 L. Ed. 2d 361 (2018) (upholding FCC's 2015 net neutrality regulations).

8 *Mozilla v. FCC*, 940 F.3d 1 (D.C. Cir. 2019), *reh'g en banc denied,* No. 18-1051 (D.C. Cir. Feb. 6, 2020) (upholding FCC's 2018 repeal of net neutrality regulations), https://www.cadc.uscourts.gov/internet/opinions.nsf/FA43C305E2B9A35485258486004F6D0F/$file/18-1051-1808766.pdf.

In response to the FCC's decision to repeal net neutrality, there were massive nationwide protests like this 2018 gathering in Ithaca, New York. Credit: Alex Chichester.

Currently, the U.S. faces an oligopoly problem in Internet access: 55% of households have just one provider that offers Internet service at 25 megabits per second, the minimum the FCC says is necessary to access the most advanced online applications.[9] ISPs now seem even less inclined to compete given that they have cut their investment in improving Internet infrastructure since net neutrality was repealed. Even in large cities such as New York, residents in many neighborhoods have only one option for high-speed Internet, and the cost can be quite high. But deregulation supporters argue that the light regulatory approach was vindicated by the Internet's admirable performance despite unprecedented demand during the COVID-19 pandemic. ISPs were able to prioritize essential web content such as online school classes on Zoom over less vital traffic such as video games — something that would have not been legal under net neutrality regulations.

During his transition to the presidency, Joe Biden expressed support for resurrecting the Obama administration's net neutrality rules. Like prior actions on this issue, such a move is likely to be challenged in the courts. What is clear is that net neutrality is a major policy issue that will continue to be discussed and debated.

ISP Regulation Overseas

During the 2000s, almost all developed countries have extended some kind of common carrier arrangement to broadband access, according to a study by the

9 Holmes, Alan and Zubak-Skees, Chris, *U.S. Internet Users Pay More and Have Fewer Choices Than Europeans*, Ctr. for Public Integrity, May 28, 2015, https://publicintegrity.org/inequality-poverty-opportunity/u-s-internet-users-pay-more-and-have-fewer-choices-than-europeans/.

Berkman Klein Center for Internet & Society at Harvard University.[10] Great Britain and France, for example, required their former monopoly telecom companies to make their infrastructure available to rival ISPs, which rent it at regulated rates and compete with other ISPs on price and speed.

The study found evidence that these common carrier policies drove prices down and speeds up for Internet users. In France, the average Internet speed is more than three times as fast as it is in the U.S. while the price is about 60% less. Meanwhile, Brits get Internet service comparable to what is available in the U.S. for nearly half the price.

In Japan, the nation's largest Internet provider was required to resell access to its facilities to competitors at wholesale prices, which resulted in thousands of ISPs reselling Internet access, all competing against each other. Consequently, Japan is often cited as a global leader in broadband technology, speed and price. The average speed of a broadband connection in Japan is 10 times that of the U.S., and the percentage of Japanese households with broadband access is around a third higher. All this, and Internet access in Japan still costs half or less of what it does in the U.S.[11]

Germany, by contrast, illustrates the drawbacks of weak regulation. Until recently, Deutsche Telekom (DT) had a monopoly over Internet access, controlling 97% of the market by refusing to open its facilities to competitors. As a result, it was able to saddle Internet users with an overpriced service that included features many consumers did not want. But in 2016 European Union officials mandated net neutrality protections in all E.U. nations, including Germany. DT now controls only 47% of the market, while better Internet technologies are being implemented and prices are going down. The Harvard study concluded that in Germany, "Regulation is seen as having promoted competition in the telecommunications market and fostering investment and growth."[12]

The Future of Network Neutrality in the U.S.

Net neutrality might make a comeback in the U.S., since the federal government's stance on net neutrality can change whenever a new president is elected. Many candidates who ran for president in the 2020 election, including eventual winner Joe Biden, campaigned on the issue, vowing to reinstate net neutrality if elected. Some candidates, such as Bernie Sanders, proposed going

10 Harvard Berkman Klein Center for Internet & Society, *Next Generation Connectivity: A Review of Broadband Internet Transitions and Policy from Around the World* (2010), http://cyber.law.harvard.edu/pubrelease/broadband.

11 Travis, Hannibal, *The FCC's New Theory of the First Amendment*, 51 Santa Clara Law Review 101 (2011), https://ssrn.com/abstract=1698091.

12 Harvard Berkman Klein Center for Internet & Society, *supra* note 10, at 280.

a step further and regulating the Internet as a public utility, saying that "High-speed Internet service must be treated as the new electricity."[13]

In addition, Congress could pass legislation explicitly stating that the FCC must impose network neutrality regulations, and possibly detailing what these regulations should say. Various members of Congress have said that net neutrality is a legislative priority and have held several hearings on the issue.

However, if history is any indication, net neutrality fans shouldn't expect Congress to come to the rescue. Since 2006, when Congress considered five different bills to reform the Telecommunications Act of 1996, U.S. lawmakers have been unable to pass any piece of legislation regarding ISP regulation, and chances for a congressional intervention appear to be dwindling further. Although both Democrat and Republican voters alike overwhelmingly support net neutrality, "Senior [FCC] staff members have essentially conceded in interviews that lobbying pressure from the monopolies is too strong," says Yochai Benkler, co-director of Harvard's Berkman Klein Center.[14]

With network neutrality in limbo at the federal level, some state and local governments are taking matters into their own hands. Several states — including California, New Jersey, Oregon, Vermont and Washington — have enacted legislation on the issue, and others have proposed such legislation. While these state laws vary, in general they require ISPs to treat all content equally and not impose special charges on specific content.

There's another alternative: about 500 communities across the nation have built their own, municipally owned broadband networks, often with the assistance of Google and other tech companies. But such projects can be costly, and telecom lobbyists have doggedly fought these attempts through lobbying and litigation. ISPs argue that it is unfair for their regulator to also be a competitor and warn that governments may charge exorbitant franchise fees to keep out private companies. In addition, critics argue, government-run services are often not as efficient as the private sector. The result is that many states now either explicitly ban communities from creating their own Internet access services or make it exceedingly difficult.

As Internet usage continues to grow, the issue of net neutrality will likely continue to be a prominent political and social issue; one that is not likely to be easily resolved in the near future.

13 Gilbert, Ben, *Bernie Sanders Has a $150 Billion Plan to Turn the Internet Into a Public Utility With Low Prices and Fast Speeds — Here's How His Plan Works*, Business Insider, Jan. 22, 2020, https://www.businessinsider.com/bernie-sanders-internet-as-utility-plan-explainer-2019-12.

14 Benkler, Yochai, *Ending the Internet's Trench Warfare*, New York Times, Mar. 20, 2010, https://www.nytimes.com/2010/03/21/opinion/21Benkler.html.

CLOSING ARGUMENTS

There has been extensive debate about whether net neutrality should be required by law. Is it an unnecessary and unwelcome imposition on the Internet that will stifle improved services online, or a necessary means to ensuring that the web remains a welcoming platform for innovators?

Additional Sources

Assion, Simon, *Net Neutrality: The 10 Key Points to Know about the BEREC Draft Guidelines*, Lexology, June 28, 2016, https://www.lexology.com/library/detail.aspx?g=789288b1-9b81-45e6-bfee-b660f85de595.

Farrell, Mike, *More Muni, More Money*, Multichannel News, Nov. 18, 2019, https://www.multichannel.com/news/more-muni-more-money.

Finley, Klint, *The Covid-19 Pandemic Shows the Virtues of Net Neutrality*, Wired, May 4, 2020, https://www.wired.com/story/covid-19-pandemic-shows-virtues-net-neutrality/

Fung, Brian, *The Supreme Court Won't Take Up Net Neutrality*, Washington Post, Nov. 5, 2018, https://www.washingtonpost.com/technology/2018/11/05/supreme-court-wont-take-up-net-neutrality-this-time/.

Guniganti, Pallavi and Grabowski, Mark, *Applying Common Carriage to Network Neutrality*, in Regulating the Web: Network Neutrality and the Fate of the Open Internet 71–94 (Z. Steigler ed., 2014).

Holtz-Eakin, Douglas, *Who Needs Net Neutrality? Internet Providers Are Handling Coronavirus Demand Just Fine*, USA Today, May 11, 2020, https://www.usatoday.com/story/opinion/2020/05/11/coronavirus-streaming-demand-light-regulation-works-column/3105366001/.

Morton, Heather, *Net Neutrality Legislation in States*, National Conference of State Legislatures, Jan. 23, 2019, https://www.ncsl.org/research/telecommunications-and-information-technology/net-neutrality-legislation-in-states.aspx.

10 Cyberthreats

> The government is going to be unable to defend this country unless the critical infrastructure owned and operated by private companies actually work with the government and ensure that their systems are protected.
>
> — Catherine Lotrionte

The modern, Internet-connected world allows us to bank, shop, talk with friends and even run appliances in our homes from wherever we are. But all that convenience has a dark side. Every connection to the Internet creates another opportunity for a hacker to get in and create havoc. The Internet is now a common crime scene, and no one is immune from being harmed. There's a high chance that you'll be a victim of a cybercrime in your lifetime, if you haven't already.

According to Gallup, 23% of Americans said they or a family member were the victim of a cybercrime on their home computer in 2018 — more than double the number in 2010.[1] The same poll also found that Americans are "much more likely to fear being victimized by cybercrimes than traditional crimes," such as muggings and shootings. Meanwhile, a majority of business executives rank cyberattacks as one of their top fears[2] and corporate spending on cyber insurance policies was estimated to balloon from $2.5 billion in 2015 to $7.5 billion in 2020.[3]

It's a justified concern. According to estimates, cybercrime is expected to cost up to an estimated $6 trillion annually worldwide in 2021.[4] And, giving

1 Reinhart, R.J., *One in Four Americans Have Experienced Cybercrime*, Gallup, Dec. 11, 2018, https://news.gallup.com/poll/245336/one-four-americans-experienced-cybercrime.aspx.

2 Whitney, Lance, *Cyberattacks Rank as the Biggest Data Protection Concern Facing SMBs*, Tech Republic, Mar. 30, 2020, https://www.techrepublic.com/article/cyberattacks-rank-as-the-biggest-data-protection-concern-facing-smbs/.

3 Reuters Staff, *Cyber Insurance to Triple to $7.5 Billion by 2020, Attracting Disruptors: Report*, Reuters, Sept. 13, 2015, https://www.reuters.com/article/us-cyber-insurance-survey-idUSKCN0RD0XO20150913.

4 Morgan, Steve, *Global Cybercrime Damages Predicted to Reach $6 Trillion Annually by 2021*, Cybercrime Magazine, Dec. 7, 2018, https://cybersecurityventures.com/cybercrime-damages-6-trillion-by-2021/.

Internet users even more to worry about, terrorists and militaries are engaging in international warfare and espionage using the Internet. In fact, organized criminal groups are behind an estimated 39% of cybercrimes, while government-affiliated hackers are involved in 23% of attacks.[5]

"There are attackers out there that work in highly organized groups that are well-funded that are working together so that they can steal that information, sell it and make money," said Kevin Skapinetz, vice president at IBM Security. "This is the essence of modern cybercrime."[6]

The best way to avoid becoming a victim is to become informed. To help, this chapter provides an overview of the common types of cybercrimes that exist, along with the challenges that law enforcement officials face in fighting crime online. We will also touch upon cyberwarfare, one of the most serious global security issues today. Finally, this chapter offers tips for keeping yourself safe online. We'll also examine the role that Internet companies have in protecting against cybercrimes.

CYBERCRIME BY THE NUMBERS[7]

- $6 trillion is stolen annually by cybercriminals.
- 25% of Americans said their family suffered a cybercrime in the past year.
- 39% of cybercrimes were committed by organized criminal groups.
- 23% of cyberattacks were committed by governments.
- 52% of cybercrimes involved hacking.
- 32% of cybercrimes utilized phishing.
- 28% of cybercrimes involved malware.

What Is Cybercrime?

The U.S. Department of Justice (DOJ) broadly defines cybercrime as "any violations of criminal law that involve a knowledge of computer technology for their perpetration, investigation, or prosecution."[8] Such crimes are also

5 Verizon, *2019 Data Breach Investigations Report*, 2019, https://enterprise.verizon.com/resources/reports/2019-data-breach-investigations-report.pdf.

6 The Dark Web: Fighting Cyber Crime (Atomic Entertainment, 2018), https://youtu.be/Xxsnu7-8D7k.

7 Verizon, *supra* note 5.

8 National Institute of Justice and Department of Justice, Computer Crime: Criminal Justice Resource Manual 2 (1989).

sometimes referred to as "computer crime" or "network crime." The DOJ divides cyber-related crimes into three categories:

1. First, crimes in which technology is the "object" of a crime. This category mainly covers theft of computer software or of hardware such as laptops and smartphones.
2. Second, crimes in which a computer is the "subject" of a crime. These are cybercrimes which make computers and other devices inoperable, or significantly degrade their usability. There is no analogous conventional crime for these criminal actions, thus special legislation is needed. This category can include the use of spam, viruses, worms, Trojan horses, sniffers, logic bombs, distributed denial of service (DDoS) attacks and unauthorized web bots or spiders.
3. Third, crimes in which a computer may be an "instrument" used to commit crimes in the real world. Such crimes include identity theft, child pornography, copyright infringement, mail fraud, wire fraud and money laundering.

Criminal Law Explained

Criminal law involves prosecution by the government of a person for an act that has been classified as a crime. A "crime" is generally defined as an act committed, or omitted, in violation of a law forbidding or requiring it. However, no act is a crime unless it has already been established as such either by law or court rulings. Since crime online is still a relatively new phenomenon, the law has some catching up to do. So, authorities are forced to sometimes use antiquated laws created for a different technological era to combat cybercrime.

Civil cases, on the other hand, involve individuals and organizations seeking to resolve disputes in court, including alleged harm by one party to another. While crimes may involve harm to an individual or entity, they are crimes because of the injury caused to society as a whole. Thus, criminal cases — prosecutions — are brought by the government, on behalf of the people.

Crimes are classified as misdemeanors (minor offenses) and felonies (more serious offenses). Felonies are usually punishable by imprisonment of a year or more and/or substantial monetary fines, while misdemeanors are usually punishable by smaller fines, surrender of property and/or confinement of less than a year, usually in a facility such as a county jail rather than a prison.

Investigations of cybercrimes are often conducted by specialized units within local or state police agencies, or within various law enforcement and other agencies of the federal government. A suspect will be identified and arrested, then eventually brought to trial in either state or federal court, depending on the nature and scope of the alleged crime.

During or after trial, those charged with crimes, including cybercrimes, may assert as part of their defenses that their constitutional rights have been violated.

In cybercrime cases, these claims usually involve either the First Amendment or the Fourth Amendment to the U.S. Constitution.[9]

The First Amendment protects freedom of speech, among other rights. Thus, a claim that the cybercrime prosecution violates the defendant's First Amendment rights alleges that the defendant's speech was protected by the free speech provisions of the First Amendment, and therefore cannot be criminal. So, for example, cyberbullying is sometimes difficult to prosecute. As discussed in Chapter 5, cyberbullying that merely involves name-calling and insults is not illegal because such words are considered opinions, which are protected under the First Amendment no matter how mean or insulting they are. But if the cyberbullying involves actual threats of harm or blackmail — which are not protected by the First Amendment — it could lead to criminal charges.

The Fourth Amendment, meanwhile, prohibits "unreasonable" searches and seizures. This applies to criminal investigations, including investigations of cybercrimes, and requires law enforcement to obtain a warrant from a court before searching things like a suspect's home computer, smartphone or e-mail dated within the last 90 days. In order to obtain a warrant, the police must go to a judge and show that they have probable cause that they will find evidence of a crime. If police conduct a search without a valid warrant, the evidence they obtain from such a search may be barred from being presented in a criminal trial.

The vast majority of defendants in criminal cases end up pleading guilty, often to a lesser charge. But in some cases, defendants may admit guilt but seek leniency by claiming they broke the law for legitimate reasons. Although cyberattacks are usually done for financial gain, they sometimes are motivated by a desire for social or political change. Such hacking activism, or "hacktivism," may be widely regarded as ethical, yet it is still considered a crime in the eyes of the law. For example, WikiLeaks founder Julian Assange was charged with computer hacking for allegedly stealing classified U.S. government documents about the controversial Iraq War, which he posted online to make a statement about government secrecy. U.S. Army soldier Chelsea Manning was convicted and imprisoned after providing documents regarding government collection of cell phone call data to reporters, even though she did so because she thought Americans should know about such government surveillance. President Barack Obama commuted Manning's sentence in 2017.

Websites and apps which provide a platform for users to post content, including social media sites, are typically immune from criminal charges for illegal content posted by a user. This legal immunity is provided by Section 230 of the Communications Decency Act of 1996. This law is based on the belief that requiring Facebook, YouTube, Craigslist and other platforms to monitor every piece of content posted by users would place an undue burden on these sites and would hinder growth of the Internet.

9 The provisions of the First and Fourth Amendments are applicable to state and local governments as a result of language in the Fourteenth Amendment.

However, there are some exceptions not covered by this immunity, such as when posts promote crimes such as sex trafficking, and when the platform actively participates in the creation and posting of the illegal content. An example of the latter was when an appeals court held that a website could be held liable for users selecting options that violated anti-housing discrimination laws, because the company created these options, not the users.[10] This is discussed in more detail in Chapter 4.

Cybercrime Laws

Congress and state legislatures have passed many pieces of legislation specifically targeting cybercrimes. The federal government can charge cybercrimes under at least 40 different federal statutes. There are also a number of traditional criminal statutes that apply to cybercrimes. Moreover, the federal government has sometimes used the U.S. Sentencing Guidelines to enhance sentences for conventional crimes committed with the aid of computers. While federal officials most often investigate and prosecute cybercrimes, state officials can also prosecute such crimes under state laws. Below are some of the most common cybercrimes addressed by federal or state statutes.

Hacking

The government has frequently used two federal laws to prosecute hackers, who illegally access computers and the data stored on them without authorization.

First, the Computer Fraud and Abuse Act of 1986 (CFAA) makes it a felony to knowingly access a computer without authorization. This federal law serves as the primary means by which the federal government prosecutes "hacking" or unauthorized access to computers and cell phones, including data access and theft cases. It has also been applied to accessing or using a website in a way that violates the site's Terms of Service. But some courts have held that violating a site's Terms of Service is not a crime under the CFAA.

Second, the Electronic Communications Privacy Act of 1986 (ECPA) makes it illegal to intentionally intercept electronic transmissions, and regulates many cybercrimes with no conventional crime equivalent. The ECPA extended laws against wiretapping of conventional landline phones to wireless communications, including cell phones and e-mail.

Note that these laws apply to only illegal, unauthorized breaches. They do not apply to so-called "white hat" hackers whom organizations hire to find and fix security holes in the organizations' websites and computer systems, because these hackers' access has been authorized.

10 *Fair Housing Council of San Fernando Valley v. Roommates.com*, LLC, 521 F.3d 1157 (9th Cir. 2008), *later proceeding after remand*, 666 F.3d 1216 (9th Cir. 2012).

A prominent early prosecution using these statutes involved a Cornell University student who released a computer virus onto the Internet in 1988. The virus, dubbed the "Morris Worm" after its creator Robert Tappan Morris, repeatedly spread itself from computer to computer, then replicated itself in infected computers until they finally crashed from the overload of data. The worm spread across the country and shut down an estimated 10% of all computers in the U.S. at the time, causing $98 million in damages.[11] In 1991, a jury found Morris guilty, making him the first person convicted under the CFAA.[12] He insisted it was an accident and was spared jail time. Instead he was fined $10,000 and sentenced to probation and 400 hours of community service. A decade later, Morris was hired as a professor by Massachusetts Institute of Technology, where he received tenure in 2016.

This disk containing the code for the "Morris Worm" is displayed at the Computer History Museum in San Francisco. Credit: Intel Corporation.

Another much publicized case occurred in 2011, when Reddit co-founder and digital activist Aaron Swartz was charged with 11 violations of the CFAA, carrying a cumulative maximum penalty of $1 million in fines and 35 years in prison, for his "hacktivism."[13] He was charged for allegedly creating a tool that downloaded a large number of academic journal articles from an online subscription database and shared them online for free, in violation of the database's

11 Orman, Hilarie, *The Morris Worm: A Fifteen-Year Perspective*, 1 IEEE Security & Privacy 35 (Sept.–Oct. 2003), https://www.cs.umd.edu/class/fall2019/cmsc818O/papers/morris-worm.pdf.

12 *U.S. v. Morris*, 928 F.2d 504 (2d Cir. 1991) (affirming conviction), *cert. denied*, 502 U.S. 817 (1991).

13 *U.S. v. Swartz*, 945 F.Supp.2d 216 (D. Mass. 2013) (resolving discovery issue after defendant's death).

Terms of Service. Swartz hanged himself in 2013, before the controversial criminal trial began.

The government was widely criticized for its handling of the case. Critics likened Swartz to a "digital Robin Hood" and said federal prosecutors overreacted in going after him when other hackers have committed far more menacing acts. Federal courts have also been inconsistent in deciding whether violating Terms of Service constitutes a crime under the CFAA. The U.S. Supreme Court heard arguments in November 2020 in a case that may settle the split by ruling on the law's scope.[14]

Since Swartz's death, hacking has become a much bigger problem and will likely only worsen as our world becomes more digitized. Early hackers' ability to penetrate networks quickly caught the interest of criminals who saw a new frontier to steal money and wreak havoc. More and more important records and documents are being digitized and stored in "the cloud" instead of locked in file cabinets. And a variety of everyday household devices, ranging from cars to refrigerators, are also being connected to the Internet. In 2017, the number of online capable devices increased by 31% from the previous year, to 8.4 billion total.[15] Known as the "Internet of Things" (IoT), this interconnection trend offers many benefits, such as convenience, improved efficiency, accuracy and economic benefits. For example, your refrigerator can be programmed to automatically detect if you're running low on soda and order more.

But such devices also raise privacy and security concerns, and bad actors can pervert these functions for mischief and worse. When hackers took aim at the Internet's backbone in 2016, impeding access to websites like Twitter and Spotify, they did so by weaponizing the IoT. Using a botnet, an Internet-connected device that runs programs ("bots") that send themselves to other devices, the hackers were able to hijack tens of thousands of devices' Internet access to overwhelm popular websites with more traffic than they could handle, resulting in the websites being temporarily inaccessible. Such DDoS attacks are difficult to stop because the incoming traffic flooding the victimized website originates from many different sources. It also makes it very difficult to distinguish legitimate user traffic from attack traffic when spread across so many points of origin.

Another hacking practice — known as "salami slicing" — utilizes a series of smaller attacks that together result in a large attack. This technique is often used for embezzling money. Such "salami attacks" played a key role in the plots of several films, including *Hackers*, *Superman III* and *Office Space*. In real life, four executives of a rental-car franchise in Florida pleaded guilty in 1994 of defrauding at least 47,000 customers by modifying a computer billing program

14 *Van Buren v. U.S., cert. granted,* No. 19-783, 140 S.Ct. 2667 (Mem), 206 L.Ed.2d 822 (U.S. argued Nov. 30, 2020).

15 DeNisco, Alison, *There Will Soon be More IoT Devices in the World Than People, Security Risks Abound,* Tech Republic, Feb. 7, 2017, https://www.techrepublic.com/article/there-will-soon-be-more-iot-devices-in-the-world-than-people-security-risks-abound/.

to add small extra charges to their rentals. The incident serves as a reminder that threats can come from anywhere. While most cybercrimes are perpetrated by outsiders, about one-third involve internal actors.

COMMON TYPES OF CYBERATTACKS

- *Botnet*: Internet-connected device that runs programs ("bots") that send themselves to other devices.
- *DDoS*: Overwhelm a website with more traffic, from many different sources, than it can handle, resulting in the sites being temporarily inaccessible.
- *Malware*: Malicious software that harms or impairs normal operations of a computer.
- *Ransomware*: A type of malware that threatens harm, usually denial of access to data stored in a computer, and demands a ransom to restore access.
- *Salami attacks*: A series of small attacks that together result in a large attack.

Meanwhile, individuals, businesses and even entire cities are increasingly falling victim to a common hacking practice known as ransomware. Ransomware is a form of malicious software (or malware) that takes over a person's computer and threatens them with harm, usually by denying them access to data stored on the computer. The attacker demands a ransom from the victim, promising — not always truthfully — to restore access to the data after receiving payment. In 2019, a ransomware attacker froze Baltimore's government network, including e-mail, and demanded the city hand over a specific amount of Bitcoin or another cryptocurrency to reverse the hack. There were similar attacks on Atlanta in 2018, Greenville, North Carolina in 2019 and Los Angeles in 2020. Ransomware attacks not only cost money but can also cost lives. A 2020 ransomware attack was blamed for a death after it paralyzed a German hospital's computers and prevented a woman from getting the urgent care she needed.

While the practice of ransomware constitutes both extortion and hacking and is therefore illegal, it is not illegal to create ransomware software itself, since such a ban would raise freedom of speech issues. However, some lawmakers are taking steps to deter ransomware. A Maryland bill would make it a crime to possess ransomware with the intent to use it. After Albany International Airport paid a five-figure ransom to restore data access after getting hit with a hack over Christmas in 2019, New York State considered legislation to ban tax dollars from being used to pay a cyber ransom.

A screenshot of a 2016 ransomware known as "Jigsaw" that made victims' data inaccessible and demanded money to restore access. Credit: Emsisoft.

Cell Phone Fraud

With most people now using their smartphones much more than laptops or desktop computers, security researchers are seeing a shift in attacks. In addition to infecting smartphones with malware, criminals are illegally "spoofing" users' phone numbers (faking the number that an incoming call is from), "porting" their numbers (moving the number from a user's phone to another phone controlled by the criminal) and even cloning SIM cards, the computer chips that identify a phone, to access users' data and steal money.

Obtaining a person's phone number may be the key to their most important financial accounts, since it is frequently used as part of these accounts' contact information. Thus, gaining access to a phone number may enable a criminal to reset the password for any online accounts connected to that number. They can also use the phone number to find other information about the individual from both legal and illicit directories. From there, the scammers can plunder the victim's financial accounts, hack their identities on social media platforms, view the victim's e-mail and call history, and harass and scam the victim and the victim's friends and family.

The federal Wireless Telephone Protection Act of 1998 prohibits "knowingly us[ing], produc[ing], traffic[king] in, ha[ving] control or custody of, or possess[ing] hardware or software knowing that it has been configured to insert or modify telecommunication identifying information associated with or contained in a telecommunications instrument so that such instrument may be used to obtain telecommunications service without authorization."[16] But experts say lax ID verification policies by cell phone carriers make customers vulnerable to hacks. In 2020, several members of Congress urged the Federal Communications

16 18 U.S.C.A. § 1029.

Commission to mandate that wireless carriers provide stronger protections for customers to truly lock down their accounts, such as requiring an in-person visit before a phone number can be ported to another device or carrier.

Wire Fraud

Another tool law enforcement has for prosecuting such crimes is the federal wire fraud statute, which prohibits the use of interstate wire communications to further a fraudulent scheme to obtain money or property. While the statute was first adopted in the era of wired telephones, courts have held that it applies equally to cellular phones and cybercrimes.

This law has been used to prosecute criminals behind the infamous "Nigerian Prince e-mail scam." In this scam, someone e-mails you claiming to be a representative of a Nigerian prince who needs to transfer millions of dollars obtained from an oil contract and wants your help. The scam continues to persist because many naive Internet users have fallen for it and shared their bank account information only to later discover their funds were stolen. Other scammers send e-mails that appear to be from financial institutions or companies, with links to fake websites set up to collect passwords and other sensitive data.

The wire fraud law was also utilized against Silk Road, a popular online marketplace for illegal drugs and other illicit products, when it was shut down in 2013 and its owner Ross Ulbricht was sentenced to 80 years in prison.[17]

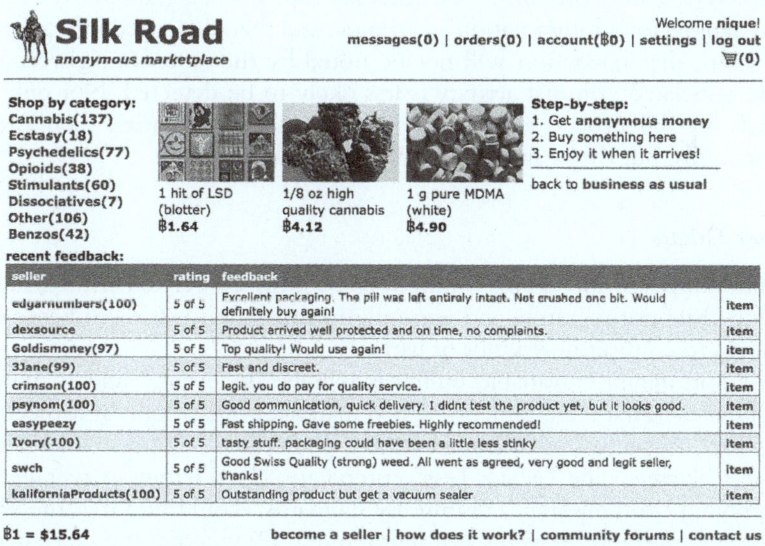

The Silk Road website was on an online marketplace for illicit products until it was shut down by the U.S. government. Credit: Dr. Monica Barratt, RMIT University.

17 *U.S. v. Ulbricht*, 858 F.3d 71 (2d Cir. 2017) (affirming conviction), *cert. denied*, 138 S.Ct. 2708, 201 L.Ed.2d 109 (U.S. 2018).

Ulbricht's capture remains a point of contention. The FBI claims that it tracked him down after he posted a Gmail address on an anonymous online forum in which he had previously used the same screenname to promote Silk Road. However, Ulbricht's lawyer argued that federal agents hacked into Silk Road's server in Iceland without a warrant and therefore their evidence was inadmissible. Prosecutors did not contest the claims, but instead said that, even if authorities did hack into the server, it was perfectly legal because the foreign location of the site's server and its reputation as a criminal haven meant that Ulbricht's Fourth Amendment protections against unreasonable searches didn't apply. Regardless of how he was captured, Ulbricht's arrest illustrates the great — and perhaps questionable — lengths federal authorities will sometimes go to in pursuing cybercriminals.

Money Laundering

When criminals acquire money by ill-gotten means, they often seek to conceal it through "laundering": transferring the money through foreign banks or legitimate businesses to hide its illicit origins. And they are increasingly turning to the Internet to do so. This is illegal under the Bank Secrecy Act, a federal law that serves as the main anti-money laundering statute. To skirt this law, criminals utilize online casinos and also cryptocurrencies such as Bitcoin, which are largely unregulated because they are not created or recognized by governments. For example, money can be deposited into an online casino and then converted into Bitcoins. The Bitcoins can then be transferred offshore and exchanged for another nation's currency, and then deposited into a foreign bank. Thus, the transaction will not be noted by the American government and the associated criminal activity is less likely to be detected. Not only can criminals use this process to hide income from illegal activities, such as drug deals or scams, but they can also illegally evade paying taxes.

Cybersex Crimes

The Internet is also increasingly utilized to commit sex-related crimes, such as accessing child pornography and engaging in prostitution. It's also being used as a means to commit new kinds of harm.

Most pornography available online is merely "indecent," and is typically legal under the First Amendment. Sexual material is illegal only if it meets the criteria for "obscenity" established by the U.S. Supreme Court in a 1973 case, *Miller v. California*. The "*Miller* Test" criteria are: (1) whether an average person, applying contemporary community standards, would find that the work, taken as a whole, appeals to the prurient interest; (2) whether the work depicts or describes, in a patently offensive way, sexual conduct or excretory functions specifically defined by applicable state law; and (3) whether the work, taken as a whole, "lacks serious literary, artistic, political, or scientific value."[18]

18 *Miller v. California*, 413 U.S. 15, 24 (1973).

But there are several categories of sexually focused speech that do not meet that *Miller* criteria that are nevertheless prohibited.

The first is child pornography: creation, distribution or possession of child pornography is a serious crime. The Prosecutorial Remedies and Other Tools to End the Exploitation of Children Today Act of 2003 (PROTECT Act) established stronger laws to combat child pornography and exploitation by strengthening the prohibition of and penalties for obscene materials that depict children. This strict prohibition also applies to "sexting," which is under-age individuals taking, posting and sharing sexual images of themselves. This has resulted in some teenagers being convicted on child pornography charges and required to register as sex offenders.

Second, a troubling online practice known as "revenge porn" is now unlawful in most states. Revenge porn is the distribution of sexually explicit images or video of individuals without their consent. Perpetrators often use the content to blackmail their victims into performing other sex acts, to coerce them into continuing their relationship, or to punish them for ending their relationship. For example, in a well-known 2017 case, model Blac Chyna was granted a temporary restraining order against her ex-boyfriend Rob Kardashian after he released a series of nude photos of her on social media without her consent.[19] But stars aren't the only victims of such a crime. It happens to a lot of ordinary people, including teens. All but four states have made the practice a crime, according to the Cyber Civil Rights Initiative.[20]

A recent, troubling development is the emergence of pornographic "deepfakes," in which an individual's face is electronically placed in pornographic pictures or videos actually depicting someone else. Several celebrities, including Daisy Ridley, Gal Gadot, Scarlett Johansson and Taylor Swift have been subject to such fake depictions. The law has not caught up with this trend, so there is often no way to prosecute the creators of this outrageous material other than perhaps seeking civil damages for infringing on publicity rights or defamation, or making a claim for infliction of emotional distress.

Cyberstalking — the repeated use of electronic communications to harass or frighten someone — is also a problem. Yet many shortcomings remain with cyberstalking laws. Typically, victims must first go to court to get a restraining order, which requires that they show an actual or legitimate threat. Then they can pursue cyberstalking charges only after the restraining order is violated.

California enacted the first cyberstalking law in 1999 after a 50-year-old former security guard pleaded guilty to using the Internet to solicit the rape of a woman who rejected his romantic advances.[21] Federal law offers some help

19 Winton, Richard, *"Devastated" Blac Chyna Wins Temporary Restraining Order Against Rob Kardashian in Sex Images Case*, Los Angeles Times, July 10, 2017, https://www.latimes.com/local/lanow/la-me-kardashian-restraining-order-20170710-story.html.

20 Cyber Civil Rights Initiative, *46 States + DC + One Territory NOW have Revenge Porn Laws*, https://www.cybercivilrights.org/revenge-porn-laws/.

21 U.S. Department of Justice, *1999 Report on Cyberstalking: A New Challenge for Law Enforcement and Industry, a Report from the Attorney General to the Vice President* (Aug. 1999).

for punishing certain aspects of cyberstalking. It is a federal crime, punishable by up to five years in prison and a fine of up to $250,000, to make threats transmitted from one state to another or to the U.S. from a foreign nation using e-mail, cell phones or the Internet.[22] But the federal law does not apply to communications within a state, so in such cases enforcement depends on state law. Another problem is that, as with cyberbullying, cyberstalking is a nebulous term that often includes other forms of disturbing behavior besides making threats, some of which may not be illegal due to freedom of speech protections.

While the law lags behind in many areas related to cybersex issues, some observers contend it sometimes goes too far. For example, in 2018, Congress enacted the Fight Online Sex Trafficking Act (FOSTA) and Stop Enabling Sex Traffickers Act (SESTA), which make it illegal for websites and apps to "knowingly assist, facilitate or support sex trafficking."[23] The laws limit the protections provided to website operators by Section 230 of the Communications Decency Act, which means websites and apps can now be held liable if their users post content related to sex trafficking.

Proponents of the new policy, which received overwhelming bipartisan support, believe it will help crack down on sex trafficking and child sex exploitation by eliminating the most popular means by which illicit arrangements are made. But critics say FOSTA-SESTA is tantamount to censorship and has hindered sex workers and driven trafficking victims further underground. "Thousands — if not hundreds of thousands — of women, LGBTQ people, gay men, immigrants, and a significant number of people of color lost their income," wrote *Engadget* tech blogger Violet Blue. "Pushed out of safe online spaces and toward street corners. So were any and all victims of sex trafficking that law enforcement might've been able to find on the open Internet."[24]

The law has already had a major impact on the Internet. Craigslist voluntarily shut down its popular personals section because it feared being held criminally liable under the new law if people used the listings for prostitution. Meanwhile, Backpage.com, a classified advertising site that included ads that were alleged to be solicitation by prostitutes and sex traffickers, shut down entirely and one owner pleaded guilty to money laundering and conspiracy to facilitate prostitution, with more criminal prosecutions by the U.S. DOJ pending.[25]

22 18 U.S.C. 875(c).

23 S.1693, Stop Enabling Sex Traffickers Act of 2017, U.S. Senate, https://www.congress.gov/bill/115th-congress/senate-bill/1693/text#id5f4efd42-850d-41e2-82ea-3d032f43e8a1.

24 Blue, Violet, *Congress Just Legalized Sex Censorship: What to Know*, Engadget, Mar. 30, 2018, https://www.engadget.com/2018-03-30-congress-just-legalized-sex-censorship-what-to-know.html.

25 *United States v. Backpage.com LLC*, 2:18-cr-00465 (D. Ariz. 2020).

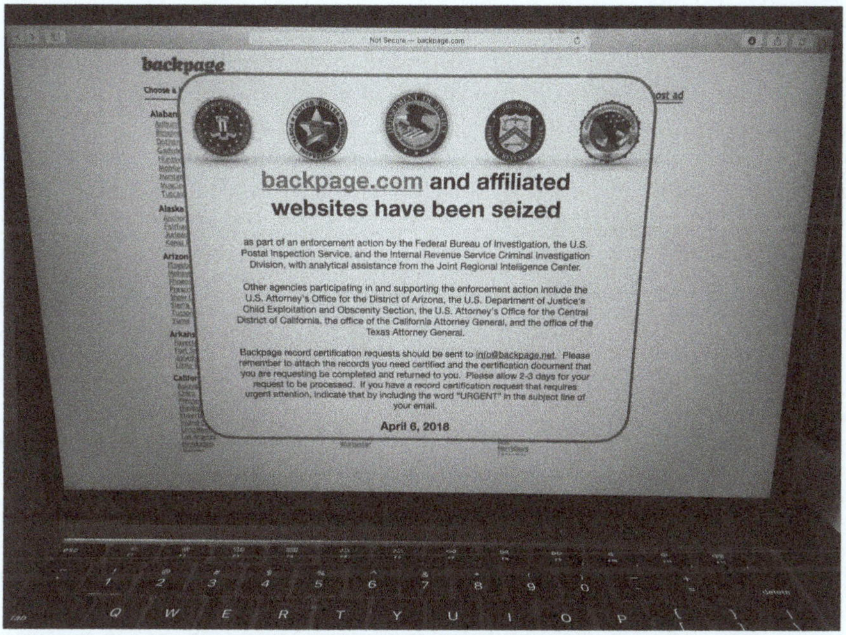

New anti-sex trafficking laws have had a significant impact on the Internet, leading to the deletion and/or prosecution of several online personals sites such as Backpage.com.

"Sugar baby" sites such as SeekingArrangement.com, which match young women with wealthy male partners, occupy a grey area of this new law. In exchange for their company, the women typically receive cash, gifts and vacations from their partners. Criminal defense attorney Sweta Patel said that while there are similarities between sex work and sugar dating, the difference in a "sugar" relationship is that sex and money may be one part of the relationship, but not all. "The sugar-daddy model is two consenting adults, while often in[volving] sex work, [but] that is not always the case," she said.[26]

While the controversy over FOSTA-SESTA rages on, even more restrictions may be enacted in the near future. As society becomes more connected and virtual, novel issues are emerging related to cybersex. There have been numerous reports of people experiencing their characters getting sexually assaulted by another player's character in multi-player video games. Some would argue that these situations are a form of rape, but our current laws may be inadequate to punish such wrongs.

26 Nagarajan, Natasha and Zhu, Janssie, *When College Students Turn to Sugar Daddies for Financial Aid*, Voice of America, Sept. 30, 2019, https://www.voanews.com/student-union/when-college-students-turn-sugar-daddies-financial-aid.

Spam

One online practice that almost every American can agree is a nuisance is "spam": unsolicited bulk commercial e-mail from someone with no preexisting business relationship with the recipients. (E-mail from businesses you have and continue to do business with is not legally considered spam.) In an effort to combat such unsolicited e-mail, Congress adopted the Controlling the Assault of Non-Solicited Pornography and Marketing Act of 2003 (CAN-SPAM Act). The CAN-SPAM Act affects people or companies that send unsolicited commercial e-mails to a large number of addresses. Specifically, the law applies to those who send more than 100 messages during a 24-hour period, more than 1,000 messages during a month, or more than 10,000 messages during a year.

In addition, the CAN-SPAM Act prohibits using deceptive subject lines, false or misleading header information, and unauthorized use of a computer to relay e-mail messages in order to prevent tracing the message back to its sender. The law also requires that a commercial e-mail include a method for the recipient to "opt-out" of or "unsubscribe" from future solicitations and that the subject line warn if the e-mail contains sexually oriented material. Both the U.S. DOJ and the Federal Trade Commission (FTC) enforce the CAN-SPAM Act. Violating the law can result in up to five years in prison, a fine, or both. The act also allows Internet service providers to sue spammers civilly over misuse of their networks.

Despite the CAN-SPAM Act, spam continues to be a persistent problem online, with estimates that it makes up more than half of all e-mail.[27] Problems include senders who operate outside from outside the U.S., and the relatively low risk of prosecution compared with the revenue from possible sales, even with very low response rates.

Piracy

Another common problem is copyright infringement, also known as piracy and bootlegging, which has been exacerbated by the Internet. It's now easier than ever before to copy and share music, movies and more with the click of a mouse.

But, as detailed in Chapter 7, doing so is typically illegal. Along with civil liability for copyright infringement, those who infringe on copyrights may also face federal prosecution for criminal copyright infringement. Copyright infringement can be prosecuted criminally when it is willful and involves one of the following: it is done for commercial advantage or private financial gain, the infringing copies have a total retail value of more than $1,000 over a 180-day period, or the infringing copies are of a "work being prepared for commercial distribution" and are made available on a publicly accessible

27 Clement, Jessica, *Spam: Share of Global Email Traffic 2014-2020*, Statista, June 24, 2020, https://www.statista.com/statistics/420391/spam-email-traffic-share/.

computer network. Criminal penalties include anywhere from one to 10 years imprisonment or, in certain circumstances, the imposition of both fines and imprisonment.[28]

The FBI has increased its efforts in fighting piracy and prosecuting criminal copyright infringement in recent years. Many of these cases were against the operators of websites that offered pirated, current movies for viewing. In the late 1990s and early 2000s, a series of websites emerged that facilitated illegal sharing of copyrighted music, and eventually TV programs and movies. Most of these sites were shut down as a result of civil and/or criminal cases both in the U.S. and abroad. Organizations of copyright holders went as far as threatening and sometimes actually suing individual Internet users, alleging that copyrighted materials had been downloaded to their IP addresses. The organizations relented in the face of negative publicity about these lawsuits. Nevertheless, there are still websites — operating out of countries with loose copyright laws — that facilitate illegal downloads, albeit with dangers such as malware.

Identity Theft

Cybercriminals aren't just stealing money, music and movies. In some cases, they're stealing people's identities. In 2019, nearly one-third of cybercrimes involved a method known as "phishing" to steal someone's identity online.[29] Targets are contacted by e-mail, telephone or text message by someone posing as a legitimate institution to lure victims into providing sensitive data such as personally identifiable information, banking and credit card details, and passwords. Fake sites that closely resemble legitimate bank and credit card sites are sometimes created to trick unsuspecting victims into sharing their account information. In phishing (as with ransomware) incidents, victims often fall prey by clicking on a link in an e-mail or on a website. In order to avoid falling victim to such an attack, e-mail return addresses and website links must be carefully scrutinized to make sure they are legitimate.

Identity theft occurs when someone uses another person's personally identifying information — such as their name, Social Security number or credit card number — without permission, to commit fraud or other crimes. The federal Identity Theft and Assumption Deterrence Act of 1998 punishes online identity theft, and also prohibits the production, transfer or possession of false or illegally issued identification documents in certain circumstances. It further prohibits production, transfer or possession of a "document-making implement," specifically including computers, with the intent to use it in the production of a false identification document. Even if someone doesn't use the Internet, they could still be a victim of cybercrime because someone could pose as them and establish online accounts in the victim's name.

28 17 U.S. Code § 506.
29 Verizon, *supra* note 5.

In addition to being prosecuted by law enforcement agencies as a form of identity theft, phishing scams are sometimes also prosecuted by the FTC because the scams also usually violate false advertising laws.

Data Security Laws

Law enforcement isn't alone in its responsibility to protect against cybercrimes. For many companies, collecting sensitive consumer and employee information online is an essential part of doing business. Those that do so have a legal responsibility to take steps to properly secure or dispose of such data. All 50 states, the District of Columbia and several U.S. territories have enacted legislation requiring private or government entities to notify individuals of security breaches of information involving personally identifiable information.[30] In light of recent major breaches involving companies such as Yahoo, LinkedIn, Experian, eBay, Target and Adobe, Congress has considered adopting a new federal data security law to protect online customers' data alongside state laws. Meanwhile, the FTC has also pursued companies for data breaches on the grounds that the companies fraudulently assured their customers that their information was protected.

At the same time, corporate victims of cyberattacks are hesitant to share information about data breaches that may result in them being sued civilly or even prosecuted criminally for their lax security. Recognizing that the private sector is at the forefront of the battle against cybercriminals and may have information valuable to the government, the federal Cybersecurity Act of 2015 was enacted to entice companies to be more forthcoming. It authorizes private companies to conduct surveillance of their networks for cybersecurity purposes and to confidentially share information with the federal government and with other private entities without liability.

"Historically, there's always been this line between the private sector and the government and there was no need to actually have these two different groups of people and entities work together because of the nature of the threats," explained Catherine Lotrionte, a cybersecurity expert with the think tank The Atlantic Council. "That's no longer the case. The government is going to be unable to defend this country unless the critical infrastructure owned and operated by private companies actually work with the government and ensure that their systems are protected."[31]

Challenges of Fighting Cybercrime

Having laws against cybercrime is only the first step in deterring it. Applying these laws is the much more difficult part. Law enforcement officials face

30 National Conference of State Legislatures, *Security Breach Notification Laws*, last updated July 17, 2020, https://www.ncsl.org/research/telecommunications-and-information-technology/security-breach-notification-laws.aspx.

31 The Dark Web: Fighting Cyber Crime, *supra* note 6.

several challenges in the investigation and prosecution of computer crimes. Although the federal government has cracked a number of high-profile cases, their resources are finite and they can't catch everyone. Also, penalties are often not enforced because of jurisdictional problems, the lack of information sharing among enforcement agencies, lack of technological resources and experience among local enforcement agencies, and resistance to devoting time and resources to a problem in which most of the victims are outside any one state. Many high-profile victims may also be reluctant to report offenses due to the potential for negative publicity.

Sophisticated criminals may encrypt data so that even if authorities seize or intercept the stolen data, law enforcement will be unable to understand its contents or use it as evidence. When that happens, law enforcement may seek help from tech companies to provide a way to access the data. But tech companies don't always comply. For example, in the aftermath of the 2015 shootings in a San Bernardino county office, the FBI sought access to the iPhone of suspect Syed Rizwan Farook. Apple said that it was unable to help, despite a federal court order to comply, because the phone's operating system did not have any "backdoor" way to access the phone's data without the password. The FBI was eventually able to access the phone's content through other means.[32] It should be noted that, although Facebook, Microsoft and other tech giants publicly supported Apple in their well-publicized fight to protect users' privacy, the reality is that all of the companies usually do what the government asks.[33]

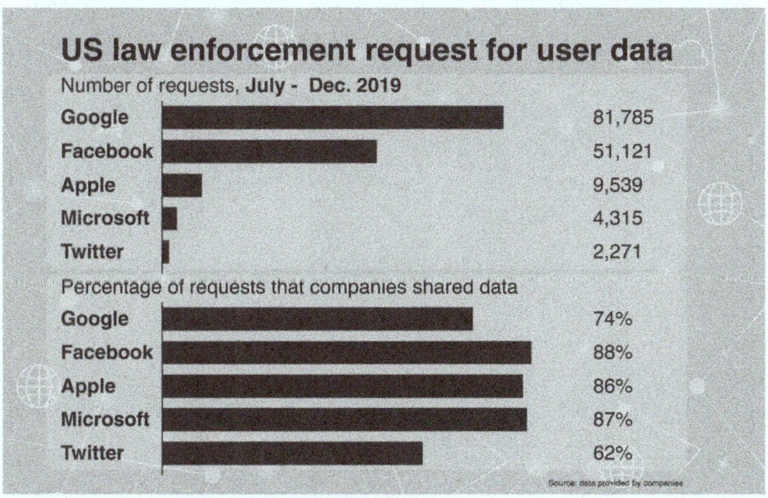

32 Rubin, Joel et al., *FBI Unlocks San Bernardino Shooter's iPhone and Ends Legal Battle With Apple, for Now*, Los Angeles Times, Mar. 28, 2016, https://www.latimes.com/local/lanow/la-me-ln-fbi-drops-fight-to-force-apple-to-unlock-san-bernardino-terrorist-iphone-20160328-story.html.

33 Wong, Joon Ian, *Here's How Often Apple, Google, and Others Handed over Data When the US Government Asked for it*, Quartz, Feb. 19, 2016, https://qz.com/620423/heres-how-often-apple-google-and-others-handed-over-data-when-the-us-government-asked-for-it/.

In investigating and prosecuting these crimes, law enforcement must comply with the privacy protections of the Fourth Amendment, which places limits on some electronic searches and surveillance. In the past decade the U.S. Supreme Court has ruled that police need a warrant before they can search cell phones or utilize a GPS tracker for long-term surveillance. These cases are discussed in Chapter 6.

Even with the cooperation of courts and tech companies, however, finding the true identity of criminals from online criminal conduct can also be a difficult task for investigators. As with the real world, in the virtual world a great deal of illegal activity occurs "underground." This dark corner of the Internet is known as the "Dark Net" or "Deep Web." The Deep Web is hidden from search engines and requires inside knowledge of obscure URLs. The Dark Net is a layer even deeper that usually requires specific authorization and software, such as the anonymous web browser Tor, to access. It is commonly used for appalling activities such as suicide forums, child pornography exchanges and ads for hitmen for hire. Lawless, offshore locations such as Sealand (a small metal platform in the North Sea off the coast of England that claims its own sovereignty) provide a haven to such sketchy actors by hosting the content on their servers.

Sealand is a platform off the coast of England that claims to be its own nation but is not recognized by other nations. It's been described by various media outlets as a "data haven." Credit: Simson L. Garfinkel (CC BY-SA 3.0).

Because of the global reach of the Internet, experts say an international solution aimed at preventing and enforcing cybercrimes is needed. Consider what happened in 2000, when Onel de Guzman sent out the "Love Bug" virus from the Philippines, causing billions of dollars in damage worldwide. The Philippine charges against de Guzman were dropped for lack of evidence, and he was never charged outside the Philippines because its law did not allow for extradition.[34] (Extradition is the official surrender of an alleged criminal by one state or nation to another having jurisdiction over the crime charged. The international extradition of suspected criminals, including suspects of cyber-crimes, is generally governed by international treaties.)

The U.S. took a step toward global cooperation on cybercrime in 2018 with the enactment of the Clarifying Lawful Overseas Use of Data (CLOUD) Act. The new law requires a communications provider based in the U.S. to give government investigators with a warrant or subpoena access to data stored off-shore. The law also allows the U.S. government to more easily share and trade its citizens' and companies' data with foreign nations when investigating crimes. But the law is not without controversy. It's been vilified by privacy rights groups who argue it will allow foreign governments to snoop on people in America that they do not like. Critics also argue it undermines basic civil freedoms by circumventing data protection and privacy laws, particularly those in Europe.

TIPS FOR PROTECTING YOURSELF ONLINE

So, how can you protect yourself from becoming one of the millions of Americans victimized by cybercrime each year? Here are some tips:

- Update your devices. Keep your computer, smartphone and other Internet-connected devices current with the latest operating system patches and updates.
- Protect passwords. Choose strong e-mail and social media passwords, keep them safe and change them regularly. And set up two-factor authentication to your accounts to provide an extra layer of security. Also protect your electronic devices (smartphone, computer, etc.) and WiFi with a strong password. Don't use information that is readily available about you as security question answers.
- Browse safely. Surf the web using "HTTPS Everywhere," or a privacy-enhanced browser that uses only encrypted connections to websites. Such connections scramble data so that it cannot be intercepted as it is transmitted. Note that the "privacy mode" of popular browsers blocks browsing history from being saved to the device being used but does not stop websites from collecting the device's IP address, which can be used to identify individual users.
- Carefully scrutinize e-mail return addresses and website links to make sure they are legitimate. The best practice after receiving a message from a financial entity is to contact the purported sender directly on your own, rather than responding to the message directly.

34 Arnold, Wayne, *Philippines to Drop Charges on E-Mail Virus*, The New York Times, Aug. 22, 2000, https://www.nytimes.com/2000/08/22/business/technology-philippines-to-drop-charges-on-e-mail-virus.html.

- Guard your devices. Be wary of allowing others to use your computer, smartphone or tablet, even if they're family members. They may inadvertently expose you to cybercrime risks and liability.
- Protect your computer with security software. Activate a firewall, use anti-virus/anti-malware software and install anti-spyware software. Consider using an "invisible" cloak or virtual private network (VPN) to protect your anonymity online.
- Protect your personal information. Set your social media accounts to private. Don't publicly announce on social media when you'll be away from home: burglars may target you. Be cautious when giving out personal information such as your name, address, phone number or financial information on the Internet. Make sure that websites are secure when making online purchases or sharing financial information.
- Protect your data. Use encryption for your most sensitive files such as tax returns or financial records. Also, make regular back-ups of all your important data and store the backups in a location separate from your computer.
- Be skeptical. Online offers that look too good to be true usually are.
- Monitor your expenses. Review bank and credit card statements regularly for any unusual charges.
- Contact the right person for help. If you are a victim, if you encounter illegal Internet content or if you suspect a scam, report it to local police. In addition, the FBI accepts cybercrime complaints online at https://www.ic3.gov. If you need help with maintenance or software installation on your computer, consult with experts such as the IT department at your school or workplace.

Cyberwarfare

Some cyberattacks are beyond the scope of law enforcement and instead require military might. Such is the case with cyberwarfare, which the U.S. Congressional Research Service defined as "state-on-state action equivalent to an armed attack or use of force in cyberspace that may trigger a military response."[35]

Cyberwarfare can involve government actors sponsoring any of the previously discussed methods of cyber misconduct. It can also involve using remote computers to impair or disable critical defense or civilian infrastructure, such as aviation control systems and electrical grids.

Cyberwar tactics can also include information warfare. For example, Russia has been accused of using various forms of cyberwarfare to interfere with the

35 Theohary, Catherine A. and Rollins, John W., *Cyberwarfare and Cyberterrorism: In Brief*, Congressional Research Service, Mar. 27, 2015, https://fas.org/sgp/crs/natsec/R43955.pdf.

2016 U.S. presidential election. In addition to purchasing ads on Facebook in an attempt to sway voters, Russians apparently managed to penetrate some U.S. states' voter registration rolls prior to the election. But there is no evidence that any of the registration rolls were altered in any fashion, according to U.S. officials.[36]

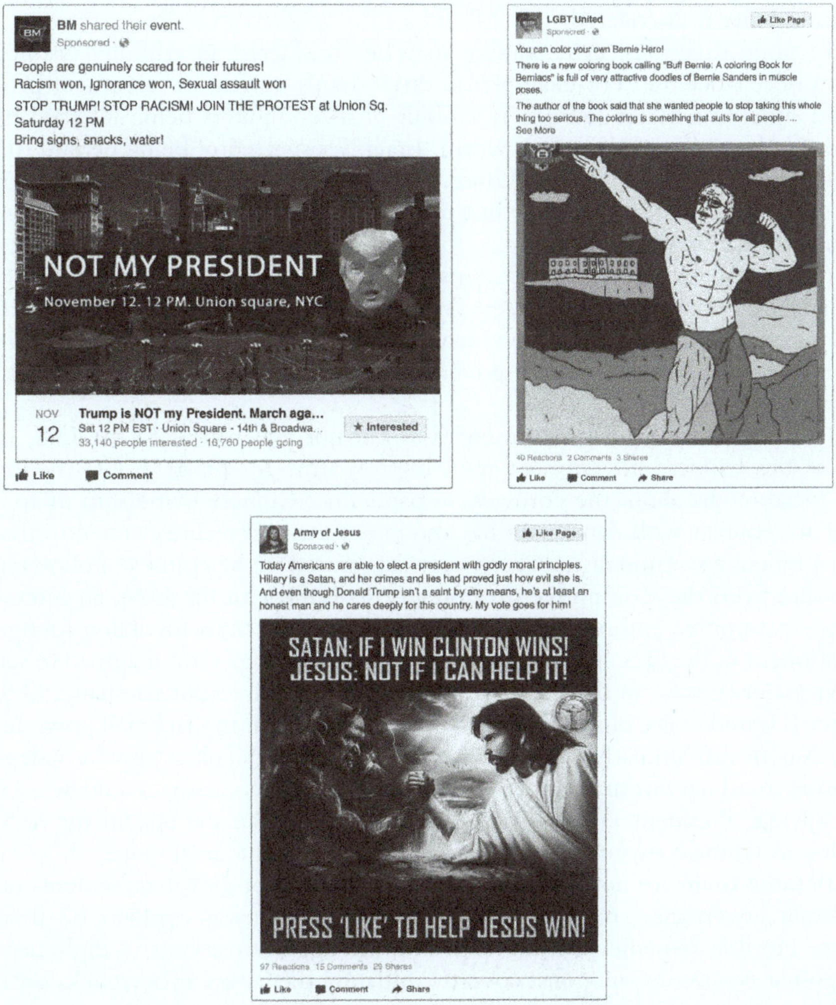

Examples of Russian ads related to the 2016 U.S. presidential race that appeared on Facebook. Credit: U.S. House of Representatives.

36 McFadden, Cynthia et al., *Russians Penetrated U.S. Voter Systems, Top U.S. Official Says*, NBC News, Feb. 7, 2018, https://www.nbcnews.com/politics/elections/russians-penetrated-u-s-voter-systems-says-top-u-s-n845721.

The U.S. is also an active participant in cyberwarfare, even establishing government units which conduct intelligence-gathering operations and support military missions through online activities. In other cases, such as the flood of false and misleading social media posts used by Russia to create chaos and sow division in the 2016 election, actors work with at least nominal independence so that the sponsoring government can maintain arms-length distance and deny responsibility if discovered.

In some situations, cyberwarfare may be considered an ethically justified form of self-defense. For example, in 2010, Iran's nuclear development program suffered a major setback as a result of its computers being infected by malware known as the Stuxnet worm. Israel is suspected of being behind this cyberespionage. In 2011, the United Kingdom reportedly infiltrated an Al Qaeda website and replaced the instructions for making a pipe bomb with the recipe for making cupcakes.

Outside of government use, terrorist organizations and rogue states have also utilized the Internet to harm their adversaries. For example, ISIS has posted its propaganda along with graphic videos of beheadings on social media sites in an attempt to spread fear, force governments to negotiate for hostages and to recruit new members.

More recently, China has emerged as a major cyberthreat to the U.S. In 2020, the Chinese government used its troll army to spread disinformation on social media about the coronavirus pandemic. Chinese ownership of apps that are popular with Americans has also raised national security concerns that the Chinese government can access user data stored in the country. Following pressure from the Committee on Foreign Investment in the U.S., an interagency committee authorized to review certain transactions involving foreign investment in the U.S., the Chinese company that owned Grindr agreed to sell their majority stake in the popular dating app to an American company. U.S. officials feared that China's government might exploit it to blackmail powerful gay Americans. Similarly, U.S. officials worried that TikTok, a popular video-sharing social networking service owned by a Chinese company, could be used for spying. President Donald Trump threatened to ban the app in the U.S. unless its Chinese owners sold it, but was blocked by a federal judge.

Because there are no international Internet police or global agreements on Internet governance, nations usually must solve cyberwar conflicts on their own. Possible remedies include expelling the aggressor country's diplomats, imposing economic sanctions, covertly initiating retaliatory cyberattacks or, if worse comes to worst, taking military action.

There have been calls for a digital version of the Geneva Convention, which would establish standards of international law for humanitarian treatment in cyberwar, along with a "Cyber Red Cross" to provide assistance and relief to netizens affected by serious cyberattack.[37] Unlike traditional war,

37 Smith, Brad, *The Need For a Digital Geneva Convention*, Microsoft on The Issues, Feb. 14, 2017, https://blogs.microsoft.com/on-the-issues/2017/02/14/need-digital-geneva-convention/.

which is guided by commonly accepted — if not always followed — Geneva Convention "rules" that date back centuries and are meant to reduce civilian suffering, netizens are not off limits in cyberwarfare and often get caught in the crossfire, or can even be the primary targets.

For example, North Korea is accused of being behind the notorious 2017 WannaCry cyberattack that froze thousands of computer systems around the world, demanding $300 in Bitcoin from each victim to remove the encryption. With frayed economic ties to most of the world, North Korea relies heavily on its cyberwarriors to illicitly generate wealth. The hackers have been used to settle scores, too. After Sony Pictures filmed *The Interview*, a movie which humorously portrayed North Korean dictator Kim Jong-un and an attempt to assassinate him, hackers looted and leaked internal company e-mails, employee records and several unreleased Sony films. Hoping to avert further damage, Sony canceled its widescreen release of the film.

Fearing that a far worse attack could someday occur against the U.S., some members of Congress have proposed giving the president control of an "Internet kill switch," which would provide a single shut-off mechanism for all Internet traffic in the event of a major cyberattack. In fact, the president may already have such power, according to some media reports. However, the implications of actually "killing" the Internet have prompted criticism of the idea. Such a switch could be abused to suppress free speech and the democratic process. For example, during the "Arab Spring" street protests in Tunisia, Egypt, Libya and other Arab countries in northern Africa and the Middle East, government officials shut off access to the Internet in an effort to prevent disgruntled citizens from organizing and protesting. In addition, in the U.S. the First Amendment legality of even having such a kill switch remains to be resolved.

CLOSING ARGUMENTS

Some Congress members have proposed giving the President control of an "Internet kill switch," which would provide a single shut-off mechanism for all Internet traffic in the event of a major cyberattack against America. (In fact, the president may already have such power.) However, such a switch could be abused to suppress free speech and the democratic process. Do you support giving the U.S. president a complete or more limited "Internet Kill Switch"? Why or why not?

Additional Sources

Abascal, Manuel A., et al., *What You Need to Know about the Cybersecurity Act of 2015*, Latham & Watkins Client Alert Commentary, Feb. 18, 2016, https://www.lw.com/thoughtLeadership/lw-Cybersecurity-Act-of-2015.

Adams, Richard, *Harvard's Aaron Swartz Indicted on MIT Hacking Charges*, The Guardian, July 21, 2001, https://www.theguardian.com/technology/2011/jul/21/aaron-swartz-indicted-hacking-charges.

Altaner, David, *Value Founder Pleads Guilty*, [Ft. Lauderdale, Fla.] Sun-Sentinel, May 10, 1994, https://www.sun-sentinel.com/news/fl-xpm-1994-05-10-9405090446-story.html.

Altman, Alex and Fitzpatrick, Alex, *Everything We Know About Sony, The Interview and North Korea*, Time, Dec. 17, 2014, https://time.com/3639275/the-interview-sony-hack-north-korea/.

Bisson, David, *DoppelPaymer Ransomware Struck City in Los Angeles County*, Security Boulevard, Apr. 22, 2020, https://securityboulevard.com/2020/04/doppelpaymer-ransomware-struck-city-in-los-angeles-county/.

Blinder, Alan and Perlroth, Nicole, *A Cyberattack Hobbles Atlanta, and Security Experts Shudder*, New York Times, Mar. 27, 2018, https://www.nytimes.com/2018/03/27/us/cyberattack-atlanta-ransomware.html.

Bob, Yonah Jeremy, *How Israel is Dealing with Cyber Warfare's New Stage*, Jerusalem Post, Mar. 17, 2014, https://www.jpost.com/Defense/Analysis-How-Israel-is-dealing-with-cyber-warfares-new-stage-345578.

Boyd, Jayson O. and Newell, Morgan, *City of Greenville Says it Has Resolved Ransomware Attack Without Having to Pay*, WCIT-TV, Apr. 25, 2019, https://wcti12.com/news/local/city-of-greenville-says-it-has-resolved-ransomware-attack-without-having-to-pay.

Brennan, Megan, *Cybercrimes Remain Most Worrisome to Americans*, Gallup, Nov. 9, 2018, https://news.gallup.com/poll/244676/cybercrimes-remain-worrisome-americans.aspx.

Cihodariu, Miriam, *Deep Web vs. Dark Web: What Is Each and How Do They Work*, Heimdal Security, Apr. 19, 2019, https://heimdalsecurity.com/blog/deep-web-vs-dark-web-what-is-each/.

Cimpanu, Catalin, *New York State Wants to Ban Government Agencies from Paying Ransomware Demands*, ZDNet, Jan. 23, 2020, https://www.zdnet.com/article/new-york-state-wants-to-ban-government-agencies-from-paying-ransomware-demands/.

Cohn, Carolyn, *Cyber Insurance to Triple to $7.5 Billion by 2020, Attracting Disruptors*: Report, Reuters, Sept. 13, 2015, https://www.reuters.com/article/us-cyber-insurance-survey-idUSKCN0RD0XO20150913.

Cosgrave, Jenny, *Online Gambling: The New Home for Money Launderers*?, CNBC, Apr. 25, 2014, https://www.cnbc.com/2014/04/25/online-gambling-the-new-home-for-money-launderers.html.

Craig, Brian, Cyberlaw: The Law of the Internet and Information Technology (2012).

DePuyt, Bruce, *Baltimore Ransomware Attack Inspires State Legislation*, Maryland Matters, Jan. 14, 2020, https://www.marylandmatters.org/2020/01/14/baltimore-ransomware-attack-inspires-state-legislation/.

FBI, *The Morris Worm*, Nov. 2, 2018, https://www.fbi.gov/news/stories/morris-worm-30-years-since-first-major-attack-on-internet-110218.

Greenberg, Andy, *Feds "Hacked" Silk Road Without a Warrant? Perfectly Legal, Prosecutors Argue*, Wired, Oct. 7, 2014, https://www.wired.com/2014/10/feds-silk-road-hack-legal/

HG Legal, *What Is the Threat of Money Laundering Associated with Bitcoin*?, 2013, https://www.hg.org/article.asp?id=31835.

Hume, Tim, *How FBI* Caught Ross Ulbricht, *Alleged Creator of Criminal Marketplace Silk Road*, CNN, Oct. 5, 2013, https://www.cnn.com/2013/10/04/world/americas/silk-road-ross-ulbricht/index.html.

Identity Theft Resource Center, *A Nigerian Prince Wants to Give Me Money!*, 2015, https://www.idtheftcenter.org/Scams/a-nigerian-prince-wants-to-give-me-money.html.

Kabay, M.E., *Salami Fraud*, Network World Security Newsletter, July 24, 2002, http://www.mekabay.com/nwss/116p--salami_fraud.pdf.

Knapp, Alex, MI6 *Hacks Al-Qaeda and Gives Them Cupcake Recipes*, Forbes, June 3, 2011, https://www.forbes.com/sites/alexknapp/2011/06/03/mi6-hacks-al-qaeda-and-gives-them-cupcake-recipes.

Krebs, Brian, *Lawmakers Prod FCC to Act on SIM Swapping*, Krebs on Security, Jan. 9, 2020, https://krebsonsecurity.com/2020/01/senators-prod-fcc-to-act-on-sim-swapping/.

Lecher, Colin, *Google Shut Out Baltimore Officials Using Gmail after Ransomware Attack*, The Verge, May 23, 2019, https://www.theverge.com/2019/5/23/18637638/google-gmail-baltimore-ransomware-attacks.

Lee, Timothy B., *Court: Violating a Site's Terms of Service Isn't Criminal Hacking*, Ars Technica, Mar. 30, 2020, https://arstechnica.com/tech-policy/2020/03/court-violating-a-sites-terms-of-service-isnt-criminal-hacking/.

Ng, Alfred, *Your Smartphones Are Getting More Valuable for Hackers*, CNET, Mar. 8, 2018, available at https://www.cnet.com/news/your-smartphones-are-getting-more-valuable-for-hackers/.

Nield, David, *How To Protect All of Your Accounts Online*, Popular Science, Mar. 21, 2017, https://www.popsci.com/protect-your-accounts-online.

Office of Legal Education Executive Office for U.S. Attorneys, Prosecuting Computer Crimes (2014), https://www.justice.gov/sites/default/files/criminal-ccips/legacy/2015/01/14/ccmanual.pdf.

O'Neill, Patrick Howell, *A Patient Has Died After Ransomware Hackers Hit a German Hospital*, MIT Technology Review, Sept. 18, 2020, https://www.technologyreview.com/2020/09/18/1008582/a-patient-has-died-after-ransomware-hackers-hit-a-german-hospital/.

Robertson, Jordan and Arnold, Laurence, Iran *Is Big on Cyberwarfare*. How Does That Work?, BloombergBusinessweek, May 11, 2018, https://www.bloomberg.com/news/articles/2018-05-11/cyberwar-how-nations-attack-without-bullets-or-bombs-quicktake.

Rouse, Margaret, *What Is Cybercrime?*, Search Security, Apr. 2018, https://searchsecurity.techtarget.com/definition/cybercrime.

Silverman, Craig, *Chinese Trolls Are n; Spreading Coronavirus Disinformation in Taiwan*, Buzzfeed News, Mar. 5, 2020, https://www.buzzfeednews.com/article/craigsilverman/chinese-trolls-coronavirus-disinformation-taiwan.

Song, Victoria, *Baltimore's Government Held Hostage by Ransomware Attack*, Gizmodo, May 8, 2019, https://gizmodo.com/baltimores-government-held-hostage-by-ransomware-attack-1834616990.

Stone, Jeff, *The CFAA Will Soon Have its Day Before the Supreme Court*, Cyberscoop, Apr. 20, 2020, https://www.cyberscoop.com/cfaa-will-soon-day-supreme-court/.

Sussman, Bruce, *As Ransomware Payments Double, Some Want Them Banned*, Secure World Expo, Jan. 27, 2020, https://www.secureworldexpo.com/industry-news/ransomware-payments-double-some-want-ransoms-payment-ban.

Weiner, Jeffrey S. *Cell Phone Fraud*, Jeffrey S. Weiner, P.A., Apr. 23, 2018, https://www.jeffweiner.com/blog/2018/april/cell-phone-fraud/.

Williams, Robert, *Grindr Sold by Chinese Owner Amid US Security Concerns*, Mobile Marketer, Mar. 9, 2020, https://www.mobilemarketer.com/news/grindr-sold-by-chinese-owner-amid-us-security-concerns/573702/.

Wilson, Clay, *Cyber Crime*, in Cyberpower and National Security (F. Kramer ed., 2009), http://ctnsp.dodlive.mil/files/2014/03/Cyberpower-I-Chap-18.pdf.

Wyden, Ron, Brown, Sherrod, Markey, Edward, Lieu, Ted W., Eshoo, Anna and Clark, Yvette, Letter to Ajit Pai, Jan. 9, 2020, https://www.wyden.senate.gov/download/010920-sim-swap-scam-letter-to-ftc.

11 Online Gaming

> The video games … It's hard to believe that at least for a percentage — and maybe it's a small percentage of children — this doesn't have a negative impact on their thought process … these things are really violent.
>
> — President Donald Trump

While it may come as a surprise to many of those who participate, gaming in the virtual world is subject to an array of laws. As the popularity of video games, e-sports, fantasy sports, online casinos and virtual reality (VR) continues to grow, so too have the legal issues that loom over them. For the most part, participating in these activities is legal. But, increasingly, lawmakers have been proposing stricter regulations. They're concerned that Internet casinos and fantasy sports can lead to gambling addictions and that video games cause violence in children. Cheating and discrimination are also common in many games, raising concerns about fairness. Let's take a closer look at the key legal and ethical issues confronting each industry.

Internet Gambling

When it comes to Internet gambling — both online casinos and sports betting online — federal laws in the United States are murky. As with offline gambling, states maintain the most control over determining which activities constitute illegal gambling online.

In the past decade, federal laws have often been unclear, and their enforcement has been unpredictable and inconsistent. At the moment, online gambling is legally available only to a small number of Americans. In 2019, the U.S. Department of Justice proclaimed that the Interstate Wire Act of 1961, which prohibits people from making bets or wagers over the phone, applies to all Internet gambling that involves interstate transactions, as well. This was a reversal of its prior position, from 2011, and possibly was done for political reasons.

Under the new policy, individual states are still permitted to legalize Internet gambling, but the gambling itself must occur wholly within state lines. Only Delaware, Michigan, Nevada, New Jersey, Pennsylvania and West Virginia offer online gambling such as playing online poker for money, and only for in-state residents. Additionally, about a dozen states allow their residents to purchase Powerball or other lottery tickets online.

Under the federal Indian Gaming Regulation Act, a Native American tribe may operate physical gaming facilities such as casinos, card rooms and bingo halls on tribal land as long as it reaches an agreement regarding operations with the state in which the facility is located. Such an agreement would also be necessary for online gambling, but the gambling would likely be limited to residents of the state where the tribe's operation is based.

Betting on professional and college sports was formerly banned in most states by the federal Professional and Amateur Sports Protection Act, but this law was found unconstitutional by the U.S. Supreme Court in 2018.[1] As a result of the ruling, 15 states — Colorado, Illinois, Indiana, Iowa, Michigan, Nevada, New Hampshire, New Jersey, New York, Oregon, Pennsylvania, Rhode Island, Tennessee, Virginia and West Virginia — as well as Puerto Rico and Washington, D.C. allow in-state, online sports betting on the outcomes of college and professional sports games via the Internet.

In order to participate in Internet gambling, users must be physically within the state where the online casino is based in order to play. Thus, Texans and Californians, for example, cannot utilize online casinos since their states do not allow them to, and federal law restricts Americans from using online casinos located outside their state. The minimum age to participate ranges from 18 to 21, with most states requiring the latter. Software pinpoints where players are located, and identity and age verification are part of the process of setting up betting accounts.

But these systems are not flawless, and many Americans and casinos are able to subvert these laws using some ingenuity. For example, some gambling websites accept untraceable virtual currencies, such as Bitcoin or virtual goods — such as "skins" used in various online games — that can then be exchanged for cash. Such workarounds are fraught with legal risks, though. Cyber law attorney James Ifrah cautioned, "Skins could ultimately be considered a 'thing of value.' If such a designation were made — either by a regulatory body, a legislature, or a court — then skin betting would fall under the auspices of gambling regulation."[2] "This is still very much a grey area" that has resulted in ongoing litigation, according to intellectual property attorney Archie Ahern.[3]

Engaging in illicit gambling carries monetary risks, too. Online casinos often shut down without warning — either because of law enforcement actions taken by authorities or exit scams by shady operators — leaving players unable to recover whatever funds they had in their accounts. "Illegal gambling proceeds are forfeited to the government," a spokeswoman for the U.S. Attorney's Office stated after authorities seized $30 million from an online casino bust in 2011. "Anyone who believes that an Internet gambling business owes them

1 *Murphy v. National Collegiate Athletic Association*, 584 U.S. ___, 138 S.Ct. 1461, 200 L.Ed.2d 854 (2018).

2 Ifrah Law, *The Ifrah Guide to eSports Law*, 2016, https://kisacoresearch.com/content/ifrah-guide-esports-law.

3 Ahern, Archie, *Skin Betting: The Multi-Billion Dollar Craze That's Taken Hold of Online Gaming*, MediaWrites, Aug. 16, 2016, https://www.mediawrites.law/skin-betting-the-multi-billion-dollar-craze-thats-taken-hold-of-online-gaming/

money can try to collect from the Internet gambling business. The government is not going to give the money to gamblers."[4]

Prediction Markets

Sports and casino games aren't the only things netizens bet on. A number of websites have popped up in recent years allowing people to bet on the occurrence of future events, such as who will win the next election.

The Iowa Electronic Market is among the pioneers of so-called "prediction markets" on the Internet. Established in 1988 by the University of Iowa, it allows students to invest small amounts of money to predict the winner of congressional and presidential elections. Another example is PredictIt.org, which was founded in 2014 by Victoria University in New Zealand and offers prediction exchanges on political and financial events.

While prediction markets have some elements of gambling, they are permitted to operate in the U.S. via a legal loophole. Instead of registering as online gambling sites, they register with the Commodity Futures Trading Commission (CFTC), the regulatory body responsible for overseeing such markets, as a futures market — in which participants "invest" in whether particular events will or will not happen in the future — for politics and current affairs. The exception is typically limited to non-profit operations that only allow small bets and share their data for academic research. However, while a letter from the CFTC that it will not act against such operations permits prediction markets at the federal level, state law still precludes them in many places.

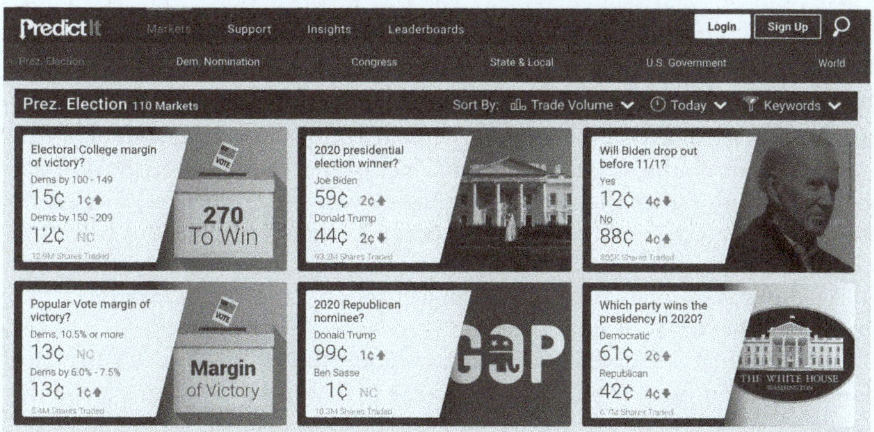

Online prediction markets such as PredictIt.org may seem like gambling, but they are considered futures markets under the law. Credit: PredictIt.org.

4 McGraw, Brian, *Police Celebrate Seized Online Gambling Funds*, Competitive Enterprise Institute, June 13, 2001, https://cei.org/blog/police-celebrate-seized-online-gambling-funds.

Fantasy Sports

A fantasy sport is a game where participants build fictional teams that compete against fantasy teams created by others, based on the statistics generated by the real individual players or teams of a professional sport. Although fantasy sports have been played for more than 70 years, they were mostly a fringe hobby until the Internet came along.

The Internet boom in the 1990s transformed fantasy sports into a popular mainstream activity. The new technology lowered the barrier to entry, as stats could quickly be compiled online, and news and information became readily available. Fantasy sports rapidly became a lucrative business for dot-com entrepreneurs, who were looking to cash in on a growing consumer market, and an obsession for participants. While many fantasy sport participants began playing for fun, numerous fantasy leagues now offer substantial prizes to winners.

Today, America's fantasy sports industry attracts more than 40 million participants and is estimated to generate billions of dollars, according to the Fantasy Sports Trade Association (FSTA).[5] Some participants wager tens of thousands of dollars on a single contest and some fantasy leagues offer million-dollar payouts, which has caused concern among anti-gambling groups, prompting calls for more stringent regulation.

While some critics consider any games that involve the exchange of money a form of gambling that should be outlawed, it is generally legal to operate and participate in fantasy sports games in the U.S. Most fantasy sports games are, by law, not considered to be a form of gambling. That's because fantasy sports contests — unlike other forms of gambling — are considered to require more skill (in choosing players, for example) than luck (such as randomly drawn cards) to win. However, a handful of states prohibit pay-for-play fantasy games.

Popular new types of short-term games, such as the daily contests offered by DraftKings and FanDuel, are legally hazy. There's controversy over the new breed of fantasy sports websites which allow users to wager thousands of dollars on an individual athlete's daily performance, over which an individual bettor has no control, rather than the performance of a "team" made of disparate players that are combined through the bettor's "skills." Only about half of all states have explicitly made daily fantasy sports games legal. The daily contests, unlike the season-long contests, are subject to a 0.25% federal excise tax that applies to other types of sports betting.

For both Internet gambling and fantasy sports, the businesses that offer such activities face far more legal risks than do the individuals who participate in the games.

Video Games

The possible link between violence in computer games and the rising trend of antisocial behavior in society has prompted calls for regulation of the video

5 Fantasy Sports Trade Association, *Industry Demographics*, 2020, http://www.fsta.org/?page=Demographics.

game industry. In 2014, for example, two 12-year-old girls claimed that "Slender Man," a video game character, inspired them to lure their friend into the woods and fatally stab her 19 times.

"The video games, the movies, the Internet stuff is so violent," President Donald Trump said following a school shooting in 2018. "It's hard to believe that, at least for a percentage — and maybe it's a small percentage of children — this doesn't have a negative impact on their thought process. But these things are really violent."[6]

However, U.S. courts have not been persuaded by such claims and have repeatedly refused to hold video game companies liable for harm allegedly caused, directly or indirectly, by their games.

In *Sanders v. Acclaim Entertainment*, for example, the plaintiff sued video game makers, alleging violent games prompted the Columbine shooters in Colorado. But a U.S. District Court found the manufacturer couldn't reasonably foresee the school shootings.[7] In *Roccaforte v. Nintendo*, a child's parents sued after their son suffered violent seizures while playing video games, but a Louisiana jury ruled in favor of the gaming company.[8]

Frustrated by these results, other activists have tried making their case by lobbying lawmakers, insisting the government has a duty to help parents shield children from violence and sexuality. In response, several U.S. cities and states passed laws banning the sale of violent or sexually explicit video games to children without parental supervision.

But federal courts have repeatedly struck down the laws, and in a landmark 2011 decision the U.S. Supreme Court ruled that such laws are unconstitutional because violent video games are protected by the First Amendment. Some of the high court's justices, who are often ridiculed for being Luddites who are unfamiliar with new technology, even played the game *Postal 2* as part of their research for the case. In the majority opinion, Justice Antonin Scalia wrote that there is no tradition of specially restricting children's access to depictions of violence in the U.S., adding that research linking video games to increased violence in children was "not compelling" and "indistinguishable from effects produced by other media."[9]

Thus, there is no law in the U.S. against the sale of violent video games to children. However, there is a system of self-regulation run by the industry-created Entertainment Software Rating Board (ESRB). The board independently applies ratings, advertising guidelines and online privacy principles adopted by the computer and video game industry. The ratings are designed

6 Disis, Jill, *The Long History of Blaming Video Games for Mass Violence*, CNN, Mar. 8, 2018, https://money.cnn.com/2018/03/08/media/video-game-industry-white-house/index.html.

7 *Sanders v. Acclaim Entertainment, Inc.*, 188 F.Supp. 2d 1264 (D. Colo. 2002).

8 An appeals court ordered a new trial due to alleged discovery abuses and ultimately awarded court costs and attorney's fees to the plaintiff. *Roccaforte v. Nintendo of Am., Inc.*, 802 So. 2d 764 (La. App. 5th Cir. 2001), *writ denied*, 811 So. 2d 884 (La. 2002).

9 *Brown v. Entertainment Merchants Association*, 564 U.S. 786, 799, 800-01 (2011).

to provide information about video and computer game content, so consumers can make informed purchase decisions. However, given that the ESRB is a private organization and not a government entity, such ratings have no legal teeth and young children are often able to purchase video games (particularly online) deemed inappropriate for their age.

In contrast to the U.S. system, most European nations require video games that depict violence, sexual activity or other content deemed inappropriate to children to be classified under the government-mandated Pan European Game Information rating system. Some countries, such the United Kingdom, have further enacted laws making it an offense to supply inappropriate games to underage consumers, punishable by a fine of up to £5,000 and up to six months in prison. Other countries, including Germany, have outright banned several games considered too offensive.

E-Sports

E-sports — the playing and watching of competitive video games as a spectator sport — is growing fast. The global e-sports market is about $2 billion and some e-sports tournaments award tens of millions of dollars in prizes. Its fundamentals are similar to "traditional" sports: skilled players compete against each other in live events, supported by passionate spectator fans and sponsors. As e-sports continues to grow, so too have the legal issues that loom over it.

E-sports have grown in popularity so much that they are now often played in arenas with plenty of room for spectators. Credit: Riot Games.

Although traditional sports are largely governed by internal self-regulation — policed by a combination of self-regulatory enforcement by leagues or conferences, with ultimate recourse to the courts only if necessary — there is also a substantial body of law governing them, whether from statute, case law or regulatory action. It is yet to be established how much of this established sports law will or should apply to e-sports. After all, a fundamental issue is whether e-sports are even sports in the first place.

The specific laws for e-sports are very nascent. While some policies exist, many issues remain unclear or unregulated. The situation is further complicated by the global nature of e-sports competitions and lack of a central governing body, such as soccer's FIFA or football's NFL, which can create uncertainty over whose regulations apply. Some colleges now offer scholarships for students to play on their e-sports teams, which raises the issue of whether the NCAA should have a role in oversight. In 2019, the NCAA's Board of Governors voted to table the issue of governing and holding championships for collegiate e-sports. But given e-sports' fast-growing revenues and popularity, that could change.

Another big problem is demographics. Because many top players are legally minors, they may lack the sophistication to deal with the myriad legal issues that arise. For example, exploitative contracts are common. Contracts, in general, are incomprehensible to most laypeople and many professional gamers do not take time to read through 20-plus pages of legalese regarding their playing, nor do they read the Terms of Service for the games themselves. Some e-sports athletes are only 13 years old when they sign professional contracts and may not understand the implications due to their inexperience combined with the excitement of having a shot at being a paid professional. For example, professional *Fortnite* player Turner Tenney, known as "Tfue," sued the gaming organization FaZe Clan to get out of what he claimed was an oppressive contract.[10] The parties eventually settled.

Owen Butterfield, a British teenager who plays e-sports professionally, detailed his contractual woes on social media in 2017. Butterfield said he was benched only months after joining his e-sports team, which resulted in his salary being significantly reduced, from $2,000 to $700 per month. Butterfield's benching effectively ended his career because his contract contained a $100,000 buyout clause which no other team was willing to pay. To make matters worse, he could not access government welfare benefits despite his mother being disabled because he was still earning a salary.

Cheating scandals are also prevalent. While traditional athletes may use performance-enhancing drugs such as steroids to enhance their strength and

10 *FaZe Clan Inc. v. Tenney*, No. 1:2019cv07200 (S.D.N.Y. 2020) (complaint).

endurance, e-sports competitors often rely on neuro-enhancing drugs to gain an unfair advantage. According to Ifrah, "It is almost an open secret that many players take prescriptions to help with focus and attentiveness, such as Adderall, during competition."[11]

Besides their bodies, participants may also manipulate their equipment to gain an edge. Much like a baseball player who corks his bat to get the upper-hand over an opponent, some e-sports players rig their hardware, such as their keyboard and mouse, or software by utilizing a bot to assist in tasks. This practice is known as "e-doping."

Other forms of cheating are common as well, such as match-fixing and cyberattacks. For example, some players have utilized distributed denial of service (DDoS) attacks in order to overwhelm a gaming network so much that it is forced to slow down or shut down, impeding other players. According to *Vice* journalist Emanuel Maiberg, DDoS attacks are common because the early rounds of competitions are often played in homes: "If you have the ability to knock one member of either team offline for more than 10 minutes, you have the power to determine the outcome of the match … This is not a difficult thing to do."[12]

Cyberattacks like these are considered a criminal offense in many nations, including the U.S. For example, an "Overwatch" hacker was punished in South Korea with one year of imprisonment and two years of probation. But other types of cheating are merely a violation of contest rules or the game's Terms of Service — not government laws — and enforcement by competition officials has been inconsistent. Players banned from competing in one tournament for cheating have been allowed to participate in other tournaments.

Finally, there have been numerous reports that racism and sexism are rampant in e-sports and not enough is being done to stop it. In traditional sports, such behavior usually results in significant punishment, such as a fine, a suspension or even a lifetime ban by the overarching sports association. For example, in 2014, the NBA permanently banned Los Angeles Clippers owner Donald Sterling, fined him $2.5 million, and forced him to sell his team due to racist comments he made privately that were leaked to the press. Although hate speech is legal under the First Amendment, such speech is only protected from government punishment. Private organizations, including sports leagues, can impose sanctions for racist speech. But because e-sports lacks an effective governing body, repercussions for discrimination tend to be much less severe.

11 Ifrah Law, *supra* note 2.

12 Maiberg, Emanuel, *eSports Has a DDoS Problem*, Vice, Aug. 7, 2015, https://motherboard.vice.com/en_us/article/vvba9m/esports-has-a-ddos-problem.

Virtual Reality and Augmented Reality

Augmented reality (AR) (which adds fictional elements to on-screen depictions of real-world scenes) and VR (which creates entirely fictional worlds) are immersive technologies that integrate virtual and real-world elements. While both are commonly used in gaming, they are also being increasingly utilized in medicine, real estate, tourism and other industries. As these technologies mature, legal questions are emerging that could trip up developers and users alike.

In a 1993 *Village Voice* article titled "A Rape in Cyberspace," journalist-turned-lawyer Julian Dibbell first raised some of these questions when he chronicled a troubling incident that rocked the online community known as LambdaMOO, a chat room and virtual world populated by early Internet adopters.[13] Using a virtual voodoo doll, an anonymous user known as "Mr. Bungle" forced simulated sex acts on another community member. The groundbreaking story brought online abuse to light and led to debates about how to regulate the early Internet, including how to potentially prosecute crimes that had never existed before. Should such behavior be considered sexual harassment or even assault? Was it protected free speech?

In the three decades since, computer scientists have added enhanced functionality to make the "reality" in VR environments highly believable. Yet, many questions raised by Dibbell's provocative article still remain unsettled. As VR becomes increasingly real, how do we decide what behavior crosses the line from an annoyance to a crime? And is there a difference in the legal standards for augmented vs. virtual reality?

"Because VR seems so real and evokes real emotions, [victims] felt just as violated as though [they] had been assaulted in real life," argues Robyn Chatwood, a technology lawyer at Dentons in Australia. "However, there are no laws that say sexual assault in VR is the same as being sexually assaulted in the real world."[14] Attorney Brian V. Finch of Keggler Brown in Ohio predicts, "It is inevitable that a virtual groping case is going to reach the courts ... such a case would be sure to turn heads in the legal community and will certainly set some kind of legal precedent regarding virtual reality."[15] Chatwood agrees: "I think within 5 to 10 years there may be an incident that draws a lot of attention to a particular problem. Or adoption may just become so widespread that society recognizes the need for regulations."[16] In the meantime, she recommends

13 Dibbell, Julian, *A Rape in Cyberspace*, Village Voice, Dec. 23, 1993 (posted Oct. 18, 2005), https://www.villagevoice.com/2005/10/18/a-rape-in-cyberspace/.

14 Harbert, Tam, *The Legal Hazards of Virtual Reality and Augmented Reality Apps*, IEEE Spectrum, Feb. 20, 2018, https://spectrum.ieee.org/at-work/innovation/the-legal-hazards-of-virtual-reality-and-augmented-reality-apps.

15 Finch, Brian, *Can Someone Commit Assault in Virtual Reality?*, Virtual Legality Blog, Dec. 28, 2016, https://www.keglerbrown.com/publications/can-someone-commit-assault-in-virtual-reality/.

16 Harbert, *supra* note 14.

VR developers help mitigate harm by including functions that allow users to set boundaries or block another user.

More recently, a wildly popular smartphone app utilizing AR, *Pokémon Go*, became the subject of a novel class action lawsuit in 2016.[17] Makers of the game, which uses location tracking and mapping technology to create an AR where users catch and train animated animals in real locations, were sued for "trespass" for causing players to congregate on lawns of private homes. Although the lawsuit was settled before trial, it raised many questions about how location-based AR experiences are legally able to interact with the real world and property laws: was the game maker responsible for trespass because it placed virtual items on private property without permission? Or were those items merely on users' phones with the players ultimately liable for where they ventured? As part of the 2019 settlement of the case, game creator Niantic agreed to pay 12 homeowners $1,000 apiece, remove Pokémon virtual gyms that were near homes and create a system for resolving nuisance complaints, among other measures.

Pokémon Go led some players to trespass onto private property, leading to lawsuits. Credit: Fabien Rafowicz.

But that wasn't the end of *Pokémon Go*'s woes. The game's record-setting success brought a range of other problems. Players were robbed at gunpoint while walking around in search of items, a driver crashed into a police car while distracted by the game, and two players even walked off a 90-foot cliff

17 *Marder v. Niantic*, Civil No. 16-4300 (N.D. Cal. filed July 29, 2016) (complaint), https://regmedia.co.uk/2019/02/15/pokemon-go-lawsuit.pdf.

while playing the game. Similar injuries may also occur with VR, which often requires the use of a headset and other equipment. Without being able to see the real-world environment one is in, falls, collisions and other injuries are likely. Can AR and VR designers such as Niantic be held responsible when users suffer harm? Experts disagree.

"The answer is probably not," according to a blog post by personal injury law firm Martinson and Beason. "Niantic warned users of the potential dangers ... The injured party is likely partially responsible for their injuries ... As part of *Pokémon Go*'s Terms of Service, a player agrees to settle any disagreement with Niantic through arbitration, not through trial-by-jury."[18] On the other hand, insurance claim and risk management consultant Kevin Quinley said, "Only time will tell whether [they] may be held liable for injuries sustained while people are playing that game ... [I]t's no stretch to envision product claims based on allegations of illness and harm from users of virtual technology products. This kind of underscores the law of unintended consequences that really applies to every tech innovation."[19]

Other Gaming Issues

Beyond these key legal issues, a host of other red flags may arise related to digital games. All of the online gaming industries must worry about a number of the legal issues covered in other chapters, including intellectual property, defamation and cybercrimes.

For example, in *O'Bannon v. NCAA*, Electronic Arts and a company that handles licensing for various colleges agreed in 2013 to pay $40 million to college athletes to settle a lawsuit alleging that the companies' products, including sports video games, used the players' likenesses without permission or compensation.[20] On the other hand, in a 2018 decision the Indiana Supreme Court ruled that use of players' names, pictures and statistics in online fantasy sports games and related advertisements are of "newsworthy value" and not actionable under Indiana's right of publicity statute.[21] These types of "misappropriation" claims are discussed in more detail in Chapter 6.

18 Martinson & Beason, *Legal Liability with Pokémon Go Accidents*, https://www.martinsonandbeason.com/legal-liability-pokemon-go-accidents/.

19 Johnson, Denise, *Industry Expert Shares Thoughts on Virtual Reality Liability Exposures*, Claims Journal, Sept. 25, 2018, https://www.claimsjournal.com/news/national/2018/09/25/286931.htm.

20 Farrey, Tom, *Players, Game Makers Settle For $40M*, ESPN, May 30, 2014, https://www.espn.com/espn/otl/story/_/id/11010455/college-athletes-reach-40-million-settlement-ea-sports-ncaa-licensing-arm.

21 *Daniels v. FanDuel, Inc.*, 109 N.E.3d 390 (Ind. 2018) (answering certified question from *Daniels v. FanDuel*, Inc., 884 F.3d 672 (7th Cir. 2018)), *answer adopted*, 909 F.3d 876 (7th Cir. 2018).

As with any interaction online or in the real world, gaming enthusiasts must watch what they say while playing or else face a defamation lawsuit. For example, participants in fantasy sports often bash players and coaches on Internet message boards and in the comments section on websites. Fortunately, professional athletes and coaches are generally considered public figures to whom one can direct a wide variety of invective without being liable for defamation since such "trash talk" is not conveyed as truthful information. Trickier, though, is the situation in which participants in a fantasy sports league or online video game start verbally attacking one another and getting personal, even making vulgar references and insults. Online game spaces are notoriously hostile to players who identify as women. Whenever the comments are made publicly, such as on a website that is accessible to many people, the rules of defamation apply.

Sometimes petty gaming disputes carry over into the real world with lethal consequences. For example, in 2017, a disagreement between two players over a $1.50 bet on the popular video game *Call of Duty* led to a Wichita man being fatally shot by a SWAT team after an Ohio man falsely reported a hostage situation taking place at the Wichita man's address. The caller was sentenced to 15 months in prison after pleading guilty to conspiracy and obstructing justice, but online anonymity and cross-jurisdictional issues often makes finding and prosecuting such bad actors difficult.

Playing games can also lead to trouble at school and work. For example, with studies showing that fantasy sports can cost billions of dollars in lost productivity, some workplaces forbid it. An employer may fire an employee found to be soliciting other employees to participate in their fantasy sports games during work hours, in violation of company policies against solicitation or gambling at work. On the flip side, many offices sponsor fantasy sports leagues as a way of building employee morale. However, an employer may be exposed to a potential hostile work environment claim if an employee who does not participate in gambling activities due to religious beliefs receives pressure to do so from coworkers.

Fantasy games and Internet gambling also can lead to legal troubles in participants' personal lives. Participants who make high-stakes bets run a heightened risk of bankruptcy based on their financially risky behavior. They can become addicted. Consequently, some lawmakers and advocacy groups oppose gambling on morality grounds.

Addiction is a growing problem for gamers, too. The lure of VR may become so seductive and powerful that users essentially lose themselves in imaginary worlds and become detached from reality. Already some teens have been hospitalized and even died from playing video games non-stop for several consecutive days without taking care of their physical needs. The World Health Organization has even declared video game addiction a mental disorder. In response, South Korea in 2011 enacted a "shutdown law" that forbids children under age 16 from playing online video games between midnight and 6 a.m. Violators face up to two years of imprisonment or a fine of approximately $9,000. China implemented a similar policy in 2019 and further limited minors to 90 minutes of video game playing time on weekdays. But in America, where legal principles such as freedom and liberty dominate, these kinds of bans seem unlikely to happen. And, even if the U.S. imposed a gaming curfew, some teens would undoubtedly figure out workarounds such as fake IDs, as South Korea discovered.

However, some schools have begun banning mobile phone games while students are on campus. In 2018, for example, the popular game *Fortnite* launched an iOS version that caused massive frustration at schools such as classroom distractions, WiFi overload and even physical altercations between students.

CLOSING ARGUMENTS

Some experts argue that video games corrupt impressionable children, cause addiction and lead to antisocial behavior. Experts are more divided on the influence that the games have on violent behavior. In response to these concerns, several nations have imposed regulations. Similar bans in the U.S. have been stymied by the Supreme Court, which has ruled that such bans violate the First Amendment. As an alternative, the video game industry has created a rating system that is meant to guide parents regarding the content of games. Is this sufficient? Or should the government be able to step in and limit children's access to such games?

Additional Sources

Alexander, Julia, *Tfue Settles Lawsuit against Faze Clan Over 'Oppressive' Gaming Contract*, The Verge, Aug. 26, 2020, https://www.theverge.com/2020/8/26/21403052/tfue-faze-clan-lawsuit-settled-streaming-events-competition-esports.

Axelson, Ben, *Pokemon Go Dangerous? Every Crime, Accident, Death Linked to Game so Far*, Syracuse.com, May 23, 2019, https://www.syracuse.com/us-news/2016/07/pokemon_go_dangerous_every_crime_accident_death_shooting_linked_to_game.html.

Barbash, Fred, *Why Two Supreme Court Justices Played a Violent Video Game to Help Decide a Major Case*, Washington Post, Sept. 18, 2015, https://www.washingtonpost.com/news/morning-mix/wp/2015/09/18/how-and-why-justices-kagan-and-breyer-faced-off-in-a-violent-video-game-to-help-decide-a-major-case/.

Blasi, Weston, *IRS Announces Daily Fantasy Tax as DraftKings Posts Second Quarter Loss*, MarketWatch, Aug. 14, 2020, https://www.marketwatch.com/story/irs-announces-daily-fantasy-tax-as-draftkings-posts-second-quarter-loss-2020-08-14.

Burtka, Allison Torres, *Liebeck v. McDonald's*, American Museum of Tort Law, https://www.tortmuseum.org/liebeck-v-mcdonalds/.

Cullins, Ashley, *Esports Pro Sues Gaming Organization FaZe Clan Over 'Oppressive' Contract*, Hollywood Reporter, May 20, 2019, https://www.hollywoodreporter.com/thr-esq/tfue-sues-faze-clan-oppressive-contract-1212124.

Entertainment Software Rating Board, *Frequently Asked Questions*, https://www.esrb.org/faqs/.

Frederikson, Eric, *Fortnite Has Invaded the Modern American Classroom Like No Other Game*, IGN, Nov. 27, 2018, https://www.ign.com/articles/2018/11/27/fortnite-has-invaded-the-modern-american-classroom-like-no-other-game.

Goldstein, Steve, *CFTC Clears Launch of Political Predictions Market*, MarketWatch, Oct. 31, 2014, https://www.marketwatch.com/story/cftc-clears-launch-of-political-predictions-market-2014-10-31.

Grabowski, Mark, *Fantasy Sports Law*, in Fantasy Sports: Perspectives from the Fields (N. Bowman and J. Sanderson eds., 2016).

Grabowski, Mark, *The Law of eSports*, *in* eSports: Understanding the World of Competitive Video Games (R. Rogers ed., 2019).

Griffin, Jonathan, *The Legality of Fantasy Sports*, National Conference of State Legislatures, Sept. 2015, https://www.ncsl.org/research/civil-and-criminal-justice/the-legality-of-fantasy-sports.aspx.

Grove, Chris, *What Are The States Where You Can Play Daily Fantasy Sports?*, Legal Sports Report, Mar. 19, 2020, https://www.legalsportsreport.com/daily-fantasy-sports-blocked-allowed-states/.

Hanna, Jason and Ford, Dana, *12-year-old Wisconsin Girl Stabbed 19 Times; Friends Arrested*, CNN, June 4, 2014, https://www.cnn.com/2014/06/03/justice/wisconsin-girl-stabbed/index.html.

Hayward, Andrew, *NCAA Votes to Note Govern Collegiate Esports*, The Esports Observer, May 17, 2019, https://esportsobserver.com/ncaa-nogo-collegiate-esports/.

Hegerman, Roxanna, *Ohio Gamer Sentenced to 15 Months in Prison for 'Swatting' Incident That Killed One Person*, Business Insider, Sept. 13, 2019, https://www.businessinsider.com/call-of-duty-gamer-swatting-prison-sentence-2019-9.

Hernández, Javier C. and Zhang, Albee, *90 Minutes a Day, Until 10 P.M.: China Sets Rules for Young Gamers*, New York Times, Nov. 6, 2019, https://www.nytimes.com/2019/11/06/business/china-video-game-ban-young.html.

Hide, Nick, *Retailers Could Be Sent to Prison for Selling 12-Rated Games*, CNET, July 31, 2012, https://www.cnet.com/news/retailers-could-be-sent-to-prison-for-selling-12-rated-games/.

Iowa Electronic Markets, *What Is the IEM*?, University of Iowa, https://iemweb.biz.uiowa.edu/media/summary.html.

Király, Orsolya et al., *Policy Responses to Problematic Video Game Use: A Systematic Review of Current Measures and Future Possibilities*, Journal of Behavioral Addictions (2018), 503–517, https://www.ncbi.nlm.nih.gov/pmc/articles/PMC6426392/.

McCarthy, Kieren, *Pokemon Go Becomes Pokemon No as Games Biz Niantic Agrees to Curb Trespassing Addicts*, The Register, Aug. 23, 2019, https://www.theregister.co.uk/2019/08/23/pokemon_go_lawsuit/.

McDonough, T., *Fantasy Football Leagues in the Workplace*, Obermayer Rebmann Maxwell & Hippel LLP, Sept. 16, 2013, http://www.hrlegalist.com/2013/09/fantasy-football-leagues-in-the-workplace/.

Paul, Ron, *Sheldon Adelson*'s *Casino Interests Ahead of States' Rights*? *Stop Trump from Filling the Swamp*, New York Daily News, Jan. 15, 2019, https://www.nydailynews.com/opinion/ny-oped-sheldon-adelsons-casino-interests-ahead-of-states-rights-20190114-story.html.

PlayUSA, *Legal US Online Gambling Guide*, Jan. 2020, https://www.playusa.com/us/.

PredictIt, *Terms and Conditions*, https://www.predictit.org/terms-and-conditions.

Price, Sadonna, *Legal Gambling Age in the US: State-By-State List*, Online United States Casinos, Dec. 10, 2018, https://www.onlineunitedstatescasinos.com/blog/legal-gambling-age-in-the-us-state-by-state-list-20385/.

Rettner, Rachel, *Video Game Addiction Becomes Official Mental Disorder in Controversial Decision by WHO*, Live Science, May 28, 2019, https://www.livescience.com/65580-video-game-addiction-mental-health-disorder.html.

Ruddock, Steve, *Which States Offer Online Lottery Sales for Mega Millions Tickets?*, Online Poker Report, Feb. 24, 2020, https://www.onlinepokerreport.com/32756/online-lottery-mega-millions-tickets/.

Staff, *Parents Beware: Retail Stores Ignore Video Game Ratings*, Council of the City of New York, Dec. 2003, http://www.nyc.gov/html/records/pdf/govpub/834gameviolence.pdf.

Zhou, Marrian, *South Korean Overwatch Hacker Sentenced to a Year in Prison*, CNET, June 25, 2018, https://www.cnet.com/news/south-korean-overwatch-hacker-sentenced-to-a-year-in-prison/.

12 Emerging Issues in Cyber Law

> AI is the rare case where I think we need to be proactive in regulation instead of reactive. Because I think by the time we are reactive in AI regulation, it'll be too late. AI is a fundamental risk to the existence of human civilization.
>
> — Elon Musk

Cyborgs and robots and drones, oh my!

As technology advances at a breakneck pace, legal and ethical problems loom.

This chapter explores some of the hottest emerging topics related to cyber law and ethics. While technologies such as cybernetics (artificial processes that mimic biological functions) have few, if any, regulations, other innovations, such as unmanned aerial vehicles (drones), may be stifled due to overly restrictive laws. And some issues, such as artificial intelligence, could play out catastrophically if the government fails to intervene. We'll cover those issues and more in this chapter. To help you keep up with legal developments regarding emerging technologies, this chapter concludes with a list of useful resources on these issues.

Artificial Intelligence

We're still probably a long way from having autonomous robots like the ones depicted in sci-fi movies and shows like *The Terminator* and *Westworld* — or are we? Experts disagree, and some warn that such apocalyptic scenarios could eventually happen. But artificial intelligence, or AI, is no longer science fiction. We're already living in an era of machine learning and cognitive computing, in which computers are completing tasks traditionally done by humans, such as cleaning, preparing food and driving cars. These machines require programming in order to operate, which raises legal and ethical dilemmas.

Science fiction writers have long pondered the implications of this. In 1942, Isaac Asimov introduced his famous "Three Laws of Robotics" to help govern future AI: (1) a robot may not injure a human being or, through inaction, allow a human being to come to harm; (2) a robot must obey the orders given it by human beings, except when such orders would conflict with the previous law; and (3) a robot must protect its own existence as long as such protection does not conflict with the previous two laws.[1] But these rules have not been formally enacted as "laws": they are more of a statement of ethics. And experts contend that these basic rules may be inadequate in modern day applications. This leads to a fundamental question in formulating ethical rules and laws regarding AI: what, exactly, constitutes harm when it comes to AI?

How should self-driving cars be programmed to deal with ethical dilemmas such as the one depicted?

For example, self-driving cars may create a modern-day version of a classic ethics experiment known as the "trolley problem," in which shifting a track-side switch could prevent the deaths of five people but result in the death of one person. To put this in a modern context, imagine that your self-driving car's brakes fail. Directly in your car's path is a group of five jaywalkers. The only place to swerve is onto the sidewalk, where a pedestrian will be killed. What should the car do: kill the pedestrian or the five jaywalkers? What if the alternative is to swerve into a utility pole, which will kill you, the car's sole occupant? Such stark choices are rare, if they occur at all, but in a future where cars drive themselves, the decision may be coded in the operating systems of millions of cars. How should the car be programmed? And who is liable for the consequences? Or, what if a glitch causes an AI system to fail and cause harm: who should be at fault? Should "My AI did it" excuse negligent or illegal

1 Anderson, Mark Robert, *After 75 Years, Isaac Asimov's Three Laws of Robotics Need Updating*, The Conversation, Mar. 17, 2017, https://theconversation.com/after-75-years-isaac-asimovs-three-laws-of-robotics-need-updating-74501.

behavior? Driverless cars have already killed people. But only a few states have enacted laws regarding who is legally responsible in such situations.

New legal issues will arise as AI advances further. In 2016, a bot known as Jill Watson served as a teaching assistant for an online course at Georgia Tech, and students were unable to distinguish "her" from human teaching assistants. A more concerning example is Amazon's recent use of an AI tool for hiring, which was scrapped after it was found to be discriminating against female applicants.

It remains to be seen if an AI will ever be created that actually possesses — or unfailingly replicates — free will and self-consciousness. Some AI, like Siri and Alexa, seems benign (although these devices do raise privacy issues). But robots and AI are already displacing workers. And some fear that ultimately they could rule over and destroy humans. Technology entrepreneur Elon Musk has urged America's governors to regulate AI before "it's too late." Although his car company, Tesla, utilizes an AI-powered autopilot system, Musk insists that AI represents an "existential threat" to humanity.[2] One theoretical example of such a threat is known as "Roko's basilisk," after the online handle of its creator. This thought experiment is based on the premise that a powerful AI agent would have an incentive to punish anyone who could have helped the agent come into existence but had not.

Others dismiss fears about such sentient, dominant machines as alarmist and believe AI can greatly improve society. Regardless of which side you agree with, it is clear that an AI revolution is coming, and society — and the law — need to get ready.

Cyborgs

When the United States Supreme Court in 2014 unanimously ruled that police officers may not search the data on a cell phone seized during an arrest without a warrant, Chief Justice John Roberts joked that "modern cell phones … are now such a pervasive and insistent part of daily life that the proverbial visitor from Mars might conclude they were an important feature of human anatomy."[3] Although Roberts likely did not intend to establish any legal precedents regarding cyborgs, the ruling in that case may serve as an indicator that the law will have to accommodate integration of technology into the human body.

The cyborgization of society is already underway. Since 1960, millions of humans have had pacemakers implanted to aid the beating of their hearts.

2 Gibbs, Samuel, *Elon Musk: Regulate AI to Combat "Existential Threat" Before It's Too Late*, The Guardian, July 17, 2017, https://www.theguardian.com/technology/2017/jul/17/elon-musk-regulation-ai-combat-existential-threat-tesla-spacex-ceo.

3 *Riley v. California*, 573 U.S. 373, 385 (2014).

Hundreds of thousands of deaf children and adults have received cochlear implants to allow them to hear.

Historically, implants were done as a medical necessity to allow infirm individuals to live a better life. But now, some people are electing to enhance their perfectly healthy bodies with cybernetic implants for added convenience. For example, in Sweden, thousands of test subjects had a chip embedded under their skin, enabling them to check in at train stations, pay for items or unlock home doors simply by swiping their hand. The Gates Foundation and Massachusetts Institute of Technology are developing a birth control microchip implant that will allow women to control contraceptive hormones in their bodies.

As cyborg technology advances, devices could be implanted to provide enhanced physical and cognitive abilities. How should the law respond when the abilities of such people surpass those of the general population? Will non-modified humans face discrimination in the workplace if they can't compete? And what legal rights should be afforded to people as they become more machine and less biology? Who should control the tech in their bodies?

Drones

Like the Internet, unmanned aerial vehicles — commonly called drones — originated for military use but are now commonly used by the public for business and pleasure. Realizing the potential nuisances that increasing public use could create, the federal government in 2012 began regulating drone operators in the U.S. By 2023, there are expected to be three million drones registered in the country, according to the Federal Aviation Administration (FAA).[4]

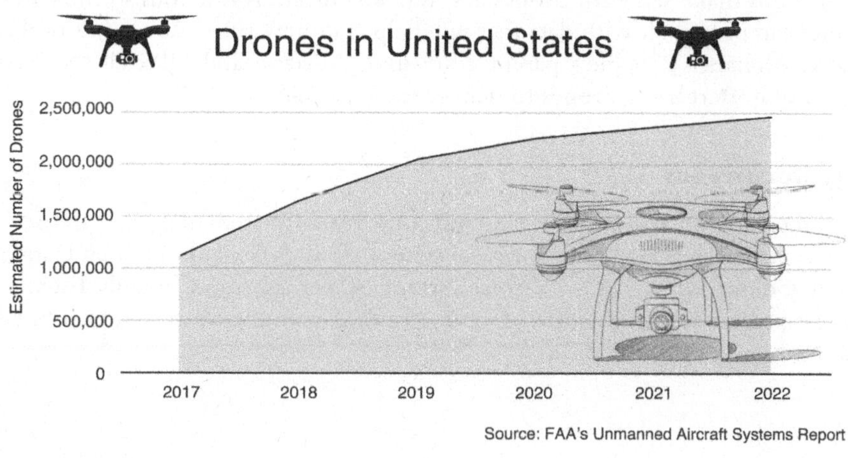

4 FAA, Unmanned Aircraft Systems: FAA's Compliance and Enforcement Approach for Drones Could Benefit from Improved Communication and Data, Oct. 17, 2019, https://www.gao.gov/reports/GAO-20-29/.

Under current rules, all civilian drones must weigh under 55 pounds, be registered with the FAA and follow a set of flying rules, including flying below 400 feet, at less than 100 miles per hour, during daylight hours only unless the drone has lights to show its location, not over people or motor vehicles, and within the line of sight of the operator. Those who want to use drones for commercial purposes, such as professional photography, must first pass an FAA test. The test will eventually be applied to non-commercial drone operators as well.

In addition to federal laws, states have enacted drone regulations of their own. For example, several states forbid using drones to record or monitor another person without their consent. Some states ban using drones for hunting while others prohibit using drones to harass hunters. An emerging legal issue is how much authority state and local governments have over drones, since aviation has traditionally been controlled by the federal government.

As technology improves, businesses are looking to utilize drones in new ways. For example, small package deliveries can be significantly more cost-effective using drones rather than trucks. But such innovations have been hindered by the FAA's rule mandating that drone operators keep unmanned aircraft within their vision at all times. In 2018 a congressionally mandated report from the National Academies of Sciences, Engineering and Medicine chided the FAA for focusing on the risks posed by drones instead of their potential benefits. "Fear of making a mistake drives a risk culture at the FAA that is too often overly conservative, particularly [with drone] technologies," the report concluded.[5]

In response, the FAA selected 10 private-sector projects to explore what regulations make sense for drones and waived current restrictions so the companies can provide it with data that will help craft new rules. As a result of this effort, Alphabet (Google's parent company), Amazon and UPS all received approval to start using drones to deliver some packages.

Cryptocurrency

Cryptocurrency is a somewhat new and controversial system of digital "money" that is challenging the legacy financial system. As U.S. Senator Thomas Carper astutely observed in 2013, "Virtual currencies, perhaps most notably Bitcoin, have captured the imagination of some, struck fear among others, and confused the heck out of the rest of us."[6]

5 National Academies of Sciences, Engineering, and Medicine, Assessing the Risks of Integrating Unmanned Aircraft Systems (UAS) Into the National Airspace System, 2018, at 2, https://doi.org/10.17226/25143.

6 Viswanatha, Aruna, *U.S. Officials: Virtual Currencies Vulnerable to Money Laundering*, Reuters, Nov. 18, 2013, https://www.reuters.com/article/us-senate-virtualcurrency-idUSBRE9AH0P120131118.

This phenomenon began in 2009, when a mysterious figure known by the pseudonym Satoshi Nakamoto invented Bitcoin and blockchain technology, which underpins the notion of cryptocurrency. "Blockchain" is a system in which individual transactions are recorded in an open-source ledger that is duplicated on several computers across the Internet, making it impossible to falsify or manipulate. Cryptocurrency can be bought, sold or transferred between parties over the Internet through the use of such technology. It can also be exchanged for traditional money and goods and services. In this sense, digital money such as Bitcoin is money the same way that dollars are.

This is a depiction of Bitcoin. There is no actual physical coin that's a Bitcoin. Cryptocurrency exists only in cyberspace — you can't hold it in your hand like a penny or dollar bill. Credit: Miloslav Hamřík.

Because it does not require an intermediary such as a bank, cryptocurrency transactions are faster and less expensive than with traditional money. This has attracted widespread adoption in the developing world, where people are more likely to have Internet access than they are to have bank accounts, as well as in the corporate world, which increasingly views cryptocurrency as the latest phase in the evolution of money. In fact, Bitcoin has been the world's best-performing financial asset during the past decade, outperforming stocks, bonds, commodities and currencies.

But cryptocurrency is also perilous. Market volatility, scams and hacks have given rise to concerns that it may be used to defraud financially illiterate users. Also, because it is pseudonymous and cannot be easily traced, cryptocurrency is often exploited by criminals for money laundering, terrorism financing and cybercrime. Hence it creates a unique regulatory quandary for governments: how can they allow access to beneficial financial services through cryptocurrencies while also preventing them from being utilized for illegal activities?

Cryptocurrency is so new that it does not fit neatly with existing laws; authorities around the world are just beginning to study its impact to determine the best way of regulating it. So far, many governments have taken one of two extreme approaches: either banning cryptocurrency altogether or condoning it with no strings attached. China has outlawed the trading of cryptocurrencies. The U.S. government, by contrast, has mostly taken a hands-off approach. While officials have enacted some policies regarding cyber currencies — such as an Internal Revenue Service notice providing that gains and losses in cryptocurrencies shall be treated for tax purposes the same as gains and losses for other forms of property — many issues surrounding digital money remain unclear or unregulated a decade after their inception. At a U.S. Senate hearing in 2018, J. Christopher Giancarlo, chair of the Commodity Futures Trading Commission, explained the lack of such regulation: "'Do no harm' was unquestionably the right approach to development of the Internet," he said. "Similarly, I believe that 'do no harm' is the right overarching approach for [cryptocurrency] technology."[7]

But times have changed. Congress has been intently studying the question: there were 52 congressional hearings on cryptocurrency in 2018, compared to 12 in 2016 and only three in 2013, when the issue first arose in Congress. In a series of tweets in 2019, President Donald Trump stated: "I am not a fan of Bitcoin and other Cryptocurrencies, which … can facilitate unlawful behavior … and [must] become subject to all Banking Regulations."[8] The Biden Administration has expressed similar concerns. Treasury Secretary Janet Yellen said, "Cryptocurrencies are a particular concern. I think many are used — at least in a transaction sense — mainly for illicit financing …I think we really need to examine ways in which we can curtail their use and make sure that money laundering doesn't occur through those channels."[9]

Facebook's announcement in 2019 that it planned to launch its own cryptocurrency, for example, caused alarm among lawmakers on both sides of the aisle, with critics warning that Facebook — already under fire following scandals related to "fake news" and data privacy — cannot be trusted with the public's finances. While Facebook later pulled back on its ambitious plans, more regulation of cryptocurrency is almost certainly coming soon.

7 McKendry, Ian, *Market Regulators on Crypto: We're On it, But May Need Help*, American Banker, Feb. 6, 2018, https://www.americanbanker.com/news/regulators-may-need-more-authority-to-catch-up-with-crypto-sec-chief.

8 Trump, Donald J. (@RealDonaldTrump), Twitter (July 11, 2019 8:15 p.m.), https://twitter.com/realDonaldTrump/status/1149472282584072192.

9 McIntosh, Rachel, *How Low Will Bitcoin Go? BTC Dives Nearly 20% over 7 Days*, Finance Magnates, Jan. 22, 2021, https://www.financemagnates.com/cryptocurrency/news/how-low-will-bitcoin-go-btc-dives-nearly-20-over-7-days/.

Sharing Economy

The "sharing economy," which includes apps such as Uber and AirBnB that enable people to utilize an item or service owned by someone else, has grown to be a major force that now challenges traditional businesses such as hotels, taxis and car rental agencies. While such sharing arrangements were not uncommon previously, the emergence of such apps has dramatically increased the number and nature of such arrangements, as well as leading to more transactions between strangers. The increasing popularity of the sharing economy brings benefits to users, but it nevertheless poses a number of legal problems.

A common criticism is that the sharing economy business model has unfair advantages over other highly regulated businesses. California lawmakers, for example, have claimed that several of these services, such as the digital ride-hailing services Uber and Lyft, abuse workers' rights by classifying full-time drivers as independent contractors instead of employees, thus keeping wages below state minimum wage levels and avoiding having to pay Social Security and payroll taxes, unemployment insurance and worker's compensation. As a result, California passed a law setting strict limits on who can be considered a contractor. But the law is having consequences for more traditional industries and companies that often utilize such workers, and a ballot proposition passed in 2020 limits how the law applies to drivers for ride-hailing services.

In New York City, a number of AirBnB hosts rent out homes in violation of New York's Multiple Dwelling Law, which restricts renting out residences for periods of less than 30 days. AirBnB has also not until recently required hosts or guests to pay hotel occupancy taxes. But in the past few years, AirBnB and other home-sharing sites have reached agreements with several cities to collect taxes from people who rent out their places through the services.

Several states have implemented reforms to mitigate such problems. Aside from its new independent contractor law discussed above, California has also established a new category of motor vehicle carriers, known as Transportation Network Companies, for ride-sharing services, requiring them to have insurance, perform background checks of drivers, and maintain drug and alcohol policies. Washington, D.C.'s "Vehicle for Hire Innovation Amendment Act" requires ride-sharing services to have background checks for drivers, and vehicle inspections, and forbids the manipulation of fare charges.

Despite these new policies, companies like Uber and AirBnB are still exempt from many of the numerous other regulations that taxicab companies and hotels are subject to. An example is guest safety: while hotels are legally required to have fire safety plans and systems such as sprinklers, residences on AirBnB are not covered by such laws. Monitoring and enforcement of the limited regulations that are applicable to sharing services also remains a problem.

U.S.–China Tech War

In recent years, tensions have escalated between the U.S. and China, with technology driving a wedge between the two superpowers. Alex Capri, a visiting senior fellow at the National University of Singapore, says the U.S.–China tech war is "the defining issue of this century."[10]

Although the U.S. and China have long been interdependent when it comes to tech, tensions have risen following continued disagreements on issues like trade, cyber stability and human rights.

Recently, the Federal Communications Commission barred state-owned Chinese telecom companies from operating in the U.S., while the Commerce Department began discouraging U.S. companies from doing business with Chinese telecom equipment-maker Huawei Technologies, both on the grounds that the Chinese government could obtain sensitive personal and commercial information. The U.S. also began restricting visas to Chinese citizens studying or working in certain tech fields in the U.S. over concerns of spying and intellectual property theft. In response, China ordered all government offices to remove all non-Chinese computers and software; a move that could cost U.S. suppliers like Dell, HP and Microsoft as much as $150 billion per year.[11] Additionally, Chinese foreign direct investment in the U.S. plunged, from $30 billion in 2017 to just $5 billion in 2018.[12]

Both sides stand to suffer from the conflict. Chinese companies are heavily dependent on U.S. suppliers for many critical parts, such as semiconductors, that are essential to products assembled in China like computers and cell phones. Meanwhile, China accounts for more than 90% of the global production of rare-earth materials used in smartphones, batteries, guided missiles and other products.[13]

In the midst of this dispute, the COVID-19 pandemic further heightened hostility between the two nations.

"The whole idea of engagement is coming under question," said Orville Schell, the Arthur Ross Director of the Center on U.S.–China Relations at the Asia Society in New York. "And that's cast an entirely different light on technology, because if you're diverging and you're heading into a world

10 Bermingham, Finbarr, *US–China Tech War to Be "Defining Issue of This Century", Despite Signing of Phase One Trade Deal*, South China Morning Post, Jan. 17, 2020, https://www.scmp.com/economy/china-economy/article/3046562/us-china-tech-war-be-defining-issue-century-despite-signing.

11 Yang, Yuan and Liu, Nian, *Beijing Orders State Offices to Replace Foreign PCs and Software*, Financial Times, Dec. 8, 2019, https://www.ft.com/content/b55fc6ee-1787-11ea-8d73-6303645ac406.

12 Hanemann, Thilo, et al., *Two-Way Street: 2020 Update US-China Investment Trends*, The US–China Investment Hub, May 2020, at 9, https://www.us-china-investment.org/us-china-foreign-direct-investments/research (noting that in 2019, the figure stayed about the same: $5 billion).

13 Bray, Chad, *Explainer: Used From iPhones to Guided Missiles, Does China's Dominance in Rare Earths Hold Potential Leverage in Trade War?*, South China Morning Post, May 21, 2019, https://www.scmp.com/business/companies/article/3011108/explainer-used-iphones-guided-missiles-does-chinas-dominance.

of antagonism — you know, conflict, possibly, then suddenly, technology is something that you don't want to share. You want to sequester, to protect your own national interest. And I think the tipping-point moment we are at now, which is what is casting the whole question of things like artificial intelligence and technological innovation into a completely different framework, is that if in fact China and the U.S. are in some way fundamentally antagonistic to each other, then we're in a completely different world."[14]

Climate Change

Our increasingly online lives are both helping and harming the environment.

On one hand, the Internet can significantly cut down on carbon emissions by allowing workers to telecommute. According to the Environmental Protection Agency, work commutes, paper waste and office buildings are among the largest sources of pollution. Several companies have significantly reduced their carbon footprint by allowing many of their employees to work from home, a trend that grew with the COVID-19 pandemic.

Unfortunately, most of the stuff we do on the Internet is not productive. In fact, it's often a waste of time and energy. Instead of reading books, playing catch or socializing with friends, many people now use their free time to scan social media, play video games or watch Netflix. The average American spends 5.4 hours a day on their smartphone, including a few hours on social media.[15] These uses of the Internet consume resources that outweigh the ecological benefits of trends like telecommuting.

Keep in mind, using the Internet involves more than just the materials to make our devices and the energy required to power them. It also requires the storing and transmission of data to and from data centers, entire buildings that house massive banks of computers on which most of the data on the Internet is stored and processed. These centers require a lot of non-renewable energy to build, power and maintain. Consequently, the Internet's use of electricity now accounts for 10% of the world's carbon emissions. This is only going to get worse as our technology takes on more advanced forms like AI and the developing 5G network, and people increasingly engage in energy-draining activities like mining Bitcoin. By 2030, the Internet will be responsible for 20% or more of the world's carbon, making its environmental impact worse than all but three countries: the U.S., China and India.[16]

14 Frontline: In the Age of AI (PBS, Nov. 5, 2019), https://youtu.be/5dZ_lvDgevk.

15 Brown, Eileen, *Americans Spend Far More Time on Their Smartphones Than They Think*, ZD Net, Apr. 28, 2019, https://www.zdnet.com/article/americans-spend-far-more-time-on-their-smartphones-than-they-think/.

16 Lozano, Kevin, *Can the Internet Survive Climate Change?*, The New Republic, Dec. 18, 2019, https://newrepublic.com/article/155993/can-internet-survive-climate-change.

In other words, as the Internet progresses, our environment will suffer more, making it increasingly clear that something has to give.

Staying Informed

Because technology is ever-evolving, cyber law and ethics are in a constant state of flux. How can you track the issues covered in this chapter and learn about new ones that may emerge in coming years? Below are several useful resources for learning about the latest developments:

- Above The Law is a legal blog that has many posts on technology issues at https://abovethelaw.com/technology/.
- The American Bar Association's magazine, *ABA Journal*, frequently posts articles on Internet law issues. It is accessible at http://www.abajournal.com/topic/internet+law.
- The American Civil Liberties Union is an advocacy group that, among other things, fights for freedom in cyberspace. Check out its blog on digital rights issues at https://www.aclu.org/news/by-issue/privacy-technology/.
- *C4ISRNET* is a publication covering emerging issues and trends in military technology and cyberwarfare at https://www.c4isrnet.com/.
- The Center for Democracy and Technology advocates for online civil liberties and has updates on trending issues at https://cdt.org/insights/.
- The Center for Digital Ethics and Policy researches ethical behavior online and its researchers frequently publish essays on timely topics at http://www.digitalethics.org/essays.
- The Center for Strategic and International Studies maintains a Technology Policy Blog at https://www.csis.org/blogs/technology-policy-blog.
- Cyberlaw Blogospace features monthly commentary from researchers at Hebrew University of Jerusalem's Cyber Law Program at https://csrcl.huji.ac.il/blog.
- The Cyberlaw Podcast is a weekly podcast on the latest events in technology, security, privacy and government hosted by a cyber attorney who is joined by expert guests at https://www.lawfareblog.com/topic/cyberlaw-podcast.
- The Electronic Frontier Foundation is an online free speech advocacy group that blogs about online speech regulation issues at https://www.eff.org/press.
- Freedom to Tinker features analysis and commentary from the staff of Princeton University's Center for Information Technology Policy at https://freedom-to-tinker.com/.
- Harvard University's Berkman Klein Center for Internet & Society has a blog on the latest issues in cyberspace at https://cyber.harvard.edu/community.

- Internet law professor Eric Goldman maintains a blog on technology law developments at https://blog.ericgoldman.org/.
- The Internet & Social Media Law Blog is maintained by Pillsbury Winthrop Shaw Pittman attorneys and addresses legal issues surrounding the latest technological developments and social media trends at https://www.internetandtechnologylaw.com/.
- Internet Cases, a blog by Chicago technology attorney Evan Brown, tracks cyberspace-related litigation at http://blog.internetcases.com/.
- The Internet Society, a non-profit that promotes Internet use and access, provides news on current Internet-related issues at https://www.internetsociety.org/news/.
- The National Conference of State Legislatures tracks proposed state laws related to the Internet and technology at https://www.ncsl.org/research/telecommunications-and-information-technology.aspx.
- Legal news site Law360 publishes cybersecurity and digital privacy news at https://www.law360.com/cybersecurity-privacy.
- Of Digital Interest, a site published by attorneys at McDermott Will & Emery, provides legal news and analysis of all things digital at https://www.ofdigitalinterest.com/.
- Pogo Was Right is a blog that tracks the latest news on privacy issues, particularly digital privacy, at https://www.pogowasright.org/.
- r/cyberlaws is an active subreddit on legal news linked to technology issues at https://www.reddit.com/r/cyberlaws/.
- Reclaim the Net reports on the latest free speech controversies involving the Internet at https://reclaimthenet.org/.
- SecureWorld is a website covering IT news and frequently reports on legal developments at https://www.secureworldexpo.com/industry-news/topic/cyber-law.
- The staff of Stanford University's Center for Internet and Society blogs about law and policy around the Internet and other emerging technologies at https://cyberlaw.stanford.edu/blog.
- On Twitter, several cyber law professors regularly tweet about the latest developments in the field. On Twitter, follow @rcalo, @jkosseff, @idokilovaty, @GusHurwitz, @yaleisp, @jessekblum and @cearta.
- The mainstream media regularly reports on cyber law issues. Do a search for terms such as "Internet law" or "digital ethics" on Google News or *The New York Times*' website.
- Several tech blogs regularly report on the latest legal developments and controversies. Check out *Ars Technica*, *Engadget*, *Gizmodo*, *Mashable*, *TNW*, *TechCrunch*, *The Register* and *The Verge*.

Be forewarned that many of these institutions, news outlets and organizations have their own political agendas and biases. But, while you may not agree with their stance on issues, reading their content will help inform you about some of the emerging issues in cyber law and ethics.

> **CLOSING ARGUMENTS**
>
> In an early chapter, we pondered whether the Internet was a net good or bad for society. Now let's conclude by considering the same issue for AI: does AI represent a promise for society or a danger? Do you agree with Elon Musk that strict regulations are needed to prevent a Terminator-like scenario or do you think such concerns are overblown? In other words, do you fear or look forward to the forthcoming AI revolution?

Additional Sources

Auerbach, David, *The Most Terrifying Thought Experiment of All Time*, Slate, July 17, 2014, https://slate.com/technology/2014/07/rokos-basilisk-the-most-terrifying-thought-experiment-of-all-time.html.

Austen, Greg, *Can There Be Any Winners in the US–China "Tech War"?*, International Institute for Strategic Studies, Jan. 20, 2020, https://www.iiss.org/blogs/analysis/2020/01/csfc-any-winners-in-the-us-china-tech-war.

Barfield, Woodrow and Williams, Alexander, *Law, Cyborgs, and Technologically Enhanced Brains*, 2(1) Philosophies 6 (2017), doi:10.3390/philosophies2010006, https://www.researchgate.net/publication/313836493_Law:Cyborgs_and_Technologically_Enhanced_Brains.

Bloomberg News, *Next China: Consequences of the Tech War*, Bloomberg, Oct. 25, 2019, https://www.bloomberg.com/news/newsletters/2019-10-25/next-china-consequences-of-the-tech-war.

Boone, Alastair. *What AirBnB Did to New York City*, CityLab, Mar. 5, 2018, https://www.citylab.com/equity/2018/03/what-airbnb-did-to-new-york-city/552749/.

Cardwell, Mark, *The Life of a Voluntary Cyborg*, University Affairs, Feb. 18, 2020, https://www.universityaffairs.ca/news/news-article/the-life-of-a-voluntary-cyborg/.

Conger, Kate, *California Sues Uber and Lyft, Claiming Workers Are Misclassified*, New York Times, May 5, 2020, https://www.nytimes.com/2020/05/05/technology/california-uber-lyft-lawsuit.html.

Daré Bioscience, Inc., *Daré Bioscience Announces Receipt of $1.5 Million under the Current Grant Supplement Award for Continued Development of User-Controlled Long Acting Reversible Contraceptive*, June 15, 2020, https://ir.darebioscience.com/news-releases/news-release-details/dare-bioscience-announces-receipt-15-million-under-current-grant.

Dastin, Jeffrey, *Amazon Scraps Secret AI Recruiting Tool That Showed Bias against Women*, Reuters, Oct. 9, 2018, https://www.reuters.com/article/us-amazon-com-jobs-automation-insight/amazon-scraps-secret-ai-recruiting-tool-that-showed-bias-against-women-idUSKCN1MK08G.

Etzioni, Oren, *How to Regulate Artificial Intelligence*, The New York Times, Sept. 1, 2017, https://www.nytimes.com/2017/09/01/opinion/artificial-intelligence-regulations-rules.html.

Fisher, Jim, *Drone Regulations: What You Need to Know*, PC Magazine, Jan 29, 2020, https://www.pcmag.com/news/drone-regulations-what-you-need-to-know.

Furness, Dyllan, *Who Controls the Tech inside Us? Budding Biohackers Are Shaping "Cyborg Law"*, Digital Trends, July 4, 2018, https://www.digitaltrends.com/cool-tech/cyborg-law-and-rights-of-augmented-humans/.

Goel, Ashok, *The Interaction Hour: Ep. 5: Who Is Jill Watson, and What Can She Teach Us about Automation?*, Georgia Tech, Jan. 23, 2019, https://www.ic.gatech.edu/podcasts/ep-5-who-jill-watson-and-what-can-she-teach-us-about-automation.

Grabowski, Mark, *Cryptocurrencies: A Primer on Digital Money* (2019).

Hao, Karen, *Should a Self-Driving Car Kill the Baby or the Grandma? Depends on Where You're From*, MIT Technology Review, Oct. 24, 2018, https://www.technologyreview.com/2018/10/24/139313/a-global-ethics-study-aims-to-help-ai-solve-the-self-driving-trolley-problem/.

He, Zack, *Risks and Regulations of the Sharing Economy*, Chicago Policy Review, Aug. 26, 2017, https://chicagopolicyreview.org/2017/08/26/risks-and-regulations-of-the-sharing-economy/.

Insider Intelligence, *Drone Flying Laws, FAA Regulations, and License Requirements You Need to Know*, Business Insider, Jan. 3, 2020, https://www.businessinsider.com/drone-license-laws-regulations.

IRS, Notice 2014–21 (Apr. 14, 2014), https://www.irs.gov/irb/2014-16_IRB#NOT-2014-21 (outlining tax consequences of transactions using Bitcoin).

Joshi, Shamani, *How Climate Change Will Kill Your Internet*, Vice, Aug. 27, 2019, https://www.vice.com/en_in/article/qvgb8b/how-climate-change-will-kill-your-internet.

Lynch, David J., *How the U.S.-China Trade War Became a Conflict over the Future of Tech*, Washington Post, May 22, 2019, https://www.washingtonpost.com/business/economy/how-the-us-china-trade-war-became-a-conflict-over-the-future-of-tech/2019/05/22/18148d1c-7ccc-11e9-8ede-f4abf521ef17_story.html.

McGregor, Jena, *Some Swedish Workers Are Getting Microchips Implanted in Their Hands*, Washington Post, Apr. 4, 2017, https://www.washingtonpost.com/news/on-leadership/wp/2017/04/04/some-swedish-workers-are-getting-microchips-implanted-in-their-hands/.

Neegaard, Lauran, *Once-a-month Birth Control Pill? Experiment Works in Animals*, Associated Press, Dec. 4, 2019, https://apnews.com/8b352ef7ac7f12855c10bf4a1d71b5d9.

Oates, Joan, *Two Can Play That Game: China Orders Ban on US Computers and Software*, The Register, Dec. 9, 2019, https://www.theregister.co.uk/2019/12/09/china_orders_ban_on_us_computers_and_software/.

Ray, Trisha, *Separation Anxieties: US, China and Tech Interdependence*, Observer Research Foundation, Apr. 9, 2020, https://www.orfonline.org/expert-speak/separation-anxieties-us-china-tech-interdependence-64369/.

Savage, Maddy, *Thousands of Swedes Are Inserting Microchips Under Their Skin*, NPR, Oct. 22, 2018, https://www.npr.org/2018/10/22/658808705/thousands-of-swedes-are-inserting-microchips-under-their-skin.

Savitz, Eric, *Uber*, Postmates Suit Says *California Law on Gig Work Is Unconstitutional*, Barron's, Dec. 31, 2019, https://www.barrons.com/articles/uber-lawsuit-challenges-californias-ab5-the-new-law-on-gig-work-51577815094.

Segal, Adam, *Year* in Review 2019: *The U.S.-China Tech Cold War Deepens and Expands*, Council on Foreign Relations, https://www.cfr.org/blog/year-review-2019-us-china-tech-cold-war-deepens-and-expands.

Stewart, Jack, *FAA Relaxes Drone Restrictions with 10 New Programs*, Wired, May 9, 2018, https://www.wired.com/story/faa-relaxes-drone-restrictions-with-10-new-programs/.

Sutton, Sara, *How Telecommuting Reduced Carbon Footprints at Dell, Aetna and Xerox*, Entrepreneur, Apr. 22, 2015, https://www.entrepreneur.com/article/245296.

Wyman, Oliver, *Why the Use of Drones Still Faces Big Regulatory Hurdles*, Forbes, Sept. 10, 2018, https://www.forbes.com/sites/oliverwyman/2018/09/10/why-the-use-of-drones-still-faces-big-regulatory-hurdles/#102534b41c0d.

Case Index

Index